H.O.T. Chess

Paul Motwani

B. T. Batsford Ltd, *London*

First Published 1996
Reprinted 2001
© Paul Motwani

ISBN 0 7134 7975 2

British Library Cataloguing-in-Publication Data.
A catalogue record for this book is
available from the British Library.

All rights reserved. No part of this book may be
reproduced, by any means, without prior permission
of the publisher.

Typeset by Petra Nunn
and printed in Great Britain by
The Bath Press, Bath
for the publishers:
B.T Batsford Ltd,
9 Blenheim Court,
Brewery Road,
London, N7 9NT

A member of the Chrysalis Group plc

A BATSFORD CHESS BOOK

Contents

Dedications

Chapter One: 'Let's F.A.C.E. It' is dedicated to my wife Jenny for all her love and support, especially in helping me to face the work of beginning this book at a time when many big changes were happening in our lives.

Chapter Two: 'A Good Way T.O.D.O. It' is dedicated to my parents, brother Joe, and sisters Mary and Cath. From their fine examples, I have learned a lot about how to live, which has also had a very positive effect on my chess work.

Chapter Three: 'The Four S's' is dedicated to four groups of people living in Dundee, where I too lived for twenty-eight years of my life so far. Jim and Jean Chalmers; Paul Fitzpatrick; Grandmaster Dr Colin McNab; and the late Bill Russell all had a great influence on my chess development as a boy. They, and indeed all my other dear friends, will always have a special place in my heart.

Chapter Four: 'C.H.A.M.P.' is dedicated to John Glendinning, the President of the Scottish Chess Association. Nearly 30 years ago, John founded the Scottish Junior Chess Association, and he has worked tirelessly to improve opportunities in Scotland for players of all standards to enjoy more chess. I thank John and the many other people who have championed such a worthwhile cause.

Chapter Five: 'N.B.' is dedicated to you, the reader. There is a long, H.O.T. chess journey ahead of you, and to reach the final chapter you will require dedication!

There is no chapter six, but I wish to give sincere and special thanks to Stefaan Six, a Belgian friend who offered numerous helpful suggestions for this book.

Introduction

Do you remember your first-ever game of chess? In my case, I still enjoy thinking back to 1973, when, as an 11-year-old schoolboy, I faced a classmate named Ann Fraser. After 1 e4 d6, she played 2 &b5+ and announced 'Checkmate'! I was stunned and asked for an explanation, to which she replied 'It's check and your king can't move.' This latter statement was absolutely correct, but neither of us understood that her bishop check could be blocked in five different ways! Over the next few weeks I encountered a wonderful variety of moves, and I began to appreciate the richness in possibilities of chess. With this realisation, there also came a strong feeling that it is important for a chess player to acquire theoretical knowledge, but that that alone is not sufficient. Chess is too vast. A player needs also to develop a repertoire of ways for handling lots of situations. I believe that this should be as individual as possible for each person. Then the player will cope more comfortably when confronted with the numerous problems which arise in the games.

In the 23 years since my first game, I have not managed to refute the Pirc Defence (even though that brief clash made it look so easy!), but, having played in 28 countries, I have built up a personal approach to chess which proved very effective in practice in helping me to become Scotland's first grandmaster. In this book I endeavour to describe my ways of thinking, in the hope that many people will find it useful in forming their own approach to chess. Of course, players may wish to modify or expand the ideas to suit their distinct needs and personalities. Some players may even create their own system of 'Highly Original Thinking chess' (H.O.T. Chess).

I know, from eleven years so far of teaching mathematics in schools, that, with the presentation of a concept, the methods of teaching should be interesting and there should be a suitable number of illustrative examples. Ever since Jurek Rzepecki and Mo Brodie, former Principal Teachers of Mathematics at St Saviour's High School in Dundee, taught me C.A.S.T. (representing Cosine, All, Sine, Tangent, which is of significance in certain problems involving trigonometry) when I was a boy, I have found such mnemonics to be particularly helpful aids to assist learning. Lots of my own mnemonics in a chess context appear in the chapters ahead, and you may well think of others which can further help your own thought processes.

In order to provide the reader with detailed and clear explanations of the ideas in this book, I felt that the most natural source for a certain part of the material was my own games (and in the end they formed about 30 per cent of all the encounters). Many of the opponents are grandmasters or international masters (in a few cases the titles were achieved some time after the games, though that is a point of only very minor importance), but I believe that if a game is annotated fully and with lucidity, then it can benefit most levels of players. All the annotations are my own. In the cases where I have previously analysed a game for any form of publication, I have now substantially increased and improved the analysis myself.

A good variety of openings feature in the games chosen, so the majority of players should find interesting lines relating to some of their favoured systems. However, I have never encouraged people to memorise screeds of information without truly understanding the content. Therefore, for clarity, all the 38 main games, and the 49 other complete references which appear in the notes or in the form of puzzles, are supplied with detailed annotations. Many partial games are included too, again furnished with lots of explanatory comments. You always have the option to skim through only the main moves (if perhaps you are in a hurry), but the much fuller accompanying explanations and analysis will always be there in the notes whenever you want to study more closely. Some people like a deep, accurate, analytical approach, while others prefer ideas put forward using words alone. I have aimed to provide the best of both worlds, and you will find that they sometimes overlap. In Game 37 for example, in the midst of the calculations (which are extensive, in order to do justice to a short but brilliant clash), a very useful mnemonic is there to be added to an armoury which will already be really strong by that stage. To equip you even more completely, an extra H.O.T. item has been included in the kit after the superb combination (one of many you will see) following the penultimate main game. The emphasis is on exciting attacking chess. Draws are not necessarily dull, but, in general, the games selected have decisive results and include 'battles' fought right up to the day I am now writing (see the stunning display of tactics in the Kasparov-Seirawan encounter within the notes to Game 18).

For a light but hopefully stimulating change, a variety of anecdotes and original puzzles are interspersed between some of the games. I think you will really enjoy them, and clear solutions are given to all of the problems. The titles which I have chosen for those examples should help them to become even more memorable and to have a lasting positive impact. Apart from providing a relaxed change of activity, the puzzles are designed to improve skills in deduction, logic, and chess. The ability to view a situation calmly and deduce conclusions in a logical way can be highly beneficial in chess (and, at least to a certain extent, in life in general).

Out of curiosity, I always look at the last line of the introduction by other authors, to see where the work was written. In my case you will see 'Brussels' mentioned. Do not delay by wondering *'I was sure he is a tall Scottish man'*. You would be correct (at least about the nationality, if not the height!), but, as I have moved now, your clock is ticking. Quickly rearranging the 28 letters in italics gives *H.O.T. Chess still awaits a main user*. This book is very 'user friendly', and it is now time for you to move into the zone of H.O.T. Chess.

Paul Motwani
Brussels, 27 March 1996

1 Let's F.A.C.E. It

'Face what?' or 'What is F.A.C.E.?' you might ask. Well, F.A.C.E. is a mnemonic which I use to help me to get into a focused frame of mind before playing any game of chess. If possible, a stroll outdoors prior to the game is a good, healthy way of refreshing the brain. So F.A.C.E. could mean Fresh Air Clears Everything. However, I use F.A.C.E. to stand for *Fear, Allegro, Consistency, Enjoyment.* I will explain the significance of those four key words.

Even before a game begins, *Fear* can seriously affect a player's future performance. In the under-13's section of the 1974 Glasgow Congress, I went into the last round leading on 5/5 ... but I was afraid of the opponent whom I was about to face. I had only recently been reading about fianchettoes, and was worried about playing David Duncan, a boy who began most of his games with the sequence ♘f3, g3, ♗g2 when playing White! My fear ensured that I lost in the final round. David Duncan won five pounds and a chess tie, while I picked up 70 pence worth of pink stamps. If I still feared fianchettoes nowadays, then I would have no chance against my friend, Grandmaster Dr Colin McNab! Fear can be caused by many factors, but I realise it is so counter-productive that I always set aside at least a few peaceful moments before my games now to remind myself to be calm. Of course, every player loses games, but, in so doing, can become stronger through the learning experiences. So my attitude is to relax and *enjoy* each game. By consciously going over this in my mind before my games, I have found that my results in chess, and enjoyment derived from it, have both improved.

Allegro is my way of reminding myself to develop my pieces rapidly. There are many examples in which even strong titled players lost quickly by sometimes neglecting to develop their army of chess men.

Consistency is also very important. In particular, I mean that a player should try to make moves that are part of an overall plan. The plan should be followed as consistently as possible. Inconsistent moves, which deviate from the plan for no good reason, generally lead to trouble.

It is time for some practical examples of F.A.C.E. in action.

The Cuban grandmaster Walter Arencibia was the reigning World Junior Champion when I faced him at the 1986 Dubai Olympiad. However, I reminded myself that anyone can be beaten, and sat down to play him ... without fear.

Game 1
W.Arencibia – P.Motwani
Dubai OL 1986
Budapest Defence

1	d4	♘f6
2	c4	e5
3	dxe5	♘g4
4	♘f3	

4 f4? ♗c5 is too dangerous for White, but he does have some good fourth-move options. For example:

a) **4 e3 ♘xe5 5 ♘h3!** intending ♘f4 with a grip on the central square d5.

b) **4 e4 ♘xe5 5 f4 ♘ec6 6 ♗e3** (6 a3!?) 6...♗b4+ 7 ♘d2 ♕e7 8 ♕c2 ♘a6 9 ♘e2 ♗c5 10 ♗xc5 ♘xc5 11 a3 ♕d6!! threatening 12...♘d3+ was W.Rutherford-Motwani, Perth 1992. 12 ♔f2 would have failed to 12...♕xd2!, while 12 ♘g3 lost quickly after 12...♕xf4.

4	...	♗c5
5	e3	♘c6
6	♗e2	0-0
7	♘c3	♘gxe5
8	♘xe5	♘xe5
9	a3	a5

| 10 | b3 | ♖e8 |
| 11 | ♗b2 | ♖a6 *(D)* |

Black could have played ...d6 earlier, but deliberately omitted it so that his queen's rook could transfer laterally from a6 over to the kingside.

W

12 ♘d5

12 ♘e4 ♗a7 reveals another point of Black's ninth move.

12	...	♖h6
13	♗d4	d6
14	♖a2	

Of course, 14 0-0? ♕h4 15 h3 ♗xh3 gives Black a crushing attack.

14	...	♗f5
15	♗xc5	dxc5
16	♖d2	♖d6

Not 16...♕c8? because of 17 ♘e7+! ♖xe7 18 ♖d8+.

| 17 | f3 | ♘g6!? |

17...c6? 18 ♘e7+!.

18 e4

This weakens White's control of the f4-square, and seems illogical now that the black knight may go there. However, 18 0-0 fails against 18...♖xe3! 19 ♘xe3 ♖xd2.

18 ...   ♗c8
19 ♘e3

19 0-0 ♘f4 is one line which illustrates Black's tactical possibilities based on the poorly defended rook on d2. Another option would be 19...♖ee6 threatening 20...c6.

19 ...   ♖d4
20 ♘c2   ♖xd2

This exchange is well-timed, now that White's knight is passively placed.

21 ♕xd2   ♕f6!

Black has succeeded in seizing the initiative. If 22 ♕xa5, then 22...♕b2 and 22...♘f4 are both unpleasant moves to meet.

22 0-0   ♖d8
23 ♕xa5?

The queen gets a fatal distraction. Necessary was 23 ♕e3, staying close to White's king.

23 ...   ♘f4
24 ♗d1 (D)
24 ...   ♗h3!
25 ♘e3

White could have resigned, as 25 gxh3 ♕g5+ is hopeless for him.

25 ...   ♗xg2
26 ♖e1

26 ♘xg2 ♕g5.

26 ...   b6
0-1

White resigned, faced with overwhelming threats, including 27 ♕a7 ♕c3.

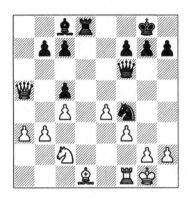

B

This victory helped me greatly towards achieving my first grandmaster norm, with half a point to spare, though I had not yet gained the title of international master. However, all the requirements for that level were satisfied after I took second place on 8/11 in an international tournament in Israel the following year. My opponent in the next game, selected from that occasion, does not manage to activate his pieces properly, and consequently he loses rapidly. Always remember *Allegro...*

Game 2
P.Motwani – M.Kotliar
Netanya 1987
Three Knights' Game

1 e4   e5
2 ♘f3   ♘c6
3 ♘c3   ♗b4

3...♘f6 would have led to a Four Knights' Game. If Black prefers to avoid that, then 3...g6 is the most popular method of doing so. The Ukrainian grandmaster Oleg Romanishin sometimes plays 3...♗c5, but, although I think he is one of the world's most creative players, in this case I do feel that White simply stands better after 4 ♘xe5! ♘xe5 5 d4. On b4, Black's bishop also just seems to become a target for White to attack.

4	♘d5	♘f6
5	c3	♗e7
6	d4!?	0-0

6...exd4 7 ♘xf6+ ♗xf6 8 cxd4 d5 9 e5 ♗e7, intending later to exert pressure on White's centre with ...♗g4 and ...f6, is playable for Black. White might prefer 7 ♘xd4, since 7...♘xe4? 8 ♘f5 is very dangerous for Black.

7	♘xe5	♘xe5
8	dxe5	♘xe4
9	♗d3	♘c5
10	♗c2	c6?

Black probably missed the force of the innocuous-looking move 12 0-0 in the game continuation. 10...d6 was better.

11	♘xe7+	♕xe7 *(D)*
12	0-0!	♕xe5
13	♖e1	♕d5

A sad necessity for Black, since 13...♕f6 would have lost instantly to 14 ♕h5, with simultaneous attacks on Black's vulnerable h-pawn and loose knight.

14	♕xd5	cxd5
15	♗f4	♘e6

W

15...♖d8 loses to 16 ♗c7 ♖f8 17 ♗d6, and an attempt to activate the undeveloped bishop on the c8 to a6 diagonal by means of 15...b6 also fails, to 16 ♗d6 ♖d8 17 ♗e7 ♖e8 18 ♗xc5 ♖xe1+ 19 ♖xe1 bxc5 20 ♖e8#.

16	♗d6	♖d8
17	f4	a5 *(D)*

W

18 ♖ad1

White's position is overwhelming. Here, the idea is to answer

18...♖a6 with 19 ♖xd5 simply to protect the bishop on d6. This is an easier route to victory than 18 f5 ♖a6 19 ♗e7 ♖e8, when Black can struggle on.

18	...	d4
19	f5	♖a6
20	♗g3	dxc3

20...♘c5 21 cxd4, 20...♘g5 21 h4 and 20...♘f8 21 ♗c7 are all hopeless for Black.

21	fxe6	fxe6
22	bxc3	d5
23	c4	♖c6
24	♗b3	d4
25	♗h4	♖dd6

25...♖d7 is no better because of 26 ♗a4.

26 c5! *(D)*

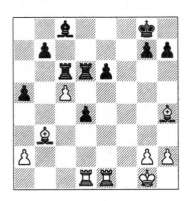

B

1-0

Black resigned in view of 26...♖xc5 27 ♗e7.

Let us do a reverse time warp now to 1974! A certain game from that year, which I played as a schoolboy, still remains one of my favourite personal efforts. Once again, it illustrates the importance in chess of not neglecting to develop one's army of pieces quickly. When Black fails to observe that vital principle, his king suffers from lack of protection, and is hunted until it is checkmated.

Game 3
P.Motwani – P.Rockwell
Dundee 1974
Sicilian Defence

1	e4	c5
2	d4	cxd4
3	♘f3	

The alternative 3 c3 is the Morra Gambit. Instead, I used to play the developing move 3 ♘f3 as in this game. However, it is really a gambit too, since Black has 3...e5. Then 4 ♘xe5?? would lose to 4...♕a5+ and 5...♕xe5. So White should prefer 4 c3. The idea is that if 4...dxc3, then 5 ♘xc3 gives White a lead in development and the d5-square as a strong outpost in return for the sacrificed pawn.

| 3 | ... | d6 |
| 4 | ♗c4? | |

In the game continuation, White gets a pretty win, but Black could have obtained an excellent position with 4...♘f6!. Then after 5 ♕xd4 ♘c6, White must move his queen again, or play 6 ♗b5 and go a tempo behind compared with the well-known variation 1 e4 c5 2 ♘f3 d6 3 d4 cxd4 4 ♕xd4 ♘c6 5 ♗b5. Therefore, instead of 4 ♗c4, White should have recaptured on d4, and both ways of doing so are perfectly sound, although very different in character.

4	...	h6?!
5	c3	

5 ♘xd4 is objectively better, but White is setting a trap...

5	...	dxc3 (D)

W

...and Black falls in! He should have played 5...♘f6.

6	♗xf7+!!	♔xf7

6...♔d7 7 ♘xc3 threatens 8 ♘e5+ ♔c7 9 ♘d5#.

7	♘e5+	♔f6

7...dxe5 8 ♕xd8 and 7...♔e8 8 ♕h5+ are obviously hopeless for Black, while 7...♔e6 8 ♕g4+ ♔xe5 9 ♕f4+! transposes to the game continuation.

8	♕f3+	♔xe5

9	♕f4+!	

A key move. The black king is forced forward, as 9...♔e6 allows 10 ♕f5#.

9	...	♔d4
10	♗e3+	♔d3

10...♔c4 11 ♘a3+ ♔b4 12 e5+ ♔a5 13 ♕c4 ♗d7 14 b4+ ♔a4 15 ♕b3#.

11	♘a3	c2

11...cxb2 12 ♖d1+ ♔c3 13 ♗d2+ ♔d4 14 ♗b4#.

12	0-0	h5

This counter-attack is a little late!

13	♖ad1+	cxd1♕
14	♖xd1+	♔e2 (D)

W

15	♕f3#	

If words like *Allegro* help players not to forget about the importance of rapidly developing their forces, then they are worth remembering. However, a single word may not be completely sufficient to highlight all the key aspects of the subject it relates to. In the case of *Allegro*, the **quality** of the rapid development is a key factor. A piece may be well-placed on a certain square in some circumstances, but the same piece on the same square could be misplaced in slightly different circumstances. For example, after 1 e4 e5 2 ♘c3 ♘c6 3 ♗c4 ♗c5, the move 4 ♕g4 merits consideration. Then 4...g6 may be better than the counter-attacking 4...♕f6, as in the latter case White has 5 ♘d5!? ♕xf2+ 6 ♔d1 ♔f8 7 ♘h3! ♕d4 8 d3. The rook on h1 can slide over to utilise the opened f-file to mount a strong attack against Black's king. Meanwhile Black's queen is also in trouble, faced with the threat of 9 c3. White's queen, in contrast, is well placed in an attacking position. Compare that with the following case.

The Wandering Queen

1	e4	e5
2	♘c3	♗c5
3	♕g4?! *(D)*	

Black can seize the initiative with 3...♘f6!, intending 4 ♕xg7 ♖g8 5 ♕h6 ♗xf2+! 6 ♔d1 (6 ♔xf2 ♘g4+) 6...d5 7 exd5? ♖g6, and this time White is the one whose queen is trapped. Even highly ranked players often neglect or misjudge the quality of development of their forces. In the following miniature, the Brazilian international master

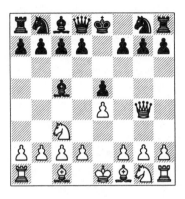

B

who played White was rated 2465 on the Elo list at that time.

Game 4
G.Vescovi – I.Sokolov
Malmö 1995
Portuguese Opening

1	e4	e5
2	♗b5	

This rare so-called 'Portuguese Opening' may resemble the much more common Spanish Opening (Ruy Lopez) 1 e4 e5 2 ♘f3 ♘c6 3 ♗b5 by virtue of the placing of the bishop on b5 in both cases. However, it is hard to recommend this development for White when Black can still play ...c6, and gain a useful tempo by forcing the bishop to retreat from b5.

2	...	c6
3	♗a4	♘f6
4	♕e2	

4 ♘c3 b5 5 ♗b3 b4 is strong for Black.

4	...	♗c5
5	♘f3	d5!

This move is very ambitious, but quite justified against White's odd opening. A tactical point is that 6 d3? would lose to 6...♕a5+ 7 ♘c3 d4.

6	exd5	0-0
7	♘xe5	

With his king and queen both on the e-file, White must have been reluctant to open that line for Black to use against them. However, 7...e4 was an unpleasant threat.

7	...	♖e8
8	c3 *(D)*	

B

Castling would have lost to 8...♗d4.

8	...	♗xf2+!

Sokolov had a far superior quality of development, so it is not surprising that such tactical strokes have become possible. Now 9 ♔xf2 would be answered by 9...♖xe5! with the idea 10 ♕xe5 ♘g4+.

9	♔f1	♗g4
10	♕xf2	♖xe5

Threatening 11...♖f5.

11	♔g1	♕e7!

0-1

White resigned in view of 12 h3 ♖e1+ 13 ♔h2 ♕e5+ 14 ♕g3 ♖xh1+ or 14 g3 ♖e2.

Consistency is really important in chess. If you have a reasonable plan in mind in any given game, and follow it consistently, then your results should, in general, be good. You will have consistency not only in your moves, fitting together well to form coherent plans, but in fine performances too. Many players find it extremely difficult to cope with an opponent who attacks consistently. Witness what happens to a super-level grandmaster in this next featured game.

Game 5
A.Vaïsser – R.Dautov
Baden-Baden 1995
Nimzo-Indian Defence

1	d4	♘f6
2	c4	e6
3	♘c3	♗b4
4	e3	

This is the Rubinstein Variation. For many years it has been one of the main focal points for practical play and theoretical discussion of the Nimzo-Indian Defence. Considering the relative popularity of

White's numerous fourth move options at the time of this game, 4 e3 seems to be second only to 4 ♕c2, the Classical Variation.

| | 4 | ... | | b6 |
| | 5 | ♘e2 | | ♗a6 *(D)* |

W

6 ♘g3!?

6 a3 ♗xc3+ 7 ♘xc3 d5 is a more common variation. Instead, Vaïsser places his king's knight in a position from where it can support the central thrust e3-e4 and can also easily participate in a kingside attack. Notice too that 6...d5?? would now be a blunder due to 7 ♕a4+.

6 ... 0-0

6...c5 merits attention. It would discourage White from playing 7 e4 on account of 7...cxd4 8 ♕xd4 ♘c6. Also, with the bishop on b4 protected by a pawn on c5, Black could follow up with ...d5 without worrying about ♕a4+. Another typical Nimzo-Indian idea which Black could opt for after 6...c5 is

...♘c6-a5 to apply pressure to the pawn fixed on c4.

	7	e4		♘c6
	8	♗g5		h6
	9	h4!		hxg5
	10	hxg5		g6! *(D)*

10...♘h7? loses quickly to 11 ♕h5.

W

11 e5! ♘h7
12 ♕g4 *(D)*

This position deserves a diagram.

B

Black is faced with the dual threats of 13 ♕h4 and 13 ♕h3. How is he to deal with both of them?

12 ...   ♔g7?

This meets with a stunning refutation. 12...♕xg5? is also bad owing to 13 ♕h3. The correct move is 12...♘xg5!, so that 13 ♕h4 can be met by 13...♘f3+! 14 gxf3 ♕xh4, when Black will have survived the main force of White's attack. Vaïsser might have planned 13 ♘e4!?, intending 13...♘xe4! 14 ♕h3 winning, but 13...♗e7 14 ♘xg5 ♗xg5 15 ♕h3 ♗h4 16 ♕xh4 ♕xh4 17 ♖xh4 may be tenable for Black. 13 f4 f5!! is certainly fine for him.

13 ♘h5+!!   gxh5

13...♔g8 is no better because of 14 ♘f6+ ♘xf6 15 gxf6 and Black is defenceless against 16 ♕h4 and mate on h8.

14 ♕xh5   ♖h8

Alternatively 14...♖e8 15 ♕xh7+ ♔f8 16 ♕h8+ ♔e7 17 ♕f6+ ♔f8 18 ♖h8#.

15 ♕h6+   ♔g8
16 ♗d3   d6

16...♘e7 also loses in view of 17 ♗xh7+ ♖xh7 18 ♕xh7+ ♔f8 19 ♕h6+! ♔e8 20 ♕h8+.

17 ♗xh7+   ♖xh7
18 ♕xh7+   ♔f8
19 g6!   ♕e8 (D)
20 ♕h4!!   1-0

Black is powerless in the face of 21 g7+! ♔xg7 22 ♕h6+ ♔g8 23 ♕h8#. For example, 20...fxg6 21 ♕f6+ ♕f7 22 ♖h8#. .

W

A brilliant display of consistent, relentless, attacking chess by Vaïsser. An even quicker loss which I once heard about for Black in the Nimzo-Indian Defence involved a drunk man picking up his king on the third move and playing the illegal 3...♔b4. White took full advantage of this, and of his opponent's condition, by replying with 4 ♕a4#!

Returning to a sober discussion of *Consistency* again, it should be stressed that consistently following a plan does not mean that one should expect to be able to carry it out free from obstacles and without any resistance from the opponent. For example, if White is castled on the kingside and decides that he wants to advance f2-f4, then it may be necessary to spend a tempo to play ♔h1 to avoid the king being harassed by Black's queen or dark-squared bishop, which might be on the g1 to a7 diagonal. Similarly, if he is castled on the queenside, then White may be forced under some circumstances to use a valuable tempo to play ♔b1, for instance to protect a pawn on a2. Such situations can be found in thousands of games in the Sicilian Defence, to mention just one opening.

The key point here is to make every move really count. Be economical. Do not waste tempi on moves that are unrelated to your main plan, unless you have some other good reason for playing them.

One recurring feature in my own games is that I rarely play moves such as the aforementioned ♔h1 or ♔b1 after castling, except when I consider them to be absolutely required. If there is any way to use the tempo more efficiently to make progress with the main plan, then I always try to find it. Also, do not forget that your king could well be needed in the centre of the board if an endgame is reached, and so I tend not to move my king further away from the centre than necessary in the opening or middlegame.

Consistency applies to all phases of the game, including the later stages. Even in the endgame, your moves should be purposeful. That does not necessarily mean that your plan must always be so obvious that your opponent can see right through it. Sometimes, masking or disguising the plan can pay

dividends. Consider the following hypothetical diagram with Black to play.

The Mask

B

1...c3? 2 ♖cxc3?? ♖c4+ results in mate next move, but 2 ♖exc3 would simply win a pawn and the game for White. However, the idea of ...c3 and ...♖c4# might suggest a plan for Black to attempt to win, without taking unreasonable risks, even if the position is probably objectively drawn with correct play. 1...♖h8 is a purposeful, but well-disguised start. The rook shifts to an opened file and attacks the pawn on h3. From White's point of view, that pawn is already protected, and ...c3 no longer looks like such a dangerous advance with only one enemy rook supporting it. He could easily play 2 ♖g2?, planning the obvious g4-g5, but thereby suddenly allowing Black's plan to work. Black would win by means of **2...c3!! 3 Rxc3** (3 b3 is met by 3...c2) **3...Rxh3!! 4 Rgc2 Rc4+! 5 Rxc4 Rb3#.**

It's time for an example from a real event again. The Latvian grandmaster Alexei Shirov is, at his best, wonderfully imaginative, but his play in the following game at the 1995 Donner Memorial tournament in Holland is very logical and consistent too.

Game 6
V.Salov – A.Shirov
Amsterdam 1995
English Opening

1   c4   e5
2   ♘c3   ♗b4

This is sometimes known as the 'Kramnik-Shirov Counter-Attack', and is the subject of a superb video presented by Grandmaster Stuart Conquest.

3   ♘d5   ♗e7

The Russian grandmaster Vladimir Kramnik, a young contemporary of Shirov, has successfully employed 3...♗c5 on a few occasions.

4   e3

Karpov's interesting idea of 4 d4 d6 5 e4!? ♘f6 6 ♘xe7 ♕xe7 7 f3 tries to keep a grip on the centre, which Black may challenge by means of ...♘h5 and ...f5, for example.

4   ...   ♘f6

5   ♘xe7   ♕xe7
6   ♘e2

Salov may have rejected 6 ♘f3 because of 6...e4, but in any case White is lagging behind in development. That is also true with the Karpov idea mentioned earlier, but then at least White controlled more space and could activate his dark-squared bishop easily.

6   ...   d5
7   cxd5   ♘xd5
8   a3

After 8 ♘c3 ♘xc3, 9 dxc3 e4! is positionally very pleasant for Black, but 9 bxc3 provides White with some dynamic possibilities. He may be able to achieve some activity with a combination of d4 and ♗a3, e.g. 9...e4 10 ♕a4+!? ♘c6 (10...♗d7 11 ♕b3) 11 ♗a3. Of course, Black could avoid this, and simply keep developing, with 8...♗e6.

8   ...   0-0
9   ♘g3   c5!

Black invests one tempo in seizing more space, before resuming with piece development.

10 b3   ♘c6
11 ♗b2   ♗e6
12 ♕c2?

12 ♗b5 was better, with the priority of getting safely castled kingside as soon as possible.

12 ...   Rfd8!

Very precise. Black reserves his queen's rook for going to the c-file, where it will be 'facing' White's queen. Such situations tend to lead naturally to future tactical possibilities.

13 &b5 *(D)*

If 13 &d3, then 13...g6 threatens 14...Ødb4! 15 axb4 Øxb4.

B

13 ... Øa5!!
14 &xe5

14 0-0 Øb6 exposes the weakness of White's b-pawn.

14 ... &d7!
15 &c3

15 &xd7 ♕xe5, attacking the loose rook on a1, shows up another drawback of White's 12th move.

15 ... &xb5
16 &xa5 Øf4

A flashy move, but justified by the situation of White's king, which has no safe haven.

17 &xd8 ♖xd8
18 ♕c3

18 0-0-0 Ød3+ 19 &b1 Øxf2 is horrible for White, as is 18 ♕e4 Ød3+ 19 &e2 (19 &f1 ♕f6 produces a double attack against a1

and f2) 19...♕f6, attacking f2 and also threatening several deadly discovered checks.

18 ... ♕e6
19 f3

19 &d1 Ød3 also subjects White to continuing pressure.

19 ... ♖d3!
20 ♕xc5

Black wins quickly after 20 ♕c2 Øxg2+ 21 &f2 Øxe3! 22 dxe3 ♕xe3+ 23 &g2 ♖d2+.

20 ... Øxg2+
21 &d1 Øxe3+
22 &c1 *(D)*

B

22 ... b6!!
23 ♕c7

23 ♕xb5 loses to 23...♕c8+.

23 ... ♖d6!

Threatening 24...♖c6+.

24 ♕b8+ &e8
25 Øe4!

25 dxe3? ♕xe3+ 26 &b2 ♖d2+ is much worse, mating White in two more moves, as is 25 ♖b1?

♖c6+ 26 ♔b2 ♖c2+ 27 ♔a1 ♕f6+, also mating quickly.

25	...	♖c6+
26	♘c3	♘d5!
27	♖a2!	♖c8!

This will free Black's queen from having to defend the bishop on the back rank so that it may participate in the attack on White's king.

28 ♕g3?

Salov has defended a very difficult position really well so far, but now, perhaps in time-trouble, he goes astray. A better chance is 28 ♕xa7, so that the pawn on a3 will be protected in lines such as 28...♘xc3 29 dxc3 ♕xb3 30 ♖b2 (30 ♖c2 ♗a4) 30...♕xc3+ 31 ♔b1. However, Black would still retain a strong attack with 31...♗b5!?, e.g.:

a) 32 ♖xb5? ♕d3+.

b) 32 ♖d1 ♗e2! 33 ♖xe2? ♕b3+.

c) 32 ♖g1 ♗f1!? 33 ♔a1 (or 33 ♖xf1 ♕d3+) 33...♕e1+ 34 ♖b1 (34 ♔a2 ♗c4+) 34...♕e5+ 35 ♖b2 ♖c1+ 36 ♔a2 ♗c4+ 37 ♖b3 ♕a1#.

28	...	♘xc3
29	bxc3	♕xb3
30	♖c2	

30 ♖b2 ♕xc3+ 31 ♔b1 ♕d3+ 32 ♔a2 ♖c3 also wins for Black.

30	...	♗a4!
31	♕f2	

31 ♖b2 ♕xa3 32 ♔b1 ♗d7 33 ♖a2 (33 ♕f4 g6) 33...♗f5+ 34 ♔a1 ♕xc3+ 35 ♖b2 ♕a3+ 36 ♖a2 ♖c1+ 37 ♖xc1 ♕xc1#.

| 31 | ... | ♕xa3+ |

32 ♔b1

32 ♖b2 ♕a1+ is an even quicker way for White to capitulate.

32	...	♗xc2+
33	♕xc2	♖xc3 *(D)*

W

0-1

White did not wait to see 34 ♕a2 ♕b4+ 35 ♔a1 ♖a3.

I remember thoroughly enjoying watching on television the 1995 World Men's 800 metres final in Sweden. The TV commentator was impressed, as I was too, by the obvious relaxation and happiness in the face of the winner even **before** the race had begun. The triumphant athlete was the Kenyan-born Wilson Kipketer, who was now representing Denmark. One important lesson which can be learned from his fine example is that, in any sport, including chess, our performances will be enhanced if we relax and *enjoy* the game. Do not fear the opponent or the result. Anyone can be beaten, but, on occasions when you are the one on the losing end, valuable experiences will be there waiting to be learned.

Personally, I always remind myself before any game to be at peace and enjoy whatever will be. After a while that peaceful state can become a permanent part of you. I have found it to be of great value not only in chess but in life in general. However, in the specific context of a chess struggle, the ability to enjoy the game does not mean that one is being too timid or not trying hard enough to win. On the contrary, it can make you so calm that you cope with any situation as well as possible instead of getting flustered under pressure. There is a wonderful prayer which has been a constant help to me daily for many years. The words are:

'Please God,
grant me the serenity to accept the things I cannot change,
courage to change the things I can,
and wisdom to know the difference'.

Of course, one should not necessarily expect instant success from prayer, but, personally speaking, I have always found that the eventual results will be for the best, and not only on the chess-board.

Each player must find his own method of approaching chess, but

another factor which can help to improve your performance is to play openings which you really enjoy. Do not feel that you must always adhere to the most popular main lines; rather play in any reasonable way which suits your style. The following nice attacking win by Danish international master Klaus Berg is a good example.

Game 7
K.Berg – B.Jacobsen
Nørresundby Bank Open 1995
Queen's Indian Defence

1	d4	♘f6
2	♘f3	e6
3	e3	b6
4	♗d3	♗b7
5	0-0	c5
6	c4	

White has adopted a rare move-order. Indeed, the earlier 3 e3, instead of the far more common 3 c4, is usually an indication that White intends to employ the Colle System. In that case, White would normally play most of the nine moves d4, ♘f3, e3, ♗d3, 0-0, ♘bd2, ♖e1, c3 and e4 in some order. For that reason, the Colle is relatively easy to learn. In connection with it, I once heard a very amusing story about a Dutch team which was missing one player. The problem was solved by finding a man with a Russian name, which made it seem plausible to the opposing team that he might be a strong chess player. In fact, this complete beginner was quickly taught to memorise the nine afore-mentioned standard Colle moves and was then placed in the Dutch team ... playing White on board one! The new hero effortlessly trotted out the moves he had learned, then offered a draw. His IM adversary readily accepted!

6 ... ♗e7

A logical alternative is 6...g6 to lessen the effect of White's bishop on the b1 to h7 diagonal. A game Berg Hansen-Motwani, Gausdal 1992, continued 7 ♘c3 ♗g7 8 d5 exd5 9 cxd5 ♘xd5 10 ♘xd5 ♗xd5 11 ♗xg6 hxg6 12 ♕xd5 ♘c6. Black followed up by developing his queen, castling queenside, and gaining a tempo by attacking the white queen with ...♖h5. The result was a quick 0-1. The Colle and related systems are potentially very dangerous, but I have found that ...g6 can be a good antidote. So far, I have never lost when using such a set-up as Black against the Colle.

7 ♘c3 cxd4

7...0-0 8 d5 exd5 9 cxd5 ♘xd5 10 ♘xd5 ♗xd5 11 ♗xh7+ ♔xh7 12 ♕xd5 ♘c6 13 ♖d1 favours White. As a late addition, I was interested to see that, in a 1996 match between teams from Slovakia and Croatia, Grandmaster Jan Plachetka fell into this variation as Black against Grandmaster Goran Dizdar. Dizdar's 13 ♗d2 was also very

strong for White. After 13...♗f6 14 ♗c3!, 14...♗xc3 would have lost quickly to 15 ♕h5+! ♔g8 16 ♘g5.

8 exd4 d5
9 cxd5 ♘xd5
10 ♘e5!

Threatening 11 ♗b5+, and also clearing a way for White's queen to get to an attacking position on g4 or h5.

10 ... 0-0
11 ♕g4 (D)

B

11 ... ♘f6

11...f5 is positionally inadvisable, as it leaves the e-pawn unprotected. 12 ♕e2 is a strong response. However, even some natural-looking developing moves can lead to disaster for Black after 11 ♕g4. For example, 11...♘d7 or 11...♘c6 both lose material to 12 ♗h6 ♗f6 13 ♕e4!.

12 ♕h4 ♘bd7

12...♘e4 13 ♕h3!? ♕xd4 14 ♗f4 gives White a dangerous initiative for the sacrificed pawn and threatens to win a piece with 15 ♗xe4 ♗xe4 16 ♖fd1 ♕b4 17 a3.

13 ♖d1!

This nullifies Black's threat of 13...♘xe5 14 dxe5 ♕xd3, since the bishop on d3 is now protected. Also, White knows that tactical possibilities could easily develop in his favour due to the rook 'facing' Black's queen on the d-file.

13 ...   ♘e4
14 ♕h3   ♘df6
15 d5!!   ♘xc3

Black loses material in the line 15...exd5? 16 ♗xe4.

16 bxc3   ♗xd5

The lines 16...♘xd5?? 17 ♕xh7# or 16...♕xd5 17 ♗xh7+ ♘xh7 18 ♖xd5 are plainly bad for Black. The last way of capturing the d-pawn, namely 16...exd5, meets the beautiful refutation 17 ♘d7!!, intending 17...♕xd7 18 ♗xh7+ ♔h8 (18...♘xh7 19 ♕xd7) 19 ♗f5+ or 17...♖e8 18 ♘xf6+ ♗xf6 19 ♕xh7+ ♔f8 20 ♗a3+ followed shortly by ♕h8#. Another line showing the force of most of White's pieces directed towards Black's kingside is 16...♕c7 17 ♗f4 ♗d6 18 ♘g4!!. 16...♕c8 17 ♗g5 exd5 (17...g6 18 ♕h4! or 17...h6 18 ♗xh6!, similar to the actual game continuation) 18 ♗f5! ♕c7 19 ♗xf6 is also terrible for Black.

17 ♗g5!

Note that 17 c4? is a mistake in view of 17...♗e4!.

17 ...   h6 *(D)*

17...g6 18 c4? ♕c7!, intending 19 ♗f4 ♗d6!, is unclear, but, instead of the 'obvious' 18 c4?, White has the powerful 18 ♕h4!. The threats then include 19 c4 and 19 ♘g4.

W

18 ♗xh6!   gxh6
19 ♕xh6   ♕b8

19...♖e8 20 ♗g6! ♖f8 21 ♖d3 is hopeless for Black. 19...♕c7 is a little more tenacious. For example, 20 ♘g4 ♘e4 keeps Black hanging on. However, the 'zigzag' manoeuvre 20 ♕g5+ ♔h8 21 ♕h4+ ♔g7 22 ♕g3+ ♔h8 23 ♘g6+ fxg6 24 ♕xc7 is sufficient to give White a decisive material advantage. Nevertheless, after 19...♕c7, the strongest continuation may be 20 ♖e1! with the idea 20...♕xc3 21 ♖ad1 intending 22 ♖e3.

20 ♘d7!   1-0

Black decides not to try for 20...♕xh2+ 21 ♔xh2?? ♘g4+. 21 ♕xh2 is better!

Chess books often give general guidelines such as advising a player against moving his queen too early, or leaving his king uncastled for long beyond the opening phase, or accepting doubled pawns if these situations can be avoided. These and many other soundly based principles should be borne in mind. However, I recall a lovely quotation from the deep-thinking grandmaster Mihai Suba. He said 'In chess, the golden rule is that there are no golden rules'. My opinion is that some kind of balance should be found. A player may *enjoy* chess more if he does not let himself be bound by too many restrictions, but particular 'rules' have evolved through the experiences of many people before us. Some rules can be ignored in particular circumstances, but, as far as possible, it is good to know when and why such cases apply.

In the next encounter, Grandmaster Dr John Nunn plays a lot of moves which are far from being routine or stereotyped. The end result is a very artistic and pleasing game.

Game 8
J.Nunn – M.de Jong
Leeuwarden 1995
French Defence

1	e4	e6
2	d4	d5

3	♘c3	♝b4
4	e5	♘e7

In my opinion, this move is slightly more flexible than 4...c5. Both moves are very common in the Winawer Variation, characterised by 3...♝b4. After White's 4 e5, the most natural square for Black's king's knight is e7. Therefore it makes sense to activate it there early on, while retaining the option of playing ...c5 or of keeping the pawn on c7 if desired. For example, if 4...♘e7 5 ♝d2!?, then 5...c5 6 ♘b5 ♝xd2+ 7 ♕xd2 0-0 8 c3 (8 dxc5 ♘d7) may be a little better for White. If Black wishes to avoid that line, in which the square d6 in his camp is particularly sensitive, then after 4...♘e7 5 ♝d2 he may opt for 5...b6.

5	a3	♝xc3+
6	bxc3	*(D)*

B

This position, which occurs very often in practice, certainly offers prospects for both sides. Black has the neater pawn structure, but, with his king's bishop gone, he is vulnerable on the dark squares. White may attempt to exploit that latter feature using his own dark-squared bishop.

6 ... b6

6...c5 is the 'main line', but 6...b6 is also quite logical. The point is that, in the French Defence, Black's light-squared bishop often has to struggle for scope since it is restricted by Black having central pawns on the light squares e6 and d5. Therefore a typical strategy is to exchange the so-called 'bad bishop' by ...b6 and ...♗a6.

7 ♕g4

White's queen develops early, but to an aggressive position.

7 ... ♘g6

7...♘f5 8 ♗d3 h5 9 ♕f4 ♕h4 10 ♕xh4 ♘xh4 11 ♗g5!, intending 11...♘xg2+ 12 ♔f1, is pleasant for White.

8 h4 h5
9 ♕d1!

9 ♕g3 may seem more natural at first sight, but White's h-pawn does not need that extra protection, since 9 ♕d1 ♘xh4 10 g3 is good for White. Another feature of 9 ♕d1 is that Black's h-pawn can turn out to be weak if attacked by ♗e2 or ♘e2 and ♘g3.

9 ... ♗a6
10 ♗xa6 ♘xa6
11 ♗g5 f6

Black chose the more solid alternative 11...♕d7 in Khalifman-Ehlvest, Rakvere 1993. That game continued 12 ♘e2 ♘b8 13 ♘g3 ♕c6 14 ♕f3?! ♘d7 15 ♗d2 (15 ♘xh5 ♖xh5! 16 ♕xh5 ♕xc3+ is too dangerous for White; 15 0-0 f6! 16 exf6 gxf6 17 ♗xf6? {if 17 ♗d2, then 17...♘xh4 demonstrates the weakness of White's h-pawn} 17...♖f8 18 ♘xh5 ♘xf6 19 ♘xf6+ ♔e7 20 ♘xd5+ ♕xd5 also favours Black: White has three extra kingside pawns, but his crippled queenside structure means that they are insufficient compensation to match Black's knight) 15...♕a4 16 ♘xh5 ♖h7 17 ♖c1 c5! with lots of activity and a fine position for Black. Subjecting that grandmaster clash to even closer scrutiny, it becomes clearer that White spent a lot of valuable time passively defending his pawn on c3 because otherwise it might have been captured by Black's queen **with check**. This provides the key to a big improvement for White: 13 0-0!, intending 13...♕c6 14 ♘g3! and then either 14...♘d7 15 ♘xh5 or 14...♕xc3 15 ♘xh5 with attacking possibilities.

12 ♕d3! ♔f7
13 ♖h3!!

White declines to capture the *en prise* knight on a6, or to move his bishop, which is also under attack. Instead, he finds a brilliant and unusual move, threatening to win with 14 exf6 gxf6 15 ♖f3!.

| 13 | ... | ♛c8 |

13...fxg5 14 ♖f3+ ♘f4 15 hxg5 ♛xg5 16 ♘h3! is clearly winning for White.

14	exf6	gxf6
15	♖f3	f5
16	♖g3	c6
17	♘f3	♘c7 *(D)*

W

18 ♗f4!!

John Nunn must have enjoyed playing this! Again it is brilliant, but also extremely logical. Black was ready to challenge White's queen with 18...♛a6, but now that would leave his knight *en prise* on c7. 18 ♗f4 also intensifies White's control of the e5-square and uncovers possibilities for his rook on the g-file or for his knight to leap into g5. A wonderfully economical move!

18	...	♘xf4
19	♘e5+	♚e8
20	♛f3	♘b5

Black could win an insignificant pawn by 20...♘xg2+, but then 21 ♛xg2 would enable White to infiltrate along the g-file even more easily than in the game.

21	♛xf4	♛c7
22	♖g6	♛d6
23	♛g5	♖f8
24	♖g7	1-0

Black is defenceless against White's threats, which include 25 ♛xh5+ ♚d8 26 ♘f7+. To quote my friend John Henderson: 'Even Perry Mason wouldn't defend this position'.

Well, I hope you have enjoyed the first stage of our chess adventure and are eager to move into the second phase. Still, patience is an excellent quality to cultivate. It can help us to notice and take in more as we continue the journey. It is natural that **after chapter one, you want to collect chess points faster.** However, one should not be in a hurry. Rearrange the 48 letters in bold to produce the following calm reminder. **Chapter One, 'Let's F.A.C.E. It', was only the start of our concepts.** It is now time to encounter the next H.O.T. idea.

2 A Good Way T.O. D.O. It

Your experience of the previous chapter tells you that T.O.D.O. is a mnemonic, but what does T.O.D.O. represent, and when and how is it useful? Well, T.O.D.O. is my personal favourite of the many concepts in H.O.T. Chess. The four letters stand for the words *Tenacious, Objective, Dangerous, Original.* These are characteristics which I always try to strengthen in my own chess style. Prior to playing any game, I also try to assess which of the four qualities my opponent possesses, and to what degree.

Before I explain how I have made effective use of T.O.D.O., I will elaborate on the meanings of our four new key words in a chess context. By the word *Tenacious,* I mean how firmly a player can hold fast, sticking to the tough struggle in progress. Tenacity is a very important quality for a chess player to develop. For example, it may mean stubbornly defending a difficult position for a long time, but eventually being rewarded with a half point, or sometimes more, if you can wear the opponent down. Conversely, you may be sitting with an advantageous position, but meeting resistance from your opponent.

Then you need to be tenacious in order to nurture your advantage patiently, keep your opponent under pressure, and finally break down his resistance. Consider the following practical example from the game Motwani-Granda at the 1988 Thessaloniki Olympiad.

Needing a Miracle

W

The fact that it is White to play does not seem to help much, since after 1 ♔c5 ♖c3+ 2 ♔d4 ♖c4+, Black will still capture the pawn on b4. I could not save the pawn, but I did save the game by tenaciously hanging on and finding 1 ♖h4!!. Black agreed to a draw after 1...♖xb4+ 2 ♔c5! because 2...♖xh4 results in stalemate. Alternatively, 2...♖c4+ 3 ♖xc4 bxc4 4 ♔xc4 or 2...♖b1 3 ♖h7+ ♔b8 4 ♔xc6 both lead to clearly drawn positions. Also, Black can make no serious progress in the lines 1 ♖h4 ♔b6 2 ♔e5 c5 3 ♖h6+ and 4 bxc5 or 2...♖c3 3 ♖g4 ♖c4 4 ♖xc4 bxc4 5 ♔d4 ♔b5 6 ♔c3 c5 7 bxc5, once again reaching a clear draw. Tenacity earned me a very precious half-point against the top Peruvian grandmaster in that encounter, and I went on to achieve my second grandmaster norm later in the Olympiad.

The second new key word is *Objective*. By this I mean the ability of a player to assess positions accurately. This quality of being able to see things the way they really are is extremely valuable to a person, and not only in chess. It can be very tempting to view things the way one wants them to be, instead of seeing them the way they actually are.

Once again, let us consider an example, this time a hypothetical position with White to play.

More Hurry, Fewer Points

Personally speaking, the first move I find myself looking at is the capture 1 dxc6. Indeed, 1...♗xc6 2 ♘d5!? ♗xd5 (or 2...exd5 3 exd5+ is winning for White) 3 exd5 is

W

strong for White. You may have already noticed that 1 ♘e2 traps the black queen, but a calm, objective player will not play that move instantly. He would not assume that 1 ♘e2 wins without at least considering Black's possible responses. Objectivity would save White from disaster, because consideration of Black's options after 1 ♘e2? should reveal that it loses to 1...♕xf3! 2 gxf3 exd5 3 exd5 ♗xh3#. This line is not so surprising since 1 ♘e2? 'boxes in' White's king and seals its fate. However, the idea of trapping Black's queen is not wrong, but it needs to be prepared by a preliminary move such as 1 ♕d3!?, threatening 2 ♘e2 as well as 2 g3 and also creating problems for Black on the d-file. Notice that 1 ♕d3 exd5 2 ♘e2! would win almost instantly for White: 2...♕xe4 3 ♘c3 or 2...dxe4 3 ♘xf4. Black is forced to move his dark-squared bishop after 1 ♕d3.

Dangerous is the third new key word. Great attacking players such as Mikhail Tal come to mind. It can be extremely difficult to cope with an opponent who attacks with such energy as the 'Magician from Riga' did. However, we can learn from his, and other, examples. The winners of all the games which featured in chapter one played in a dangerous, attacking style and only one of their opponents lasted more than 30 moves.

Original comes from the last letter of T.O.D.O. It is obviously a great asset if a player can produce his own ideas, particularly in the opening, instead of always relying on documented theory, which the opponent may have studied too. Players are often concerned with knowing about the latest published 'novelties'. Such moves are not always strictly original, as they may have been played before in games which perhaps never reached the attention of the chess media. However, a player can be original in his own way just by, say, choosing the Caro-Kann Defence when playing an opponent against whom he has always previously used the Sicilian Defence. That is originality of a kind, and it is sure to surprise the opponent. Originality can nullify your opponent's opening preparation and force him to go down a route he did not expect. When trying to inject some originality into

certain games, care must be taken not to get into territory which is unfamiliar to oneself. Personally, I often select openings which are known to me and to theory but which are rarely seen in practice. So it is likely that the opponents will have little or no experience of facing such systems. Consequently, they then find themselves in original and difficult situations.

After 1 e4 e6, Chigorin's 2 ♕e2!? is a good example. Although 2 ♕e2 is mentioned in many books, it tends to be given very little attention in comparison to 2 d4, yet the early queen move is not illogical. The point is that most people who adopt the French Defence expect to play 2...d5, but 2 ♕e2 is designed to make that more difficult for Black. A tremendously talented and creative Scot, International Master Roddy McKay, put his opponent, rated around 2100 at that time, in an original situation in the following miniature gem.

Game 9
R.McKay – I.Lamont
Glasgow 1978
French Defence

1	e4	e6
2	♕e2!?	d5?

2...c5 or 2...♗e7 are examples of sounder moves. White can develop his kingside forces with g3, ♗g2, ♘f3 and 0-0, perhaps preceded by f4. Exponents of the Closed Sicilian or the King's Indian Attack will be especially familiar with such configurations.

3	exd5	♕xd5
4	♘c3	♕d8
5	♘f3	c5 (D)

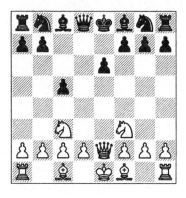

W

6 d4!

White energetically opens up more lines to expose Black's lack of development.

| 6 | ... | cxd4 |
| 7 | ♘b5 | ♘c6 |

7...♗b4+ 8 c3 dxc3 9 bxc3 ♗a5 (9...♗c5 10 ♕e5!) 10 ♗a3! is even more difficult for Black than the game continuation.

| 8 | ♗f4 | ♗b4+ |
| 9 | c3! | |

White gambits a pawn, but gains a valuable tempo by attacking the bishop on b4.

9	...	dxc3
10	bxc3	♗a5
11	♖d1	♕f6

12 ♕d2! ♕g6

12...♘ge7 loses by force to 13 ♗g5 ♕g6 (13...♕f5 14 ♘d6+) 14 ♘d6+ ♔f8 15 ♘h4! ♕h5 16 ♗e2. The same moves are sufficient for White to win after 12...a6. 12...h6 is not much of an improvement for Black due to 13 ♗c7 (threatening 14 ♗xa5 ♘xa5 15 ♘c7+) 13...a6 14 ♘d6+ ♔f8 15 ♘e4 ♕g6 (15...♕e7 16 ♗d6) 16 ♕d6+ ♔e8 (16...♘ge7 17 ♕d8+! ♘xd8 18 ♖xd8#) 17 ♗d3 ♕xg2 18 ♔e2 and Black is hopelessly under-developed. A typical conclusion is 18...♘ge7 19 ♗xa5 ♘xa5 20 ♗b5+! and soon ♕d8#.

13 ♗c7! (D)

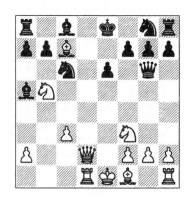

B

13	...	a6
14	♘d6+	♔f8
15	♗xa5	♘xa5
16	♘f5!	

White chooses the most elegant way to win, but 16 ♘xc8 ♖xc8 17 ♕d6+ ♘e7 (17...♔e8 18 ♕d7+) 18 ♕d8+! would also suffice.

16 ...　　　　♕f6

Black also loses after 16...♗d7
17 ♕d6+ or 16...f6 17 ♕d6+ ♔e8
(17...♔f7 18 ♕c7+) 18 ♕d8+ ♔f7
19 ♘d6#.

17　♕d8+　　　♕xd8
18　♖xd8#

So far, the key words *Tenacious,
Objective, Dangerous, Original*
have been described individually.
In practice, I consider all the four
elements of T.O.D.O. when trying
to evaluate my opponents before
each game. Let us assume, for the
moment, that I know my prospec-
tive opponent, or have access to information about his style of play,
such as some published games.
Then, from my knowledge of the
opponent, I make a personal assessment about which parts of
T.O.D.O. are relatively strong or
weak in his style. For example, the
great Mikhail Tal was an extremely
dangerous and original player. In
fact, he was a very powerful all-
round player, but, in my opinion,
the D.O. parts were even stronger
in his style than the T.O. parts of
T.O.D.O. Therefore, if I were about
to play an opponent such as Tal, I
would make a conscious decision
to aim to play particularly Tenaciously and Objectively. In other
words, I would attempt to steer the
game into types of positions where
my opponent will feel least 'at
home'.

Actually, I try not to neglect any
parts of T.O.D.O., but I have found
that if I can identify the relative
weaknesses in my opponent's style
then I can start by choosing an
opening which I think will provide
me with good prospects of expos-
ing his weaknesses later in the
game.

If I know little about my opponent, then I just try to play in a
good, all-round, way. Of course,
you should always play in a style
which **you** feel comfortable with.
However, if you can be a bit flexible in your opening repertoire,
then, in my opinion, you will have
much better chances of directing
games into channels where your
opponents will have difficulties.

There is another interesting way
of trying to find out something
about an opponent's style: from the
person's face! I am being perfectly
serious when I say that. It is not for
any of us to start judging other people, but, personally speaking, the
early impressions which I normally get from a face whenever I
encounter someone for the first
time are usually confirmed as I get
to know the person more. So in
practice, if I am facing a new opponent, I find that I can often make a
good guess from his or her type of
face about which qualities he or
she possesses. Please do not start
staring at all of your opponents,
but, if discreet use of my idea

works for you, then why not consider it!? As a late note, I will mention that I had never met, or seen any previous games of Juan de Roda before my encounter with him in game 35. After a few minutes, I developed the impression that he was more tenacious and objective than dangerous or original. When the game was over, Juan and one of his friends enquired about this book, which they had heard I was writing. I explained briefly about my favourite T.O.D.O. concept. They then asked if I had managed to form any opinion about Juan in relation to T.O.D.O. The views I gave really surprised them. 'That is a very accurate assessment, particularly after just one game' was the reaction of Juan's Dutch friend. In fact, Juan's face had told me as much about him as his moves did. Still, I must emphasise that I am not in favour of judging people, and especially not by appearances. What I am saying is that if one gains an impression about a person, and if one can then make use of that over the chessboard, then I see no wrong in that.

It is time for more examples of T.O.D.O. in practice. I have great respect for English grandmaster William Watson as a friend and as a chess player. He is particularly strong in the D.O. elements of T.O.D.O. So, when I faced the 1994 British Champion in a British Club Team Championship match, I endeavoured to play with particular emphasis on the T.O. parts.

Game 10
W. Watson – P. Motwani
Darlington 1995
Reversed Pirc

1 g3

There are some subtle differences between this move and 1 ♘f3. For example, 1 g3 d5 2 ♗g2 c5 3 f4!? is possible, like playing a Leningrad Dutch system with an extra tempo. Note that, in that variation, 2 f4 could be answered aggressively by 2...h5!? 3 ♘f3 h4 4 ♘xh4 ♖xh4 5 gxh4 e5, with a dangerous initiative for the sacrificed exchange.

1 ...   e5
2 ♗g2

During 1990, I had a long conversation with the deep-thinking grandmaster Mihai Suba, including discussion of this opening. He felt strongly that White should play 2 c4 instead of allowing Black to establish two pawns in the centre so easily with 2...d5. However, as grandmasters like Azmaiparashvili and Chernin have demonstrated frequently, the Modern Defence is playable, so, when White employs it with an extra tempo, it should not be taken lightly.

2 ...   d5
3 d3   ♗e6 *(D)*

W

Recommended by Suba. Black develops his light-squared bishop to the best square while remaining flexible with the rest of his army.

4 ♘f3

4 c4 is comfortably answered by 4...c6.

4 ... f6
5 c3 ♕d7!

So that 6 ♕b3 can be met by 6...c6 or 6...c5.

6 ♘bd2 ♘h6
7 e4

Four months later, McNab-Mannion, Grangemouth 1995, deviated with 7 0-0. The game continued 7...♘c6 8 b4 a6 9 ♘b3 ♘f7 10 ♗e3 ♗h3 11 a4 ♗e7 12 ♘c5 ♗xc5 13 bxc5 0-0 14 ♖b1 ♖ab8 15 ♖b2 ♗xg2 16 ♔xg2 f5 17 ♕b1 ♘fd8! 18 ♗d2 ♘e6! 19 ♖xb7 ♖xb7 20 ♕xb7 ♘xc5 (20...♖b8? 21 ♘xe5!) 21 ♕b1 ♘xa4 22 ♕a2 ♘b6 23 ♕xa6 e4 24 ♘g1 (24 ♘d4 ♖a8 25 ♕b7? ♘d8 and Black wins, but even 25 ♕b5 ♘xd4 26 ♕xd7 ♘xd7

27 cxd4 ♖a2 is uncomfortable for White) 24...♘e5 25 ♗f4 ♘g6 26 ♕a2 ♘xf4+ 27 gxf4 ♕c6!, and Black stood better.

7 ... ♘f7
8 0-0 ♗e7
9 ♘h4

An alternative is 9 d4 ♘c6, and Black should have no serious problems, since he is well-developed with a harmonious position.

9 ... g6
10 ♘b3

Realising that 10 f4 exf4 11 gxf4 dxe4 12 dxe4 ♘c6 leaves Black with excellent piece play and the safer king, White changes plan.

10 ... ♘c6
11 ♗e3 0-0-0 *(D)*

W

White's last move might have discouraged me from 'castling long' if I had started to worry about the pawn on a7. However, objectively White has no serious threats, and therefore I tenaciously stuck to my previous castling intentions, and to my overall 'T.O. game-plan'.

12 ♘c5?!

Missing a tactical point. 12 ♕e2 was better.

12	...	♗xc5
13	♗xc5	dxe4
14	♗xe4 *(D)*	

The point is that after 14 dxe4 ♕xd1 15 ♖fxd1 ♖xd1+ 16 ♖xd1, Black can take the a-pawn safely.

B

14	...	g5!
15	♘g2	f5
16	♗f3	g4
17	♗e2	♘g5

White's position is suddenly critical, having lost three tempi in being pushed back on moves 15-17.

18 ♕a4 ♗d5!

Threatening 19...♗xg2 20 ♔xg2 ♕d5+.

19 ♗xa7?

This loses by force, but White was under extreme pressure. However, 19 b4 b6 20 ♗e3 f4! 21 gxf4 ♘h3+ 22 ♔h1 exf4 23 b5 f3! is also hopeless for White.

| 19 | ... | ♘xa7 |
| 20 | ♕xa7 *(D)* | |

B

| 20 | ... | ♕c6! |
| | **0-1** | |

White resigned, since his knight cannot be satisfactorily shielded or defended, and moving it to e3, e1 or h4 would allow 21...♘h3#.

The top Norwegian grandmaster, Simen Agdestein, is also a renowned footballer. I do not know much about his playing style on the pitch, but I feel that he is especially strong in both the Objective and Original departments of T.O.D.O. on the chess-board. So, without neglecting those areas myself, I decided to attempt to be particularly Tenacious and Dangerous when facing him.

Before we study in detail one of my typically tough battles with

Simen Agdestein, you may be wondering precisely how I arrive at my pre-game assessment of a player's style. Well, it is based mainly on what I know from previous encounters with the player, or from some of his published games. You can then glean clues about his style from the types of openings he favours, and how he handles the positions resulting from them. In the specific case of Simen Agdestein, against 1 e4 he often chooses Alekhine's Defence 1...♘f6, or the unusual variation 1...e5 2 ♘f3 ♘c6 3 ♗b5 a6 4 ♗a4 b5 5 ♗b3 ♘a5!? in response to the Ruy Lopez. This begins to paint a picture of someone who is quite an original thinker and who prefers to avoid the most popular, heavily analysed main lines. Also, delving a bit deeper and playing through even just a few of his games, I gained the strong impression that Agdestein is not easily bluffed. In other words, he is very objective, and in order to cause him any real difficulties my moves would have to be truly dangerous, not just superficially so. I knew this too from an earlier duel in which he had reacted in a very cool, impressive manner to a theoretical novelty of mine. However, I also noticed that when his opponents did manage to generate genuinely dangerous threats, then he sometimes 'caved in' quickly. This perhaps indicated

a slight lack of tenacity when confronted with real danger.

All this may sound a little long-winded, but I have found T.O.D.O. extremely helpful before clashes in forming 'game-plans'. It is reassuring to have such a plan, and normally it does not take me long to decide on the approach I am going to use. In any case, my results when using T.O.D.O. have been very encouraging.

It is time for the 'kick-off' of the next game.

Game 11
S.Agdestein – P.Motwani
Isle of Lewis 1995
Nimzo-Indian Defence

1	d4	♘f6
2	c4	e6
3	♘c3	♗b4
4	♕c2	d5

This was my first time playing 4...d5 against the Classical variation 4 ♕c2. Previously I had had some success with 4...♘c6 and 4...c5, the latter choice being much more of a 'main' line. After **4...c5**, the game G.Flear-Motwani, Isle of Man 1992, continued **5 dxc5 0-0 6 a3 ♗xc5 7 ♘f3** (7 ♗g5? ♗xf2+!) **7...♘c6 8 ♗g5 b6 9 ♖d1 ♗e7 10 e3 ♗b7 11 ♗e2 ♖c8 12 ♕a4?!** (12 0-0 ♘a5 13 ♘d2 is safer) **12...♘a5! 13 ♘e5** (13 ♗xf6 ♗xf6 14 ♖xd7 ♗xc3+ 15 bxc3 ♕f6 is excellent for Black) **13...♕c7! 14**

♘xd7? ♗c6 15 ♘b5 ♗xd7 16 b4
♘xc4 17 ♗xf6 ♗xf6 18 ♗xc4
♗c3+! and **White resigned**.

5 cxd5   ♕xd5 *(D)*

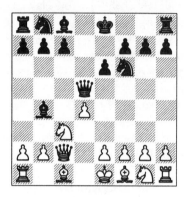

W

6 a3

After 6 ♘f3, 6...♕f5!? is an idea
of Ukrainian grandmaster Oleg Romanishin, a highly creative player.
Then 7 ♕xf5 exf5 gives Black a
half-open e-file to use, and, in particular, makes it difficult for White
to achieve the push e2-e4. The latter point is one of Black's principal
objectives in the Nimzo-Indian
Defence, so he is happy to accept
doubled f-pawns. A different route
was taken in the game Kasparov-
Anand, New York World Championship (2) 1995. That clash went 6
e3 c5 7 ♗d2 ♗xc3 8 ♗xc3 cxd4 9
♗xd4 ♘c6. Then 10 ♗xf6 was a
novelty, but it contributed to a quiet
draw in which there were multiple
exchanges of pieces.

6 ...   ♗xc3+

7 bxc3

7 ♕xc3 ♘c6 8 e3 e5 or 8 ♘f3
♘e4 provides Black with active
piece play.

7 ...   c5
8 e3

Ideally, White would like to play
f3 then e4, so, instead of 8 e3, 8
♗b2!? merits attention.

8 ...   0-0
9 ♗b2   ♘bd7
10 f3!   ♘b6
11 c4   ♕c6
12 ♖c1!

Supporting his c-pawn and making ♗a1 possible in reply to ...♘a4.

12 ...   ♗d7
13 ♗d3   ♖ac8
14 ♘h3   ♖c7

14...♕a4 is also reasonable.

15 ♔f2!?

Castling is more obvious, but
White wants to have the pawn on
e3 protected. This is important in
many lines involving dxc5 when
Black recaptures with ...♕xc5.

15 ...   ♖fc8 *(D)*
16 ♕b1

A very sharp alternative is 16
e4!? cxd4 17 e5 ♘fd5! 18 ♗xh7+
♔f8, when the situation is rather
unclear. Note that 18...♔h8 is inferior in view of 19 ♕e4, threatening
20 cxd5 or 20 ♕h4.

16 ...   ♕d6
17 ♖hd1   ♗a4
18 dxc5   ♕xc5
19 ♗xf6?! gxf6

19...♗xd1? 20 ♗d4.

W

20	♗xh7+	♔g7
21	♖d4	f5

I had tenaciously tried to maintain a sound position, but with a lot of tactics involved too. Now the black king has lost some of its pawn-cover protection, but White is in danger of losing his bishop.

| 22 | ♘g5 | ♖d7! *(D)* |

W

| 23 | ♕a1 | e5 |

After 23...♖xd4 24 exd4 ♕e7 25 d5+, 25...♕f6! 26 dxe6 ♕xa1 27

♖xa1 f6! favours Black, and is superior to 25...f6 26 ♘xe6+ ♔xh7 27 ♕b1!, which allows White dangerous play.

24	♗xf5	exd4
25	♗xd7	♗xd7
26	♘e4	♕e5
27	exd4	♕f4
28	d5+	f6
29	♕d4	♕e5

29...♕xc1 30 ♕xf6+ gives White at least a draw.

| 30 | ♕xe5 | fxe5 |

Both players only just manage to reach the time-control within their allotted 90 minutes, and now have a further half-hour each to complete the game.

31	♘d6	♖c7
32	♖b1	

Now 32...♘xd5 no longer works, and, of course, 32...♘xc4? fails to 33 ♘xc4 ♘xc4 34 ♖xb7.

32	...	♔f8!
33	h4	♔e7
34	♘xb7	♖xc4

34...♖xb7 35 c5.

35	d6+	♔f6
36	h5	♖c2+
37	♔g3	♘d5!

While White's knight is virtually out of play, Black's counterpart heads for the kingside with decisive effect.

38	♘d8	♘e3!
39	♖b7 *(D)*	

39 ♖g1 ♘f5+ is also hopeless.

39	...	♖xg2+
40	♔h4	♖h2+

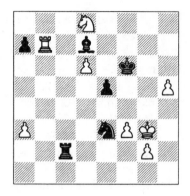

B

41 ♚g3   ♘f1#

A new record was set when eight consecutive draws occurred at the start of the 1995 Intel PCA World Championship in New York. Then, on Monday 25 September, hurricane Anand swept across the queenside of Kasparov's Scheveningen Sicilian in game nine. However, there was no calm after the storm. The next day, the defending champion unleashed a whirlwind attack of devastating force against his challenger's Open Ruy Lopez to level the score at 5-5.

I know that by the time you read this all the games of the match will have been published in hundreds of places around the world. Nevertheless, game ten is so breathtaking that I felt I really wanted to include it in this, my first Batsford book. I analysed the game in detail the day after it was played, and the annotations are entirely my own.

As a school teacher, I am aware of the fact that many people rush for the nearest calculator to work out problems which they are quite capable of solving themselves. In the same way, we can easily become too dependent on computers. Certainly, they are great time-savers and are very worthwhile, or even necessary, in numerous situations. However, there still remains something nice and healthy about a truly human effort. In the following encounter, and indeed throughout the whole book, I have enjoyed trying to discover lots of stimulating variations. Of course they are not completely exhaustive like those of a computer, but the reader will, I think, get a clear, accurate picture of what was going on from the analysis and comments supplied.

Kasparov went into this battle trailing Anand 4-5 in the match. His opponent had been playing confidently and typically quickly in the nine earlier games. So something really dangerous and original was needed to slow down the Indian hurricane. Kasparov was not slow to D.O. it!

Game 12
G.Kasparov – V.Anand
New York Wch (10) 1995
Ruy Lopez

1   e4   e5
2   ♘f3   ♘c6

3	♗b5	a6
4	♗a4	♘f6
5	0-0	♘xe4
6	d4 *(D)*	

B

This position looks similar, but is quite different in character, to one arising from the Berlin Defence after the moves **1 e4 e5 2 ♘f3 ♘c6 3 ♗b5 ♘f6 4 0-0 ♘xe4 5 d4**. In that case, Black can attack the bishop on b5 by **5...♘d6**. Then the fun line 6 dxe5 ♘xb5 7 a4 d6 8 e6 fxe6 9 axb5 ♘e7 is known to theory, but regarded as a dubious gambit for White. The main road after 5...♘d6 is **6 ♗xc6 dxc6 7 dxe5 ♘f5 8 ♕xd8+ ♔xd8**. This course has the reputation of being very solid for Black. An example of its reliability can be seen in Anand-Motwani, Thessaloniki Olympiad 1988, which continued **9 ♘c3 ♔e8 10 b3 a5 11 ♗b2 h6 12 ♖ad1 ♗e6 13 h3 ♗b4 14 a3 ♗xc3 15 ♗xc3 a4 16 b4 ♖d8 17 ♘d4 ½-½**.

To avoid such rock-solid paths after **1 e4 e5 2 ♘f3 ♘c6 3 ♗b5 ♘f6 4 0-0 ♘xe4**, some players prefer **5 ♖e1** instead of 5 d4. A game Moultrie-Condie I recall from the 1970s continued **5...♘d6 6 ♘xe5 ♘xe5 7 ♖xe5+ ♗e7 8 ♘c3 ♘xb5?** (better is 8...0-0) **9 ♘d5! 0-0 10 ♘xe7+ ♔h8 11 ♕h5!** (threatening 12 ♕xh7+! ♔xh7 13 ♖h5#) **11...g6 12 ♕h6 d6 13 ♖h5!** and **Black resigned**, in view of 13...gxh5 14 ♕f6#.

6	...	b5
7	♗b3	d5
8	dxe5	♗e6
9	♘bd2	♘c5
10	c3	d4 *(D)*

W

11 ♘g5!?

This surprising move was introduced by Anatoly Karpov in his World Championship match against Victor Korchnoi in 1978. Korchnoi responded with the same move as Anand chooses, refusing to capture the knight, in view of 11...♕xg5 12 ♕f3 with huge complications.

11 ... dxc3

11...♗d5!? was uncorked by grandmaster Ivan Sokolov in the game in which he beat Anand with Black at Lyons 1994. Kasparov would have been well aware of that idea before his match against Anand. I wonder if he might have intended 12 ♕h5!?, threatening 13 ♘xf7 or 13 e6. Then 12...♘xb3 13 ♘xb3 dxc3 14 ♖d1 or 14 e6 gives White a dangerous lead in development and a powerful attack in spite of his 'Spanish bishop' having been exchanged off.

12 ♘xe6 fxe6
13 bxc3 ♕d3

Opening the e-file by 13...♘xe5 is probably too risky for Black. Let us consider some possibilities after 14 ♖e1:

a) 14...♗d6? 15 ♖xe5! ♗xe5 16 ♕h5+ is a thematic tactic.

b) 14...♘cd3 15 ♖xe5!! ♘xe5 16 ♕h5+ ♘f7 (16...♘g6 17 ♘f3 threatening 18 ♘e5, 18 ♘g5 and 18 ♗g5 is very strong for White) 17 ♗xe6 ♕f6 (17...g6 18 ♕f3 ♘e5 19 ♕e4 or 18...♘g5 19 ♕c6+ is terrible for Black) 18 ♕d5 ♖d8 19 ♕c6+ ♔e7 20 ♗a3+ ♘d6 21 ♗b3 is a nightmare for Black in which he is faced with ♖e1+, ♘e4 or ♕xc7+ among other threats!

c) 14...♘ed3 15 ♖e3 ♗e7 16 ♕f3! gives White a strong attack, keeping Black's king in the centre.

14 ♗c2! *(D)*

A powerful novelty. After 14 ♘f3 in game six, 14...0-0-0!? was itself an innovation from Anand.

B

14 ... ♕xc3
15 ♘b3! ♘xb3

As a late note, I will mention a game from February 1996 which I spotted later the same month when I had almost finished this book. Khalifman-Hraček, played at the Paul Keres Memorial Tournament in Pärnu, saw the (unsuccessful) attempt **15...♖d8** to improve Black's play. The continuation was **16 ♗d2 ♖xd2** Black dare not expose his uncastled king more on the e-file by making the capture 16...♕xe5, since ♖e1 will gain White a further tempo for his attack. **17 ♘xd2 ♘xe5 18 ♘b3 ♘ed7** 18...♗d6 19 ♖c1 is also very unpleasant for Black. **19 ♘d4!** Preventing the black queen from returning to relative safety on the kingside, where she could have also protected her king. **19...♗d6 20 ♖c1 ♕b2 21 ♗b3 ♘xb3 22 axb3 0-0** 22...e5 23 ♘f5 is unbearable for Black. **23 ♖c2!** Avoiding 23 ♘xe6?? ♕e5. **23...♕a3 24 ♘xe6 ♕xb3** Desperation, but 24...♖c8 25 ♕g4 ♗e5 26 ♘c5 ♘b6 27 ♕e6+ is an even worse nightmare for Black. **25 ♘xf8 ♘xf8 26 ♕b1 ♕xb1 27 ♖xb1 ♘d7 28 ♖d1 ♘c5 29 ♖d5 ♘e4 30 ♖c6 1-0** Black never got a chance to start rolling his extra pawns forward, and now they are ripe for picking by White's rooks.

16 ♗xb3 ♘d4

16...♕xa1 17 ♕f3 ♔d7 18 ♖d1+ or 17...0-0-0 18 ♕xc6 ♕xe5 19 ♕xa6+ ♔d7 (19...♔b8 20 ♗e3 ♗d6 21 ♗a7+ ♔a8 22 ♗d4+ wins for White) 20 ♗f4! (intending 20...♕xf4? 21 ♕xe6#), with ♖d1+ to follow, illustrates the enormous defensive problems which Kasparov posed Anand in this game. The television commentary on BBC2 confirmed my initial view that 17 ♕f3 is the right way to continue after **16...♕xa1**. It was only later that I considered 17...♘d8! 18 ♕xa8 ♕xe5. I now believe that **17 ♕h5+!** is best. Here are some key lines:

a) 17...♔d7 18 ♗xe6+! ♔xe6 19 ♕g4+ ♔f7 20 ♕f3+ ♔g8 21 ♕d5#.

b) If 17...g6 18 ♕f3, then most variations proceed in similar fashion to those resulting from 17 ♕f3.

However, an important difference is that Black is more vulnerable on the a1-h8 diagonal, and after 18...♘d8 White has 19 ♕f6!?. One beautiful finish is 19...♖g8 20 ♗xe6 ♗g7 21 ♗f7+! ♘xf7 22 ♕e6+ ♔f8 23 ♗a3+ winning. 20...♗e7 21 ♗d7+! ♔xd7 22 e6+ ♘xe6 23 ♕xa1, though less clear, is nevertheless better for White.

Still, a good alternative to 19 ♕f6 is 19 ♗f4!? ♕d4 20 ♖d1 ♕a7 21 ♗g5 ♗g7 (21...♗e7 22 ♗xe7 ♔xe7 23 ♕f6+; 21...c5 22 ♗xd8 threatening 23 ♕c6+) 22 ♖xd8+! ♖xd8 23 ♕c6+ ♔f8 (23...♖d7 24 ♕xe6+ ♔f8 25 ♕xd7 also mates quickly) 24 ♗e7+! ♔xe7 25 ♕xe6+ ♔f8 26 ♕f7#. White is two rooks down in the final position!

17 ♕g4! ♕xa1

17...♘xb3 18 ♕xe6+ ♗e7 19 ♗g5! is clearly bad for Black.

18 ♗xe6!

Preventing ...0-0-0 and keeping Black's king in the centre. This is the simple, yet very effective, main theme of White's play. Many of his moves are brilliant, but are also undoubtedly the result of much pre-game preparation, because, even when sacrificing a rook on move 17, Kasparov had only taken about five minutes compared with an hour and ten minutes used by Anand. Note that the line 18 ♗e3? ♘e2+! 19 ♕xe2 ♕xe5 is good for Black.

18 ... ♖d8 (D)

Or:

a) 18...♘xe6 19 ♕xe6+ ♗e7 20 ♗g5 loses quickly for Black.

b) My favourite lines are possible after 18...♕c3. White then has 19 ♗d7+ ♔f7 20 ♗e3! ♗c5 21 e6+ ♔g8 22 ♕e4! (22 e7 g6) 22...c6 23 e7 ♔f7 (23...♘e2+ 24 ♔h1 ♗xe7 25 ♕xe7 h6 26 ♗e6+ ♔h7 27 ♗f5+ ♔g8 28 ♕e6+ ♔f8 29 ♗g6 ♕f6 30 ♗c5+ winning) 24 ♗xd4 ♕xd4 25 ♕e6#. When I first analysed these variations, I considered 22 ♗xd4 instead of 22 ♕e4. I noticed that 22...♗xd4 23 ♕f5 ♗f6 (23...♖f8 24 e7! or 23...h6 24 e7!) 24 ♕d5 c6? (24...g6!) 25 e7+! cxd5 26 ♗e6# and 22...♕xd4 23 ♕f3 ♖f8? 24 e7!! ♖xf3 25 ♗e6+ win nicely. However, during a second analysis session I found the surprising defence 22...♕xd4 23 ♕f3 h6!! 24 ♕xa8+ ♔h7 with ...♖f8 to follow, and a counter-attack for Black. Therefore 22 ♕e4! is the correct winning line.

W

19 ♗h6! ♕c3

19...♕xf1+ is met by 20 ♔xf1 and then 20...gxh6 21 ♕h5+ ♔e7 22 ♕f7# or 20...♘xe6 21 ♕xe6+ ♗e7 22 ♗g5! ♖d7 23 ♗xe7 ♖xe7 24 ♕c8+ loses for Black, as does 19...♘e2+ 20 ♕xe2 ♕d4 21 ♗xg7! ♗xg7 22 ♕h5+.

20 ♗xg7 ♕d3

20...♗xg7 21 ♕h5+! mates next move.

21 ♗xh8 ♕g6

21...♘e2+ 22 ♔h1 ♘g3+ 23 hxg3 ♕xf1+ 24 ♔h2 ♖d1 (or 24...♕xf2 25 ♕h5+ ♔e7 26 ♗f5! with the terrible threat of 27 ♗f6#) 25 ♕h5+ ♔d8 26 ♗f6+ ♗e7 27 ♗xe7+ ♔xe7 28 ♕f7+ ♔d8 29 ♕f8#.

22 ♗f6 ♗e7
23 ♗xe7 ♕xg4

23...♔xe7 24 ♕h4+! ♔e8 25 ♗g4 guards against ...♘f3+ while threatening 26 ♗h5.

24 ♗xg4 ♔xe7
25 ♖c1!

This accurate move secures victory for White. Black is prevented from gaining any activity with ...c5. Notice how efficiently the white bishop simultaneously stops ...♘e2+, ...♖d7 and ...♖c8.

25	...	c6
26	f4	a5
27	♔f2	a4
28	♔e3	b4
29	♗d1!	a3
30	g4	♖d5
31	♖c4	c5

32	♔e4	♖d8
33	♖xc5	♘e6
34	♖d5	♖c8

34...♖xd5 35 ♔xd5 ♘xf4+ 36 ♔c4 also wins easily for White.

35	f5	♖c4+
36	♔e3	♘c5
37	g5	♖c1
38	♖d6	1-0

Black resigned in view of the line 38...b3 39 f6+ ♔f8 40 ♗h5! ♘b7 41 ♖a6 bxa2 42 ♖a8+.

Since the time that I wrote most of the following passage about my happy experiences in Gausdal, I have heard that Mr Arnold Eikrem, a friendly man and a tremendous organiser of events in Norway, died early in 1996. He will be greatly missed.

For guaranteed tough opposition in an open tournament, Mr Eikrem's competitions at the Høyfjellshotel ('High Mountain Hotel') were hard to top. An accelerated system of pairings produced very testing clashes right from the start. At the Arnold Cup competition in April 1992, when I was still an international master, I faced a grandmaster opponent in round one. Later, in round five, my adversary was the top-ranked player, Russian grandmaster Sergei Tiviakov. He knows lots of opening theory. For example, he is a dangerous exponent of the sharp Sicilian Dragon. However, he seemed to me to be quite set in his repertoire. Other noticeable characteristics are that Tiviakov is a tough fighter on the chessboard, but he sometimes takes big risks. Putting these observations together gives a profile of a highly dangerous and tenacious player who is, relatively speaking, less objective or original. Of course, that assessment is my personal opinion. Consistent with my ways of using T.O.D.O., I sat down to play Tiviakov with the intention of being particularly objective and original. As I have stressed before, that does not means that I should forget about tenacity and danger. In fact, those features were very much present in the next game.

Game 13
P.Motwani – S.Tiviakov
Gausdal 1992
Sicilian Defence

1	e4	c5
2	c3	

Black will not get a chance now to demonstrate his vast theoretical knowledge of the Dragon variation.

2	...	d5
3	exd5	♕xd5
4	d4	♘c6 *(D)*
5	♗e3!?	

I have discussed this interesting idea with IM Johan van Mil, a Dutch friend of mine. White threatens 6 dxc5. Another point is that he

W

avoids 5...♗g4. The 'normal' move, 5 ♘f3, allows the pin by Black's queen's bishop, and then 6 ♗e2 e6 7 h3 ♗h5 8 c4 ♕d6 9 g4 ♗g6 10 d5 ♘b4 11 0-0 exd5! (11...♘c2 12 ♘a3! ♘xa1 13 ♘b5 ♕b6 14 ♗f4 ♖c8 15 ♕a4 ♔d8 16 ♘xa7 gives White a decisive attack) 12 cxd5 0-0-0! 13 ♘c3 ♘f6 14 ♕a4 a6 15 a3 ♗c2! 16 b3 ♘bxd5 17 ♘xd5 ♕xd5 was very good for Black in the game Short-J.Polgar, Isle of Lewis 1995.

| 5 | ... | cxd4 |
| 6 | cxd4 | e6 |

6...e5!? 7 ♘c3 ♗b4 is also playable.

7	♘c3	♕d8
8	♘f3	♘f6
9	a3	

This is a standard move in isolated queen's pawn (IQP) positions. White prevents the blockading manoeuvre ...♘b4-d5. However, 9 ♗e2 ♗e7 10 0-0 0-0 11 ♘e5 ♘b4 12 ♗f3 ♘bd5 13 ♕b3, with some

queenside pressure, merits consideration.

9	...	♗e7
10	♗d3	0-0
11	0-0	b6
12	♕e2	♗b7
13	♖ad1	♖c8
14	♖fe1 (D)	

B

White has achieved a complete harmonious development. In one sense the IQP is a weakness, but it also gives White some important central control.

| 14 | ... | ♘a5 |

The position after 14...♖e8 was reached by a different move-order after 16 moves in the game Motwani-Pritchett, Scottish Centenary Championship 1993. That game continued 17 ♗b5!? ♘d5 18 ♘e4 ♘xe3?! 19 fxe3! (strengthening the centre and opening the f-file) 19...♗f8 20 ♖f1! ♖e7 21 ♘fg5 h6 22 ♕h5! ♖cc7 23 ♗d3 ♕d5 24 h4! (threatening 25 ♘c3 ♕d8 26

🜚xf7! 🜚xf7 27 ♕g6! winning)
24...🜚d8 25 🜚d2 (protecting the
pawn on g2 and intending, among
other ideas, 26 🜚df2 and 27 ♕g6!!)
25...f5 26 ♕g6! and **Black resigned**, in view of 26...hxg5 27
🜚f6+ and mate next move. I went
on to tie for first place in the tournament with Grandmaster Dr Colin
McNab.

15 ♗g5! 🜚d5?

Black overlooked or underestimated White's reply. Maybe he was
unsettled when he discovered that
15...♗xa3 fails to 16 ♗xf6 ♕xf6
17 🜚e4! ♗xe4 18 ♕xe4, threatening 19 ♕xh7# and 19 bxa3. Note
that 16...gxf6 17 d5! exd5 18 🜚d4,
intending 19 ♕g4+ ♔h8 20 ♕f5, is
also terrible for Black.

16 ♕e4! 🜚f6

16...g6 17 ♕h4 is also unpleasant for Black.

17 ♕h4 g6

17...h6 18 ♗xh6! gxh6 19 ♕xh6
♗xf3 20 🜚e5 is a crude, but effective, sacrificial attack by White.

18 d5! *(D)*

18 ... ♗xd5

Objectively, Black is already in
a lost position. If the opening had
been a Sicilian Dragon, he would
still be following his theoretical
preparation at this stage. Instead,
he finds himself in an unfamiliar
situation facing original problems.
Of course, White had to be tactically alert, especially over moves
15-18, to create chances that are

B

dangerous to Black. However, White
cannot afford to slacken off the
pressure or to become complacent.
This should apply irrespective of
whether the opponent is highly
rated or not. The game is not over
yet, and Tiviakov searches for the
path of maximum resistance.

One should assume that the opponent will find the most tenacious
moves in defence. For example, I
know from personal experience
that people often try to 'blitz' a
player who is in time-trouble. That
is a serious mistake. The minds of
certain players are ultra-focused
and razor-sharp in their analysis
even when short of time. So it is
wise always to respect the other
person.

Both 18...exd5 19 🜚xe7! and
18...🜚xd5 19 🜚xd5 ♗xg5 20 🜚xg5
lose very quickly for Black.

19 🜚xd5

19 ♗a6 also wins. For example,
19...🜚c7 20 🜚xd5 🜚xd5 21 🜚xd5!

♕xd5 22 ♗xe7 or 19...♖c5 20 ♘e4!! or 19...♖xc3 20 bxc3, threatening 21 c4.

19	...	♘xd5
20	♗a6!	f6

20...♖c7 21 ♖xd5! transposes to a line already given.

21	♗xc8	♕xc8
22	♖xd5!	fxg5
23	♘xg5	♖f7
24	♕h3	♗xg5
25	♖xg5	♕c2
26	♕g3	

26 ♕xe6!? is worth considering as, after 26...♕xf2+ 27 ♔h1, Black cannot win with 27...♕f1+ 28 ♖xf1 ♖xf1# because the last move is not legal! The black rook is pinned on f7.

26	...	♘c6

Black hurries his knight back towards the kingside, seeing that White intends the assault h4-h5.

27	h4	♘d4 (D)

W

28	h5!	♘f5

Black loses after 28...♘e2+ 29 ♖xe2 ♕xe2 30 hxg6 hxg6 31 ♖xg6+ ♔f8 (alternatively 31...♔h7 32 ♖g4 ♖f6 33 ♖g7+ ♔h8 34 ♖g8+ ♔h7 35 ♕g7#) 32 ♕d6+! ♖e7 (32...♔e8 33 ♖g8+ ♖f8 34 ♖xf8#) 33 ♕d8+ ♔f7 (33...♖e8 34 ♕f6#) 34 ♕g8#. If, instead of 30...hxg6, Black attempts to cover the d6-square with 30...♕d1+, there follows 31 ♔h2 hxg6 32 ♖xg6+ ♔f8 33 ♕b8+ ♔e7 34 ♕xa7+ ♔f8 35 ♕b8+ ♔e7 36 ♕c7+ ♕d7 37 ♕xd7+ ♔xd7 and White is two pawns ahead in the rook endgame. However, the greedy 37 ♕xb6?? would allow Black to turn the tables and win with 37...♖h7+ 38 ♔g3 ♕d3+.

29	♕b8+	♔g7
30	♕e5+	♖f6
31	♖g4	♕d2
32	♖c4	gxh5
33	♕c3	

White was in time-trouble here.

33	...	♕d5
34	♖c7+	♔g6
35	♖xa7	h4
36	♕c7	h5
37	♕d7	♕b3
38	♕e8+	♔g5
39	♖h7	♕xb2

39...♖g6 40 f4+ ♔f6 41 ♕f8#.

40	♕xh5+	♔f4

The time control is reached, and White now forces a win quickly.

41	♕f3+	♔g5
42	♖h5+	♔g6
43	♕g4+	♔f7
44	♖h7+	♔f8 (D)

W

45 ♖d1! 1-0

Tiviakov is threatened with 46 ♖d8#, and he also gets mated after 45...♔e8 46 ♕g8+ ♖f8 47 ♕xf8+ ♔xf8 48 ♖d8#. Other variations leave him hopelessly behind on material.

On 30th August 1995, Grandmaster Lev Polugaevsky died in Paris at the age of 60. He will be remembered fondly by generations of chess players world-wide. Polugaevsky was a friendly, popular, well-balanced man.

I think that, to some extent, a chess player's style reflects his personality. Lev Polugaevsky's best games exhibit a beautiful equilibrium, combining many elements in a wonderful, balanced way. In the following 1975 game, in the then Soviet Union, Polugaevsky wins elegantly against Boris Gulko. All the aspects of T.O.D.O. are present in this gem.

Game 14
L.Polugaevsky – B.Gulko
USSR 1975
English Opening

1 c4

Polugaevsky is famous for his superb handling of Sicilian positions. 1...e5 is one of Black's most common responses to 1 c4, but, if Gulko had chosen that reply, then he would, in effect, have allowed Polugaevsky to play a Sicilian Defence with an extra tempo.

1 ...   ♘f6
2 ♘c3   e6
3 ♘f3

A major alternative is 3 e4. Then S.Williams-Howell, British Championship 1995, continued 3...d5 4 e5 d4 5 exf6 dxc3 6 bxc3 ♕xf6 7 d4 (I have seen grandmasters Viktor Korchnoi and Margeir Petursson omitting the d2-d4 advance, and instead playing 7 ♘f3 e5 8 ♗d3!?, with the intention of castling kingside then following up with ♖e1 and/or ♕c2 to exert pressure against the pawns on e5 or h7) 7...e5 8 ♘f3 exd4 (8...♘c6!?) 9 ♗g5 ♕e6+ 10 ♗e2 f6 11 ♘xd4 ♕f7 12 ♗h6! g6 (12...gxh6? 13 ♗h5) 13 ♗xf8 ♔xf8 14 h4! h5 15 0-0 ♔g7 16 f4!, with some initiative for White.

After 3 e4, another popular move is 3...c5. Korchnoi-Barle, Europa Cup 1995, continued 4 e5 ♘g8 5 ♘f3 ♘c6 6 d4 cxd4 7 ♘xd4 ♘xe5

8 ♘db5 a6 9 ♘d6+ ♗xd6 10 ♕xd6 f6 11 ♗e3 ♘e7 12 ♗b6 ♘f5 13 ♕c5 d6 14 ♗xd8 dxc5 15 ♗c7 ♗d7 16 0-0-0 ♗c6 17 ♗xe5 fxe5 18 ♖e1 0-0 19 ♖xe5 ♘d4 20 f3 ♖f5 21 ♖e3, and White enjoyed a slight structural advantage in the endgame due to Black's isolated e-pawn.

| 3 | ... | b6 |
| 4 | e4 | ♗b7 *(D)* |

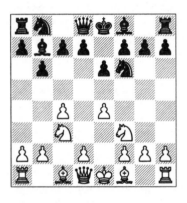

W

A significant comparison should be made with this position and the one arising after 1 c4 ♘f6 2 ♘c3 c5 3 ♘f3 b6 4 e4 ♗b7. Then 5 e5! is strong, because 5...♘e4? loses material to 6 ♘b1!, threatening 7 d3.

5 ♗d3

Here 5 e5 is less dangerous. For example, 5...♘e4 6 ♘b1? ♘g5 is very pleasant for Black.

5	...	d5
6	cxd5	exd5
7	e5	♘fd7

7...♘e4 8 0-0 (8 ♕a4+ ♕d7) 8...♘c5 9 ♗c2 d4! is nice for Black,

but White can improve with 8 ♗c2, preparing to play d4 if needed.

| 8 | ♗c2 | d4! |
| 9 | ♗e4 | ♗xe4 |

I prefer 9...c6 10 ♘xd4 (10 ♘e2 ♘c5) 10...♘xe5 11 ♘f3 ♘d3+.

| 10 | ♘xe4 | ♘c5 |

10...♘c6 11 ♕a4! is good for White.

| 11 | ♘xc5 | ♗xc5 |
| 12 | 0-0 | |

12 d3 ♗b4+ 13 ♗d2 ♗xd2+ 14 ♕xd2 0-0 is more comfortable for Black than the actual game continuation. He has exchanged an extra pair of minor pieces and can follow up with ...c5 and ...♘c6.

| 12 | ... | 0-0 |

12...d3!? merits consideration, but note that, after 13 b4, Black should play 13...♗e7. 13...♗xb4?? is a blunder on account of the reply 14 ♕a4+.

13	d3	♕d5
14	♖e1	♘c6
15	♖e4!	♖fe8
16	♕e2	♖e6
17	♗f4	h6
18	a3	♗f8
19	h4!	♖ae8
20	♖e1	g6 *(D)*

Altering his kingside pawn formation. An alternative plan is to play on the other wing with 20...a5, perhaps to gain more space with ...a4 and ...b5 later.

| 21 | ♕d2 | h5 |

This creates further dark-square weaknesses around his king, but

W

Black hopes that the protection needed for the e-pawn will keep White's pieces tied down to that task. Black could have played 21...♔h7.

22 ♗g5!?

There is a saying 'Fortune favours the brave'. Polugaevsky courageously leaves his e-pawn with less protection in an attempt to get at Black's fresh weaknesses.

22 ... ♗g7

22...♘xe5!? 23 ♘xd4 ♖d6 24 f4?! ♘g4! 25 ♖xe8 ♕xd4+, with ...f6 to follow, favours Black, so White might diverge from that line with 24 ♕e2. Then 24...♕xd4!? 25 ♖xd4 ♘f3+! 26 ♕xf3 ♖xe1+ 27 ♔h2 ♖xd4 also looks good for Black at first sight, but White has 28 ♕a8! ♔g7 29 ♗h6+! ♔xh6 30 ♕xf8+ ♔h7 31 ♕xf7+ ♔h6 (not 31...♔h8? 32 ♕f6+) 32 ♕f6 ♖d7! and a draw by perpetual check with 33 ♕h8+ ♖h7 34 ♕f8+ and so on.

23 ♗f6! ♗xf6

23...♘xe5? 24 ♖xe5 ♖xe5 25 ♗xe5 ♗xe5 26 ♕g5! is winning for White.

24 exf6

Threatening 25 ♕h6.

24 ... ♕f5

25 ♘g5! ♖xe4?

Black must play 25...♖e5!. If 26 f4, then 26...♖xe4 27 ♘xe4 and the diagonal path for White's queen to h6 has been blocked. Alternatively, 26 ♖xe5 ♖xe5 27 ♘e4 ♘d8 28 ♕h6 ♘e6, intending 29...♕f4, is much healthier for Black than the game continuation.

26 ♘xe4 ♘d8

27 ♕h6 ♘e6 *(D)*

W

28 ♘d6!! 1-0

After 28...cxd6 29 ♖xe6! it is mate in at most two moves. A typically instructive game by the great Polugaevsky. His original and dangerous play was rewarded with a full point. He tenaciously adhered to his plan of probing the black kingside weaknesses, without losing his objectivity at any stage. Under the pressure, Gulko's critical error came three moves from the end, and met with a stunning refutation.

The young Dutch grandmaster Jeroen Piket is exceptionally well-versed in the latest theory. He is also very original and flexible in his choices of opening lines. For example, as Black against the Ruy Lopez it seems to me that he has explored more systems than Captain Kirk! However, one of the openings which I have never seen Piket employ in reply to 1 e4 is the Caro-Kann Defence. Yet, in the next game from the 1995 Donner Memorial tournament, clever and creative play in the opening by grandmaster Alexander Khuzman led to a transposition from a Slav Defence to the Panov-Botvinnik Attack against the Caro-Kann.

Just before that, as a late extra especially for those supporters of the Caro-Kann who feel it should be given a higher profile, we have...

The Caro-Kann on TV!

In Brussels on 12 March 1996, I saw a chess position in a programme called *Acapulco H.E.A.T.* on a Dutch TV channel. I started to think about how the position might

have been reached, then realised that it can arise after ten moves from a neat trap in the Caro-Kann Defence. However, I must warn C-K fans... White delivered mate on the next move!

The miniature goes like this: **1 e4 c6 2 d4 d5 3 ♘d2 dxe4 4 ♘xe4 ♘f6 5 ♕d3!? e5? 6 dxe5 ♕a5+ 7 ♗d2! ♕xe5 8 0-0-0! ♘xe4** Black would only last a little longer after 8...♕xe4 9 ♖e1. **9 ♕d8+! ♔xd8 10 ♗g5++** This was the picturesque moment when the cameras homed in on the game, though the lenses spent more time focusing on the beautiful face of actress Catherine Oxenberg (who, unfortunately, was playing Black)! **10...♔e8** 10...♔c7 11 ♗d8# is also pretty. **11 ♖d8#**

Game 15
A.Khuzman – J.Piket
Amsterdam 1995
Slav Defence

1	d4	d5
2	c4	c6
3	cxd5	cxd5
4	♘c3	♘c6
5	e4!? *(D)*	
5	...	e6

5...dxe4 6 d5 ♘e5 (6...♘b4? 7 ♕a4+ or 6...♘a5? 7 b4) 7 ♕a4+ ♗d7 8 ♕xe4 ♘g6 9 ♘f3 ♘f6 10 ♕d4 is very pleasant for White. He has more space to activate his pieces freely, whereas Black will experience difficulties in trying to

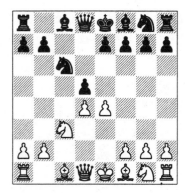

B

complete his kingside development.

6	exd5	exd5
7	♗b5	♘f6
8	♘f3	♗e7

This position can also arise from the move-order 1 e4 c6 2 d4 d5 3 exd5 cxd5 4 c4 ♘f6 5 ♘c3 e6 6 ♘f3 ♗e7 7 cxd5 exd5 8 ♗b5+ ♘c6. However, most players prefer 7...♘xd5 as Black. The point is that the pawn structure is symmetrical in the ...exd5 positions, but White still has some initiative because he is always half a move ahead of Black. Piket does not normally choose to defend passively, but Khuzman's very original play has resulted in this situation.

9	♘e5!	♗d7
10	0-0	0-0
11	♖e1	h6

Played mainly to prevent White from playing ♗g5.

12 ♕a4! (D)

| 12 | ... | ♗d6!? |

13 ♗f4

Threatening 14 ♘xf7! ♖xf7 15 ♗xd6. Note that 13 ♘xc6 bxc6 14 ♗xc6 ♗xh2+! 15 ♔xh2 ♕c7+ is fine for Black.

| 13 | ... | ♗e8 |

14 ♗g3

Now ♘xc6 really is threatened.

| 14 | ... | ♘e7 |

15 ♕b3!

The queen's work on a4 is done. Hence the switch to b3 to exert pressure against the pawns on d5 and b7.

15	...	♕b6
16	♗xe8	♖fxe8

If 16...♕xb3?, White wins a pawn with the *zwischenzug* 17 ♗xf7+ before recapturing on b3.

17	♕xb6	axb6
18	♘b5	♘f5
19	f3	♗b4

19...♘xg3? 20 ♘xd6.

20 ♖ed1

To prevent Black from playing the manoeuvre ...♗d2 and ...♗e3+.

If allowed, in conjunction with
...♘xg3, Black could undermine
the protection of White's knight on
e5 by ...♗xd4.

20	...	**♖ec8**
21	**♘d3**	**♘xg3?!**

Black's knight on f5 was one of
his most actively placed pieces,
and so 21...♗f8 was preferable in
order to retain it. Also, by preserv-
ing the knight, Black could have
used it to challenge White's counterpart outposted on b5. For example, 21...♗f8 22 ♗f2 ♘d6. Note
that 22 ♗c7? ♖a5 23 a4 ♖xb5 24
axb5 ♖xc7 allows Black to win.

22	**hxg3**	**♗f8**
23	**a3**	**h5**

If 23...♖c2, then 24 ♘c3 incar-
cerates Black's rook in White's
camp and threatens ♖ab1 and ♘e1.
24...♗xa3 would not help, because
of 25 ♘b5 winning material, but
24...♗d6! is unclear. Thus White
could first play 24 ♖ab1, intending
♘c3 and ♘e1.

24	**♖ac1**	**♖xc1?!**

This leaves White with control
of the c-file. A more consistent follow-up to 23...h5 is 24...g6, intending ...♗h6 to activate the bishop
and challenge White on the open c-
file. Black must be alert to tricks in
lines such as 24...g6 25 ♘c7 ♖a4?
26 ♘xd5! ♖xc1 27 ♘xf6+ ♔g7 28
♘e8+. However, 25...♖ab8, with
the threat of ...♗d6, is certainly
playable.

25	**♖xc1**	**♖a5**

26	**♘c3**	**♗d6**
27	**♔f2**	**♔f8**
28	**♘e2**	**♖a8** *(D)*

W

29	**♖c3!**	**♔e7**
30	**♖b3**	**♗c7**
31	**♘c3**	**♔d7**
32	**♘b5**	

32 ♖b5 ♖a5 holds for Black, at
least temporarily.

32	...	**♗b8**
33	**♘e5+**	**♗xe5**
34	**dxe5**	**♘e8**
35	**♘d4**	**♖a6**
36	**f4**	**g6**
37	**♘b5**	**♖a4?**

In time-trouble, Piket collapses
under pressure. He might, under-
standably, have been afraid of the
invasion ♔e3-d4. Instead of the
text-move, the alternative 37...♔c6
is a more tenacious defence, although White can improve his position on the kingside by means of
♔f3 and g4.

38	**♘c3**	**♖d4**

39	♔e3	♖c4
40	♘xd5	1-0

Black overstepped the time limit, but he faces the loss of at least a second pawn. White's play in the game was tenacious, although not particularly flashy. Some originality, in the opening especially, combined with persistent and patient probing of Black's weaknesses, gained him an advantage on the clock, which contributed to his victory on the board.

The next game will be the penultimate one of this chapter, but first there is something a little bit different, and lighter too. A doctor friend of mine called me today (8 October 1995) and asked how I was getting on with writing this book. I told her that about one quarter of it had been completed. She then said 'Well done Paul. The last time we spoke, you had only done a third'! You can probably imagine my reaction, but, after all, laughter is the best medicine.

I am, at this time, in the process of moving with my wife Jenny to live in Belgium, so I will leave you with a puzzle to ponder. As a preamble to it, I should just point out that many people would say there are 64 squares on a chess-board. However, 64 is, in fact, somewhere between one quarter and one third of the **total** number of squares on the board.

Squares, Scores and Ages

Two of the main characters in the puzzle are a young adult and a boy. Let us call them A and B respectively. They have finished playing in a five-round weekend open tournament (with normal scoring rules: 1 point for a win, ½ point for a draw, 0 for a loss), and B has a higher score than A, but both players are happy because it is their birthday. A third person, C, who knows the ages of A and B, asks them about their scores in the tournament. A and B only tell C how many points they have each scored. C is then able to deduce that A and B could not have played each other in the tournament. He also calculates correctly that the product of their scores and the age (in years) of B is exactly equal to the age (in years) of A plus the total number of squares on a chess-board.

Your puzzle is to work out the scores and the ages of A and B. The solution will be revealed after the forthcoming game.

In the cascade of elegant sacrifices which you are soon to witness, the necessity of objectivity can easily be forgotten. However, particularly when deciding to give up material as an investment in an attack, the objective element in one's play is essential. There is no shortage of examples in which players got carried away with throwing wood on to the fire to fuel their plans, only to find that the dreams are all suddenly extinguished due to a failure to be objective, accurate, and take proper account of the defensive or counter-attacking options available to the opponent. The need for objectivity is underlined by the following example.

Not Just a One-Horse Race

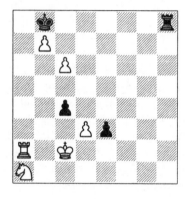

B

This hypothetical, but plausible diagram, with Black to move, exemplifies beautifully the resources which can exist for both sides. White threatens ♖a8+, but Black earlier sacrificed a piece and has calculated correctly well in advance. Now 1...♖h2+ 2 ♔b1 ♖xa2 3 ♔xa2 e2 would be correct, although Black must be content with a draw after 4 ♘c2 cxd3 5 ♘b4

e1♕ 6 ♘a6+ ♔a7 7 b8♕+ ♔xa6 8 c7 ♕d2+ 9 ♔b3 ♕c2+ 10 ♔b4 ♕b2+ 11 ♔c4 ♕c2+ 12 ♔d4 ♕f2+, and White's king cannot escape the checks, irrespective of whether he captures the d-pawn or not. Deep objectivity is required to see that the tempting 3...cxd3 (instead of 3...e2) actually leads to a forced loss for **Black**! A small sample of variations can show why: 4 ♘b3 e2 5 ♘c5 e1♕ 6 ♘d7+ ♔c7 7 b8♕+ ♔xc6 8 ♘e5+ ♔d5 9 ♕b7+! ♔d6 10 ♕d7+! ♔c5 11 ♘xd3+ ♔c4 12 ♘xe1; alternatively 4...d2 5 ♘c5 d1♕ 6 ♘d7+! ♔c7 7 b8♕+ ♔xc6 8 ♘e5+ ♔c5 9 ♕c7+ ♔b5 10 ♕b7+ ♔c5 11 ♕c6+ ♔b4 12 ♕b6+ ♔a4 (12...♔c3 13 ♕b2#) 13 ♘c4! (threatening 14 ♕a5# or 14 ♘b2#) 13...♕d5 14 ♕b3#.

A few observations can give a good impression of how tough the 1995 World Junior Championship in Halle, Germany, was. Scotland's Jonathan Rowson gained his third international master norm with a score of 7/13 against highly rated opposition. In fact, just two of the twelve best-placed competitors at the finish were rated less than 2450, and only one among that top dozen did not have the title of IM or GM.

The exciting clash between the very talented young IMs who represented The Czech Republik and Brazil is indicative of the kind of daring attacking chess which occurred in the tournament. You will see that White's approach was also original and, at the same time, deeply objective.

Our third game in this book featuring the ever-popular Sicilian Defence may not look like a close encounter, but, facing such powerful and dangerous play, Black was scarcely given a chance to be extra tenacious (E.T.)!

Game 16
T.Oral – G.Vescovi
Halle 1995
Sicilian Defence

1	e4	c5
2	c3	d6
3	d4	♘f6
4	♗d3	

If 4 dxc5, then 4...♘xe4?? is a blunder due to 5 ♕a4+. However, 4...♘c6! 5 f3 d5! 6 exd5 ♘xd5, intending ...e5, gives Black excellent piece play in compensation for a pawn, while 5 cxd6 ♘xe4 presents Black with no difficulties either.

4	...	g6

After 4...cxd4 5 cxd4 g6 6 ♘c3 ♗g7, I have twice played 7 e5 in official tournaments. A tactical point is that 7...dxe5 8 dxe5 ♘d5? loses to 9 ♗b5+. Black avoided this pitfall in the game Motwani-Chiong, Bern 1992, by playing 8...♘fd7. Nevertheless, 9 f4 ♘c5 10 ♗b5+ ♗d7 11 ♗e3 ♗xb5 12 ♕xd8+ ♔xd8 13 ♘xb5 ♘d3+ 14 ♔e2 ♘xb2 15 ♘f3! ♘c6 16 ♘g5 a6 17 ♘d4! ♔e8 18 ♘xc6 bxc6 19 ♖hc1 h6 20 ♘e4 f5 21 ♘c5 ♔f7 22 ♖ab1 ♖hb8 23 ♗d4 soon resulted in victory for White, and illustrates the unpleasant cramping effect which the advance 7 e5 has on Black's position. That win in Switzerland helped me towards my third grandmaster norm and a joint second place on 7/9 in the Open tournament, half a point behind the winner, GM Andrei Sokolov. My international rating reached the 2500 level ten weeks later, at the start of May, and I was officially awarded the title of International Grandmaster on 1 July 1992, when the next FIDE rating list was published (although Chris Morrison, the Scottish team captain at the Manila Olympiad, made me a very happy man on 17 June, when he brought the news that I was already a grandmaster, subject to confirmation of the 2500 rating).

A distinctive feature of the big annual Bern event is that players from the same nation are allowed to form teams of four (if they can). At the end of the main competition for individuals, the scores of the four team members are added together. Then the team with the highest aggregate wins a substantial prize. I was delighted when my friends Mark Hebden, Chris Ward and Peter Wells asked me to form a

'Great Britain' quartet with them. Initially it was nicknamed 'England plus one'. Later, when a certain seven points helped us to secure one of the better team rewards, the nickname was changed (not by me) to 'Scotland plus three'! Sincerely though, we all played well, developed tremendous team spirit, and had great fun too.

    5 dxc5   dxc5
    6 e5 *(D)*

B

    6 ...   ♘fd7

Also at Bern, the Hungarian international master Emil Szalanczy played 6...c4 against me. The intention was to answer 7 ♗xc4 by 7...♕xd1+ 8 ♔xd1 ♘g4. However, the game continuation 7 ♕a4+ ♘c6 8 ♗xc4 ♘g4 9 ♘f3 (9 f4 is highly risky because of 9...♕b6) 9...♗g7 10 ♗xf7+!! virtually refuted Black's sixth move. After 10...♔xf7, there followed 11 e6+. Then 11...♗xe6 12 ♘g5+ would

have been terrible for Black, yet all of his king's alternative choices at move 11 can be met simply and strongly with 12 ♕xg4.

    7 e6!?

After 7 f4, White would enjoy a safe spatial plus while at the same time restricting the future scope of Black's dark-squared bishop. Instead, the enterprising gambit chosen is designed to weaken the opponent's kingside pawn formation. It is also justified by the fact that Black's extra pawn will only be part of a doubled isolated pair.

    7 ...   fxe6

7...♘e5 8 exf7+ ♔xf7? 9 ♗xg6+! wins the lady on d8.

    8 ♘f3   ♘c6
    9 ♕e2   ♗g7
    10 ♘bd2

If 10 ♕xe6??, then 10...♘de5, and White is the one who must part with his queen or light-squared bishop.

    10 ...   ♘de5
    11 ♗e4

Note that the e4-square is an effective outpost for White's pieces to use, since Black can no longer play ...d5 or ...f5. This highlights another spin-off resulting from the pawn sacrifice on move seven.

    11 ...   0-0 *(D)*

Castling does not always improve the safety of the king, and here the Black monarch soon faces an assault on the h-file. He should have prepared to castle on the other wing, starting with 11...♗d7. Then 12 ♘xe5 ♗xe5? 13 ♗xc6 wins a piece for White, but 12...♘xe5 13 ♗xb7 ♖b8 14 ♗e4 0-0, threatening ...♗b5, offers Black much more active piece play than in the game.

W

12 h4!   **♗d7**

Trying to block White's attack by 12...h5 not only hands over the g5-square as another outpost for White, but also critically weakens Black's g-pawn. For instance, 13 ♘xe5 ♘xe5 14 ♘c4 ♕e8 15 ♘xe5 ♗xe5 16 g4! ♗g7 17 gxh5 gxh5 18 ♖g1, with numerous threats, including 19 ♗g6 and 19 ♗h6, is terrible for Black.

13 h5   **♗e8**
14 ♘g5   **♕d6 (D)**

14...♕d7 15 ♘b3! is also very unpleasant for Black.

15 ♘xh7!

The potential of White's attacking pieces had reached its climax and had to be released. In other

W

words, White was ready to strike, and the sacrifice to expose Black's king by removing its pawn-cover is a logical conclusion.

15 ...   **♔xh7**
16 ♘c4!!

Exploiting the position of the black queen to gain a tempo and unlock the bishop on c1. Precision is required, especially when sacrificing material, and note that 16 hxg6+ ♔g8 17 ♕h5? would fail badly after 17...♖f4.

16 ...   **♘xc4**

16...♕c7 17 hxg6+ ♔g8 18 ♕h5 ♖f6 (18...♗xg6 19 ♗xg6 ♘xg6 20 ♕xg6 ♖f6 21 ♕h7+ ♔f7 22 ♕h5+ ♖g6 23 ♖h3! is extremely unpleasant for Black, who is faced with threats such as 24 ♖g3 and 24 ♗f4!?, while 23...♖h8 loses quickly to 24 ♖f3+ ♗f6 25 ♕xh8) 19 ♕h7+ ♔f8 20 ♗h6! ♗xh6 21 ♕h8# illustrates the significance of White having freed his dark-squared bishop on move 16.

17 hxg6+ &g8 *(D)*

B

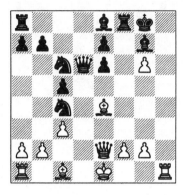

W

18 &h8+!!

This beautiful move is also necessary, as 18 &h5? would be met by 18...&f4!, allowing Black to win.

18 ... &xh8

18...&xh8 19 &h5+ mates Black quickly.

19 &h5 &xg6

In spite of his huge surplus of material, Black has no satisfactory defence. 19...&f4 20 &h7+ &f8 21 &xh8# demonstrates the point of White's 18th move.

20 &xg6+ &g7
21 &h7+ &f7
22 &h5+! &f6

Another possible finish was 22...&g8 23 &h7+ &h8 24 &g6+ &g8 25 &h7#.

23 f4! *(D)* 1-0

Black resigned, staring at 24 &g6#, and in view of 23...&6e5 being answered by 24 fxe5+ &xe5 25 &g5#.

Solution to Puzzle (posed after game 15)

The **adult** is **21** years old and scored **4½** points; the **boy** is **10** years old and scored a perfect **5/5**.

This requires some explanation.

We were told that the boy had a *higher* score than the adult in the five round tournament. So the boy's score must be somewhere between ½ and 5, while the adult's score must lie in the range 0 to 4½. However, the third person, C, was able to deduce, from being told only the actual scores, that the adult and boy *could not* have played each other in the tournament. This is a crucial fact, which narrows the options for the scores of the adult and boy to either 4½, 5; or 0, ½. The latter case can be quickly ruled out, as it would make the *product* of the scores equal to zero. This would be inconsistent with the statement concerning 'product' mentioned in the puzzle. Therefore the adult, A, scored 4½ points, and the boy, B, scored 5 points (because B did not concede any points, he would have had to have won if he had played A, but, since A dropped only half a point, A and B could not have played each other).

The *total* number of squares on a chess-board is *204* (64 squares of size 1x1; 49 of size 2x2; 36 of size 3x3; 25 of size 4x4; 16 of size 5x5; 9 of size 6x6; 4 of size 7x7; 1 of size 8x8, this final one being the whole board).

It is also significant that, in the puzzle, it is the *birthday* of A and B. So we can safely assume that the ages of A and B are both exact *whole* numbers of years. If B was less than 10 years old, then the product of the two scores and his age could not be more than 4½x5x9 =202.5, which is less than the number of squares on a chess-board. So B must be at least 10 years old. 4½x5x10 =225 =204+21, which gives the answers which were stated earlier. It only remains to show that there are no alternative answers where B is more than 10 years old. 4½x5x11 =247.5, which is not a *whole* number. 4½x5x12 =270 =204+66, but it was mentioned in the puzzle that the adult is *young*. I hope I am not offending anyone by not describing 66 as a young age! Clearly, if we started to

consider ages more than 12 for B, then it would not help A to feel younger! Therefore the answers given are the unique solution.

The ability to think logically can, as with most skills, be cultivated through practice, and is a great asset in solving puzzles such as my lengthy one we have just considered. Personally, I have tried to improve my capacity for logical thought, and, in so doing, I feel that my chess strength has increased too.

Certain players seem to possess all the elements of T.O.D.O., with the result that their games flow beautifully, and have sufficient logic to impress even Mr Spock! Such players can be very difficult to cope with, and consequently they often defeat their adversaries in rapid fashion. For instance English grandmaster Julian Hodgson frequently wins in under 25 moves, including numerous miniature victories against other grandmasters. Let us see two instructive examples from the 1989 European Team Championship in Israel.

Game 17
J.Hodgson – W.Schmidt
Haifa 1989
King's Indian Defence

| 1 | d4 | ♘f6 |
| 2 | ♘f3 | |

'Jules' is renowned as a deadly exponent of the Trompowsky Attack 2 ♗g5, a typical example being his game against Zsuzsa Polgar in Haifa. That encounter continued **2...e6 3 e4 h6 4 ♗xf6 ♕xf6 5 ♘f3** (nowadays I have noticed that Julian prefers 5 ♘c3, leaving his f-pawn free to advance to f4, perhaps after preparing this by ♕d2 and 0-0-0) **5...d6 6 ♘c3 c6 7 ♕d2 e5** (Black prevents White from playing e5, and attempts to acquire some control of the central dark squares, especially in the absence of the bishop which White has parted with) **8 0-0-0 ♗e7** (8...♕f4? 9 dxe5 dxe5 10 ♘xe5!, intending 10...♕xe5? 11 ♕d8#) **9 ♔b1 ♘d7 10 h4 exd4?!** (she should have preferred the solid regrouping manoeuvres ...♗d8, ...♗c7, ...♕e7, ...♘f6 instead of relinquishing her strong-point in the centre) **11 ♘xd4 ♘e5 12 f4 ♘g4 13 h5!** (it is true that the g4-square is an outpost for Black, but she is still suffering from a serious spatial disadvantage, and the position of her knight is rather insecure now that White has stopped it from being supported by ...h5) **13...♗d8?! 14 ♘db5! cxb5 15 ♗xb5+ ♗d7** (White also obtains a very powerful initiative after 15...♔f8 16 e5!) **16 ♗xd7+ ♔xd7 17 ♕e2! ♕xf4 18 ♖hf1 ♕g5 19 ♖f5 ♕h4 20 ♕b5+ ♔c8 21 ♖xf7 ♗e7 22 ♘d5**, and **Black resigned**.

2 ...   g6
3 ♘c3

Black would probably have faced 3 c4 far more often than White's rare move, which is an especially appropriate choice against players who are 'booked up' with reams of theory in the fashionable main lines of the Grünfeld or King's Indian Defence.

3 ...   d5

After 3...♗g7 4 e4 d6, Black would find himself playing a Pirc Defence, which is not part of his normal repertoire of openings.

4 ♗f4   ♗g7
5 e3 *(D)*

B

5 ...   0-0

In Hebden-E.Spencer, Scottish Open 1993, Black resigned after 5...♘bd7? 6 ♘b5!, already faced with unavoidable loss of material. 5...♗g4 is a much safer route for Black. The game Hebden-W.Watson, British Championship 1994 then continued 6 h4 c6 7 ♕d2 ♗xf3 8 gxf3 ♘bd7 9 e4 e6 10 0-0-0 ♘b6 11 ♗e2 ♕e7 12 ♔b1 0-0-0 13 ♗h2 (threatening 14 ♕f4) 13...♘h5! 14 exd5 ♘xd5 15 ♘e4 e5! 16 ♕a5 ♔b8 17 ♗c4 f5 18 ♘c5 ♔a8 19 ♗xe5? ♗xe5 20 ♖he1 ♕c7, and Black converted his material advantage into a victory. The permanent nature of his superior pawn structure after capturing on f3 outweighed the temporary activity which White obtained by opening up the position to increase the scope of his bishop pair.

6 ♗e2 b6?!

6...♘h5 7 ♗g5 f6 8 ♗h4 g5 9 ♗g3 (9 ♘d2!?) 9...♘xg3 10 hxg3 leaves Black seriously weakened on the light squares, especially at the sensitive, exposed h7 point. Note that the e7-f6-g5 pawn chain also impairs the scope of the fianchettoed bishop.

7 ♘e5!

White's sixth move looked innocuous, but suddenly it becomes clear that his army is harmoniously placed to support a kingside assault with his g- or h-pawns. In other words, Black has unwittingly castled into an attack (as was the case in Game 16 too).

7 ... ♗b7
8 h4! ♘bd7

After 8...h5, White prises open Black's castled position by means of 9 g4!, which underlines the usefulness of 6 ♗e2.

9 h5 ♘e4?!

Reducing White's attacking force by first exchanging knights on e5 offered Black improved chances of survival.

10 hxg6 hxg6

10...fxg6? 11 ♘xe4 dxe4 (or 11...♘xe5 12 ♘g5 is also disastrous for Black) 12 ♗c4+ ♔h8 13 ♘xg6#.

11 ♘xe4 dxe4 *(D)*

11...♘xe5 12 ♘g5 is also unpleasant for Black.

W

12 ♘g4!

12 ♘xg6? hxg6 13 ♗c4+ ♖f7, intending ...♘f6 and ...♗d5, favours Black.

12 ... ♖e8
13 ♘h6+?!

There is a saying 'The threat is stronger than its execution'. In this instance, I would have preferred 13 ♗c4, threatening 14 ♘h6+. Then if 13...e6, White can develop naturally with 14 ♕e2, intending to follow up with 0-0-0, ♖h3 and ♖dh1. 14...♘f6? would land Black in really hot water after 15 ♗g5, which shows one of the benefits of keeping the knight on g4. On h6, the white knight blocks the h-file, needs protection, and is slightly out of play.

> **13 ...   ♔f8**
> **14 ♗c4**

Notice that White gains time for his attacking operations by making his move really count. This bishop move not only carries a threat to the vulnerable f7 spot, but also clears a diagonal pathway for the queen to lift off from d1.

> **14 ...   e6**
> **15 ♕g4   ♗d5?**

Black may have rejected 15...♘f6 due to 16 ♕g3. However, 16...♘h5! 17 ♖xh5 gxh5 18 ♗xc7 ♕f6 19 ♗d6+ ♖e7 20 ♗xe7+ ♕xe7 (not 20...♔xe7? 21 ♕c7+) 21 ♕f4 ♕f6 (avoiding 21...♕b4+ 22 c3 ♕xc4?? 23 ♕xf7#) illustrates the point I made earlier about White's knight being poorly placed, and requiring protection, on h6.

> **16 ♗b5!   a6**

16...c6 allows 17 ♗d6+, and also leaves the bishop on d5 trapped and endangered by the possibility of White soon playing c2-c4.

> **17 ♗g5!**

Gaining a valuable tempo.

> **17 ...   f6**
> **18 ♗xd7   ♕xd7** *(D)*
> **19 ♗xf6!!   ♗xf6**

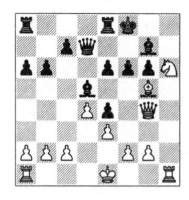

W

> **20 ♕f4!   ♔e7**

After 20...♔g7 21 ♘g4 ♖f8, 22 ♕h6+ ♔f7 23 ♕h7+ ♔e8 (23...♗g7 24 ♘e5+) 24 ♕xg6+ wins even more easily for White than 22 ♕xf6+!? ♖xf6 23 ♖h7+! ♔xh7 24 ♘xf6+ and 25 ♘xd7.

> **21 ♘g4   ♗g7**
> **22 ♘e5!!**

22 ♖h7 ♔d8 23 ♘f6 ♕e7 24 ♘xe8 ♔xe8 is not convincing for White.

> **22 ...   ♕a4**

22...♗xe5 23 ♖h7+! is another way for Black to capitulate.

> **23 ♕f7+   ♔d8**
> **24 ♕xg7   ♔c8**
> **25 0-0**

This elegant, calm move, following the earlier display of fireworks, stresses the hopelessness of Black's situation.

> **25 ...   ♔b8**
> **26 c4!   ♗b7**

26...♗xc4 27 ♘xc4 ♕xc4 28 ♖ac1.

27 c5	bxc5

1-0

Black resigned without waiting to see 28 ♘d7+ ♚a7 29 ♘xc5 or 28 ♖fc1 cxd4 29 ♛xc7+ ♚a7 30 ♘c6+.

We finish this section with a puzzle in which you are invited to play White. It is your turn to move, and to achieve the best possible result. My solution will appear early in chapter three, but here is the position, with an attempt to inspire you!

A Cornered King

W

You're playing White and are down one pawn,
But don't take fright or start to yawn,
Prepare to fight for it could be drawn,
Without adjourning tonight and getting up at dawn,

I mean goodness gracious you're no stranger,
To words like tenacious, original and danger,
These collectively could save the game,
But remember 'objectively' all the same,
Don't think the most you'll get is a half,
And we'll see who has the very last laugh!

Incidentally, I certainly would not claim to be a true poet, but I know that even a simple poem can be a useful aid to recalling facts. For example, I first heard the following verse in the Department of Mathematics at St Saviour's High School in Dundee. Some people like it as a means of remembering the formulae $C = \pi D$ and $A = \pi r^2$ for calculating the circumference and area of a circle given the diameter or radius (and knowing that $\pi = 3.14$ approximately). The poem goes like this:

Tweedle dum and tweedle dee,
Round the circumference is pi times D;
But when the area is declared,
What you use is pi r squared.

Well, one could go round on a topic forever, just like a circle, but enough attempts at poetry for now ... a new chapter awaits!

3 The Four S's

In a sense, the first two chapters looked primarily at *the player*, and considered qualities which can improve performance, and increase enjoyment derived from chess. In the third phase of our H.O.T. adventure, we shall focus on certain features relating specifically to *positions on the chess-board*.

I hope it does not come as a disappointment that my four S's are not sun, sand, sea and ... something else! They are: *Safety, Scope, Space, Structure*.

A natural example to illustrate a lack of safety of a king is the puzzle I left you investigating at the end of Chapter two. Black's monarch was incarcerated, and clearly uncomfortably placed, on h1. 'Open the h-file' is a logical thought for White to have. In fact, he can achieve this and force a quick win. The main variation is **1 g4! fxg4 2 h4! gxh3 e.p. 3 ♖xh3#**. Notice that the poor scope of the rook on g6 prevented Black from organising any counterplay. If the rook had been on, for instance, g8 in the initial position of the puzzle, then its scope for manoeuvring would have been much greater, and after 1 g4 ♖a8!, intending ...♖a1+, Black

would have had little difficulty in drawing the game.

As a boy, I particularly loved game collections of some really strong players, such as Tigran Petrosian, the 1963-9 World Champion. He had a reputation for producing very sound, solid, but sometimes tedious chess, although I found it to be exceptionally rich in content, and far from dull. Certainly, he rarely took risks regarding pawn structure, but the lessons I learned from his fine examples have served me well. I, too, try to avoid having isolated, doubled or trebled pawns, **without good reason,** since they tend to be difficult to defend. For instance, Black's doubled, isolated e-pawns in game 16 were undoubtedly weak. In game 2, a similar frail duo on the d-file caused headaches for their owner. However, it would be far from correct to automatically label all doubled or isolated cases in a negative way. In Game 8, John Nunn obtained a bishop pair and pressure on the kingside when his opponent parted with the dark-squared bishop to isolate White's a-pawn and leave him with doubled c-pawns. Those pawns never became seriously exposed in the course of the game. In the first main encounter in this book, I gained a useful open d-file in return for accepting doubled c-pawns. In other words, sometimes positive features of one's position can outweigh aspects concerning structure. I stress the word 'sometimes', since defects in structure are often permanent, whereas compensating factors might only be temporary.

Petrosian had an excellent sense of when the exceptions applied. Consider the following position from a 1974 encounter against Balashov in Moscow. Petrosian, playing White, is to move.

Weak or Strong?

W

White's d-pawn is isolated, but, being on the fourth rank, it gives White some advantage in space, because Black has no pawn beyond his own third rank. Also, Petrosian's pieces have great freedom, while Balashov's army is relatively cramped and lacking scope to manoeuvre. Furthermore, Black's king is looking very insecure with most of White's forces pointing menacingly towards it.

Petrosian's energetic **1 d5!!** virtually wins on the spot (recall the devastating effect which the sudden d4-d5 advance of an isolated queen's pawn, or IQP, had on the black position in games 7 and 13). It is curious that precisely the same position occurred in two games in the same round of a tournament in Maribor – 14 years after the great Petrosian's example! One of the 1988 clashes, Barle-Grosar, continued **1...exd5 2 ♗g5 ♘e4** (2...g6 3 ♖xe7! ♛xe7 4 ♘xd5 should win for White) **3 ♘xe4 dxe4 4 ♛xe4 g6 5 ♛h4 h5 6 ♗b3! ♛c7 7 ♛e4! ♔g7 8 ♗xf7!! ♔xf7 9 ♗h6** (threatening 10 ♛e6#) **9...♛d7 10 ♛c4+ ♔f6 11 ♛c3+ ♘d4** (11...♔g7 12 ♛g7# or 11...♔f5 12 ♖e5+! ♘xe5 13 ♛xe5+ ♔g4 14 h3#) **12 ♘xd4 ♖ac8** (12...♔f7 13 ♘f3 ♗f6 14 ♘g5+ ♗xg5 15 ♛g7#) **13 ♘c6+** and **Black resigned**.

A beautiful illustration of how an IQP can sometimes be utilised for attacking purposes. Note that that specific case can very easily arise from several different openings, including the Caro-Kann Defence and the Queen's Gambit Declined. For example, the move-orders **1 e4 c6 2 d4 d5 3 exd5 cxd5**

4 c4 ♘f6 5 ♘c3 e6 6 ♘f3 ♗e7 7 cxd5 ♘xd5 (7...exd5 8 ♗b5+ ♘c6 transposes to Game 15) **8 ♗d3 ♘c6 9 0-0 0-0 10 ♖e1 ♘f6 11 a3** (to stop the manoeuvre ...♘b4-d5, blockading the IQP) **11...b6** (11...♘xd4?? 12 ♘xd4 ♕xd4 13 ♗xh7+ and 14 ♕xd4 should definitely be avoided by Black) **12 ♗c2 ♗b7 13 ♕d3 ♖e8?** (natural looking, but bad, as is 13...♕d7? due to 14 d5!! ♘d8 15 ♗g5 g6 16 d6! 1-0 A.Karlsson-J.Fridjonsson, Icelandic Ch 1995) **14 d5!!** *and* 1 d4 d5 2 c4 e6 3 ♘c3 ♘f6 4 cxd5 ♘xd5!? (an interesting alternative to the more commonly seen 4...exd5) 5 ♘f3 (5 e4 ♘xc3 6 bxc3 c5 has received some attention in master chess practice) 5...c5 6 e3 ♗e7 7 ♗d3 cxd4 8 exd4 ♘c6, and so on as before, can lead Black straight into the mouth of the tiger (maybe I should say 'Tigran')!

By now it must be obvious that I am a fan of Petrosian, yet I have an even greater fascination for Karpov's games. He makes the vast majority of them look easy. Karpov possesses a superb feel for where each member of his army should be deployed on the chess-board so that every piece has plenty of scope, and co-operates in harmony with the rest of the forces. Also, he seldom has a weak pawn structure or a cramped position. In fact, regarding the latter point, it is often the case that Karpov manages to achieve a spatial advantage. He is particularly renowned for having a highly developed sense of danger, which means that his king is normally very safe. In short, he is extremely difficult to beat!

I was amazed when I saw the following game, with the great Karpov floored in a mere 18 moves. Read on and see the incredibly quick punch, or IQP!

Game 18
U.Andersson – A.Karpov
Enköping 1995
Queen's Gambit Accepted

1	♘f3	d5
2	d4	♘f6
3	c4	dxc4
4	e3	e6

The variations 4...b5 5 a4 c6 6 axb5 (or 6 b3) 6...cxb5 7 b3 and 4...♗e6 5 ♘a3 demonstrate that Black does not have a good way of keeping an extra pawn.

| 5 | ♗xc4 | c5 |

A standard freeing move, before continuing piece development, so that Black is not too cramped.

6	0-0	a6
7	♕e2 *(D)*	
7	...	cxd4

Andersson's move 7 ♕e2 may not look very threatening, but, in my opinion, it carries some sting and must be handled with caution. For example, 7...b5 seems a logical follow-up to Black's sixth move. However, after 8 ♗d3 White is

B

well-placed to undermine Black's queenside by advancing a2-a4. If that situation occurs, Black will encounter a difficult choice: ...bxa4 would leave his a-pawn isolated; pushing on with ...b4 would let White manoeuvre his knight from b1 via d2 to the new outpost at c4 (this illustrates an important aspect of leaving the knight at home on b1 for a while); ...c4 would normally be answered simply by ♗c2, when White's pawn centre is no longer under pressure from the c-pawn, so it will be relatively easy to achieve the thrust e3-e4.

Personally, I don't like Karpov's choice 7...cxd4 either, because it opens up the position when Black is lagging behind in development. It is true that the recapture 8 exd4 makes the white d-pawn isolated, but it also increases the scope of his queen's bishop.

My preference would be for **7...♘c6** 8 dxc5 ♗xc5 9 e4 b5 (here

this has a specific tactical point behind it, namely 10 ♗d3 ♘b4!) 10 ♗b3 ♘d4!? 11 ♘xd4 ♕xd4 12 ♘c3 ♕e5, intending ...♗b7 to exert pressure on White's e-pawn and towards his king.

A common alternative is **7...♕c7** 8 dxc5 ♗xc5 9 e4 ♘g4 (planning ...♘c6 and ...♘d4 to eliminate the knight defending h2, a trick which I once used to win a game in 16 moves in an Olympiad) and now:

a) 10 h3?! is not best, in view of 10...♘xf2 intending 11 ♖xf2 ♗xf2+ 12 ♔xf2 b5.

b) 10 e5! ♘xf2 11 ♘c3 really does give White dangerous prospects for his sacrificed pawn due to the big lead in development. The fact that GM Ivan Sokolov has been playing this line prompted me to investigate it further. In home analysis on 14 March 1996, I found some pretty variations which I decided to squeeze in before sending the book off to Graham Burgess at Batsford. Here are a few examples: 11...♘e4+ 12 ♔h1 ♘f2+ (after 12...♘xc3 13 bxc3, White can follow up with ♘g5 or ♕e4-g4, with a promising attack) 13 ♖xf2! ♗xf2 14 ♘e4 (see the very end of this note for an interesting alternative) 14...♗c5 *(D)*.

At this point I stopped and said to myself 'Black is an exchange and a pawn ahead, but he is lagging behind in development and so the extra material cannot be used in the

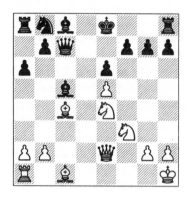

W

short term'. This gave me confidence in White's position. Nevertheless, White should act quickly. At first I was pleased with the following variations:

b1) 15 ♗f4 0-0 16 ♗d3 (threatening ♖c1, but 16 ♘fg5 is also tempting) 16...♗e7 17 ♘f6+!! leading to conclusions like:

b11) 17...♗xf6 18 ♕e4 g6 19 exf6 ♕d8 20 ♗xb8 ♖xb8 21 ♕f4! ♗d7 (21...♕xd3 22 ♕h6) 22 ♘e5 ♗e8 23 ♖f1 ♔h8 24 ♕h6 ♖g8 25 ♖f3 ♕d6 26 ♕xh7+ ♔xh7 27 ♖h3#.

b12) 17...gxf6 18 ♘g5! fxg5 (or 18...f5 19 ♕h5 ♗xg5 20 ♕xg5+ ♔h8 21 ♕f6+ ♔g8 22 ♗h6) 19 ♕h5 f5 20 exf6 ♗d6 21 ♗xd6 ♕f7 22 ♕xg5+ ♔h8 23 ♗xf8 ♕xf8 24 ♕h5 ♕g8 (24...h6 25 ♕g6) 25 f7 ♕g7 26 f8♕+ ♕xf8 27 ♕xh7#.

Then it struck me that the reply 16...f5! deadens most of White's attack, a key tactical point being 17 exf6 ♕xf4. Even earlier, 15...h6 is a reasonable defensive move

which virtually rules out ideas involving ♘g5. So I went back to the drawing board! I began to realise that in variations 'b11' and 'b12' it was White's powerful queen which caused much of the damage to Black. That led me to consider the idea of immediately re-routing the lady to the kingside as follows:

b2) 15 ♕e1!?, intending ♕g3, with possibilities such as:

b21) 15...0-0 16 ♘f6+!! *(D)*.

B

16...gxf6 (16...♔h8 17 ♕h4) 17 ♗h6 ♔h8 18 ♕h4 ♘d7 19 exf6 ♖g8 20 ♗d3 ♖g6 21 ♗xg6 fxg6 22 ♖f1 ♗f8 23 ♘g5 (threatening ♗g7+) 23...♘xf6 (23...♗xh6 24 ♕xh6 ♘xf6 25 ♕f8+ ♘g8 26 ♘f7+) 24 ♗xf8 (24 ♖xf6?? ♕c1+) 24...h5 25 ♗d6! ♕c6 (25...♕xd6 26 ♘f7+) 26 ♗e5 winning. A long variation, but one which flows very naturally after the piece sacrifice at move 16 prises open the cover around the black king.

b22) 15...♗e7 16 b3!?, intending ♗b2. Sometimes a well-timed ♘d6+ can lead to the a1-h8 diagonal opening up for White's dark-squared bishop. However, if Black has already castled, then from b2 White's bishop supports the familiar sacrifice ♘f6+. Still, I would not be surprised if you found this line of argument a lot less convincing than the concrete analysis in variation 'b21'. OK, read on!

Murdo Morrison, a friend of mine in the Isle of Lewis, once said to me that he prefers comments in words rather than very deep variations. In my writing I tend to give a lot of analysis, but nearly always with explanations to show that what may otherwise look just like a mass of moves is actually a logical sequence. Furthermore, since the moves have a logical basis, it is quite possible to flow with them for a long way, often resulting in beautiful finishes. By the time one has journeyed as far as one is able to, the valuable experience which has been gained sometimes stimulates a return to the starting point to begin again, but perhaps with a new approach. In variations 'b11' and 'b21', I could not help noticing that the dark squares around Black's king were highly sensitive. This strong feature (and also the fact that variation 'b22' is not as convincing as I would like) led me to think about the fresh approach of

eliminating Black's dark-squared bishop with **14 ♕xf2!?** (instead of 14 ♘e4). A plausible continuation is 14...♕xc4 15 ♕g3 ♕f1+ (15...0-0 16 ♗h6) 16 ♘g1 ♖g8 17 ♘e4, when the threats include 18 ♘d6+ or 18 ♘f6+ gxf6 (18...♔f8 19 ♕a3#) 19 ♕xg8+.

In conclusion, I find the 14 ♕xf2 idea particularly convincing for White, but the earlier analysis is relevant too. I found the process of searching for the best moves to be highly instructive and enjoyable. Many nice variations discovered on the way show what is possible when pieces co-operate with each other in harmony.

For those who are hard to convince, I have a special addition. The Kasparov-Seirawan game played on 27 March 1996 in Amsterdam started off as a Queen's Gambit Declined, but transposed into a Queen's Gambit Accepted at move five. Kasparov sacrificed the exchange at move 12, and his follow-up, right to Seirawan's resignation at move 34, had the powerful theme of an assault on the dark squares around Black's king. That is basically the same idea that my earlier 14 ♕xf2 move was based on. Here are the complete moves of Kasparov-Seirawan, illustrating the 'dark-square attack': 1 d4 ♘f6 2 c4 e6 3 ♘f3 d5 4 ♘c3 ♘bd7 5 ♕c2 dxc4 6 e4 c5 7 dxc5 ♗xc5 8 ♗xc4 a6 9 a4 ♕c7 10 0-0! ♘g4 11

h3! (11 ♗b3 ♘de5! is very dangerous for White) 11...♘xf2 12 ♖xf2
♗xf2+ 13 ♕xf2 ♕xc4 14 ♕g3 f6
15 ♕xg7 ♕c5+ 16 ♔h1 ♕f8 17
♕g4 ♕f7 18 e5! (threatening ♘e4)
18...♖g8 19 ♕c4 f5 20 ♗g5! (the
dark-square plan is taking shape)
20...h6 21 ♗h4 ♕g6 22 ♖g1 ♘f8
23 ♕b4! ♖g7 24 ♘e2! (heading for
the dark square f4 on the kingside)
24...b5 (desperately seeking some
active play) 25 axb5 ♖d7 26 ♘f4
♕f7 27 ♖c1 ♗b7 28 bxa6 ♗xf3 29
gxf3 ♖da7 30 ♖g1! ♖xa6 31 ♘h5!!
(threatening to invade on f6 or g7,
and the knight is immune because
of 31...♕xh5?? 32 ♕e7#) 31...♕c7
32 ♖g7 ♖a1+ 33 ♔g2 ♕c2+ 34
♗f2 1-0 (in view of 34...♖1a7 35
♘f6+ ♔d8 36 ♕xf8#).

After that marathon, it is time to
return to Andersson-Karpov.

8	exd4	♗e7
9	♘c3	b5
10	♗b3	0-0
11	♗g5	♗b7
12	♖ad1	♘c6
13	♖fe1	

White is fully mobilised, and all
of his pieces are actively placed
with ample scope to manoeuvre.
The immediate push 13 d5 of the
IQP also deserves consideration,
but 13...♘xd5! 14 ♗xd5 (14 ♘xd5
♗xg5!; alternatively 14 ♗xe7?
♘cxe7) 14...exd5 15 ♖xd5 ♕c7 is
fine for Black. Note, however, that
13...exd5? 14 ♘xd5 ♘xd5 15
♗xd5! would get Black into dire

straits, since he loses material after
15...♗xg5 or 15...♕c7 to 16 ♗xc6
in both cases.

13 ...   ♘b4? *(D)*

Karpov perhaps assumed that he
had prevented the IQP from advancing, because he has five sepa-
rate units controlling the square d5.
Is 13...♘d5 an improvement? 14
♗xe7 ♘cxe7?! 15 ♘e4!, intending
to occupy an outpost with ♘c5, is
nice for White, but Black should
insert 14...♘xc3! 15 bxc3 (15 ♗xd8
♘xe2+ is fine) 15...♘xe7. White's
isolated a-pawn and backward c-
pawn are then factors contributing
to Black having an excellent position.

However, after 13...♘d5, White
has a much stronger continuation
than 14 ♗xe7, as was demonstrated by English grandmaster Peter Wells when he qualified for the
'Interzonal' stage of the World
Championship cycle after defeat-
ing Spanish GM Jordi Magem in
the final round of the 1995 Linares
Zonal tournament (to be precise,
Peter also had to survive a quick-
play eliminator, but he made it!).
The course of their clash was 14
♗xd5! ♗xg5 15 ♗e4! ♗h6 16 a4!
bxa4 (16...b4 17 d5! exd5 18 ♘xd5
threatens ♘xb4, and 18...♕a5
loses to 19 ♘e7+! ♘xe7 20 ♗xb7
♖ae8 and then 21 ♖d7 or 21 ♗c6!
♘xc6 22 ♕xe8 ♖xe8? 23 ♖xe8#)
17 ♘xa4 ♖a7 18 ♘c5 ♗a8 19
♘xe6! fxe6 20 ♗xc6 ♗xc6 21

♕xe6+ ♖af7 22 ♕xc6, and White was two pawns ahead (1-0 in 40 moves).

W

14 d5!

The IQP refuses to be restrained! Black's superficially safe position is suddenly beyond saving. Actually, this is not really surprising, and can be traced back to a lack of development in the opening.

14 ...   ♘fxd5

14...♘bxd5 15 ♘xd5 ♗xd5 (or 15...♘xd5 16 ♗xe7 ♕xe7 17 ♗xd5 ♗xd5 18 ♖xd5 costs Black a piece) 16 ♗xd5 ♘xd5 17 ♗xe7 ♕xe7 18 ♖xd5 also loses for Black, as does 14...♗xd5 in a similar manner.

15 ♘xd5   ♗xg5

15...♘xd5 16 ♗xe7 ♕xe7 17 ♗xd5 ♗xd5 18 ♖xd5 transposes to a line already mentioned.

16 ♘xb4   ♕e7
17 ♘d5   ♗xd5
18 ♗xd5 (D)   **1-0**

B

In case you are starting to get too fond of isolated pawns, I now have a puzzle for you to put things right!

Going for Mate

First, you are allowed to place more of *Black's pawns* on the board, so that, *if* it were then Black to move, he would already be stalemated.

Having put the required pawns on the board, suppose that it is actually White to move. The second part of your puzzle is to find the forced way of checkmating Black in six moves. The solution awaits you at the end of Game 19.

All four S's star in our next feature, from the 1995 Rubinstein Memorial event in Poland.

Game 19
G.Sosonko – S.Tiviakov
Polanica Zdroj 1995
Queen's Indian Defence

	1	d4	♘f6
	2	♘f3	e6
	3	g3	b6

In view of the location of the tournament, Black might have opted for 3...b5, which is often referred to as the Polish Defence! However, Tiviakov's results when employing the Queen's Indian Defence are, in general, excellent. That fact adds weight to Sosonko's achievement in this particular game.

	4	♗g2	♗b7
	5	0-0	♗e7
	6	c4	0-0 (D)
	7	d5!?	

This move, linked with the follow-up 8 ♘h4, is known as Polugaevsky's Gambit, named after the great Lev Polugaevsky, who popularised it in the early 1980s. White ambitiously tries to establish a spatial advantage, while at the same time reducing the scope of his opponent's fianchettoed bishop.

W

Apart from Polugaevsky's pawn sacrifice, another interesting deviation from the 'main' line 7 ♘c3 ♘e4 8 ♗d2 is **7 ♗f4!?**, as the game Hebden-Cooksey, Islington 1994, demonstrated. That clash continued **7...d6** (after 7...d5 8 ♘e5 ♘bd7 9 ♘c3, White also enjoys more freedom for his pieces) **8 ♘c3 ♘e4?!** (Black tries to revert to the plan normally followed in the main line, but 8...♘bd7 appears more natural and consistent with his 7th move) **9 ♖c1 ♗f6 10 ♕d3 ♘xc3 11 ♖xc3 ♘d7 12 ♘g5! ♗xg5 13 ♗xg5 ♕xg5 14 ♗xb7 ♖ab8 15 ♗c6 ♕e7 16 b4!** (with the simple but strong plan of playing ♖a3 to win the pawn on a7) **16...♖bd8 17 b5!** (17 ♖a3 ♘b8 18 ♗b7? c5! unnecessarily allows Black dangerous counterplay) **17...♘b8 18 ♗b7 c5** (perhaps missing White's 21st move in the game continuation, but 18...♖d7 fails to 19 ♖a3, provided White moves his bishop before

playing ♖xa7, because otherwise
...c6 would cost him material: bxc6
could be met by ...♘xc6!, and if
♗xc6 then ...♖xa7) **19 bxc6 ♕c7
20 ♕f3!** (20 d5 ♘d7!?, intending
...♘c5, would give Black some
chances of salvaging a draw after
21 cxd7 ♕xb7 22 dxe6 fxe6 23
♕xd6 ♕xd7, in spite of his deficit
of one pawn) **20...d5?** (this accelerates the end, though, objectively,
Black was lost anyway) **21 ♕f4!**
and **Black resigned** (because he
will no longer be able to maintain
the blockade on c7, which was
holding up the march of the c-pawn
to promotion).

7	...	exd5
8	♘h4	c6
9	cxd5	♘xd5

9...cxd5 would allow the knight
to remain on f6, defending the
kingside; otherwise the safety of
Black's king can be threatened by a
subsequent attack based on ♕g4,
as we shall see. The down-side of
choosing to capture with the pawn
on d5, instead of with the knight, is
that Black gets saddled with a serious structural weakness, namely
doubled isolated d-pawns. In the
1983 Glasgow Herald Congress, I
saw International Master Craig
Pritchett defending this difficult
situation against Roddy McKay,
another of Scotland's best-ever
chess talents. The ensuing course
of their encounter demonstrates the
passive nature of Black's position,
caused by his damaged structure,
and shows that White can quickly
recover a pawn for the one he has
sacrificed. The game went **10 ♘c3
♘a6 11 ♘f5 ♘c7 12 ♗g5 ♗c6**
(12...♘e6 is relatively best) **13
♕d4! ♘e6 14 ♘xe7+ ♕xe7 15
♗xf6 ♕xf6 16 ♕xf6 gxf6 17
♘xd5 ♗xd5 18 ♗xd5 ♖ac8 19
♖fc1! ♖fe8** (19...♘d4 20 ♔f1) **20
e3 ♔f8 21 ♔g2 ♔e7 22 ♔f3 h6 23
h4 f5 24 b4!** (seizing more space,
and restricting the scope of Black's
knight) **24...a5 25 a3 axb4 26 axb4
♖xc1 27 ♖xc1 ♔d6 28 ♗c4 ♖c8
29 ♖d1+ ♔e7 30 ♗b5 d6 31 ♖a1!
♖c3 32 ♖a7+ ♔f6 33 ♔g2** (33
♖b7?? ♘d4+!) **33...♘c7** (33...♖b3
34 ♗e8! ♘d8 35 ♖d7 or 34...♘g7
35 ♖xf7+ ♔g6 36 h5+! ♘xh5 37
♖d7+ ♔g5 38 ♖xd6 ♖xb4 39 ♖g6#
and 36...♔h7 37 ♖b7 ♖xb4 38
♗g6+ ♔g8 39 ♖b8+ all illustrate
the lack of safety of Black's king,
even in this endgame with few
pieces remaining on the board) **34
♗e2 ♖c2 35 ♗d1 ♖c1 36 ♗h5!
♖c4 37 ♖b7 ♖c6 38 ♗f3 d5 39 b5!
♘xb5 40 ♗xd5 ♖d6 41 ♖xf7+ ♔e5
42 ♗c4 ♘c3 43 f4+** and **Black resigned**, in view of 43...♔e4 44
♖e7+ ♔e6 45 ♖xe6#.

10	♘f5	♘c7
11	e4	d5
12	♖e1 *(D)*	
12	...	♘e6

White has a dangerous initiative,
so it would be quite natural for
Black to try to exchange queens by

B

opening the d-file with 12...dxe4. There are many interesting replies, including 13 ♕g4 and 13 ♗xe4. As a late note, I will mention that the former case was the choice of Norwegian GM Jonathan Tisdall in a game I spotted from the 1996 Hallsberg Open, but I also like the latter option, which threatens 14 ♘xe7+ ♕xe7 15 ♗xh7+ and 16 ♖xe7. The attempt to avoid that trap by playing 13...♗b4 can be refuted in stunning fashion with 14 ♘h6+! gxh6 (14...♔h8 15 ♘xf7+! ♖xf7 16 ♕xd8+) 15 ♕g4+ ♔h8 16 ♕f5 ♔g7 17 ♗xh6+! ♔xh6 18 ♕xh7+ ♔g5 19 ♕h4#.

13 exd5   cxd5
14 ♘c3

A typical recurring problem for the attacking side in such situations is the need to decide when, and if, he should recoup some material. For instance, a player of Sosonko's calibre would usually consider 14 ♗xd5 in his calculations. However,

this move was probably rejected in view of 14...♗xd5 15 ♕xd5 ♘d7 (not 15...♕xd5?? 16 ♘xe7+), after which Black has virtually completed his development and defused most of White's initiative through exchanges. Indeed, the further attempt to revive the attack with 16 ♖xe6? is unsound, and would be refuted easily by 16...fxe6 17 ♕xe6+ ♖f7.

14 ...   ♗b4
15 ♕g4!   ♗xc3

15...♘c6? 16 ♖xe6! fxe6 17 ♕xg7#.

16 bxc3

17 ♖xe6 is now a clear threat. What is far from clear, however, is how Black might find a satisfactory defence.

16 ...   ♕f6

If 16...g6, then 17 ♘h6+ ♔g7 18 ♘xf7 ♖xf7 19 ♕xe6 ♕f6 20 ♕xf6+ ♖xf6 (20...♔xf6 21 ♗b2, intending c4+) 21 ♖e7+ ♖f7 22 ♖xb7! ♖xb7 23 ♗xd5 wins for White, and provides a good illustration of the powerful potential of a bishop pair in operation on an open board.

17 ♗a3   ♘c5

17...♖c8 18 ♘e7+, 17...♖d8 18 ♗e7 and 17...♖e8 18 ♘d6 ♖e7 19 ♘xb7 ♖xb7 20 ♗xd5 are all hopeless for Black.

18 ♗xc5   bxc5 *(D)*
19 ♘e7+   ♔h8
20 ♖ab1!

White seizes the opportunity to gain a valuable tempo by harassing

W

the black bishop before capturing the d-pawn.

20 ...   &c6
21 &xd5   &d8

21...&g6? 22 &xg6 hxg6 23 &c7.

22 &bd1   &a5

White can win material by force after 22...&d7. The clearest route is 23 &e3 &xg2 (23...&c7 24 &xc6 &e5 25 &f4! or 25 &d5! also finishes Black off) 24 &xd7, when Black's queen and bishop are simultaneously *en prise*. Less convincing is 23 &e7, on account of 23...&xg2 24 &xd7 &f3! 25 &f5 &e8 26 &c7 &d8 or 24 &xg2 &f6!. The point is that, from the e3-square, White's knight can defend his queen, thereby ensuring a gain of material in all variations.

23 &e7!   &a6

23...&xa2 24 &xf7! &g8 (or 24...&xf7 25 &c8+) 25 c4!, intending 26 &e7 &xg2 27 &g6+! hxg6 28 &h4#, is a nice line. Notice that

the move 25 c4! is important, to avoid the long-range retreating capture ...&xf7. Also, 24 &xf7! is much stronger than 24 &c7, which can be answered with 24...&xg2 25 &xg2 &c6!.

24 &f5!

The situation of Black's king becomes more precarious with each powerful blow by White. Actually, it is hardly surprising that Tiviakov's position caves in now, since his queen has been forced far away from the kingside, where she is desperately needed for defence. The lack of reinforcements in that region of the board explains why Black is so helpless in variations such as 24...f6 25 &e4 g6 26 &xh7+! &xh7 27 &xg6+ &h8 28 &h7#.

24 ...   &xd5
25 &xd5   &ad8
26 &xa7   c4 *(D)*

W

27 &g2!

This is a very useful prophylactic move, intended to avoid 'back rank' checks. After 27...♕xa2, for example, Sosonko could win instantly with 28 ♗e4! g6 29 ♕f6+. There is also the immediate threat of 28 ♖xf7 ♖xf7 29 ♗xf7!!, exploiting Black's awkward back-rank situation.

27	...	h6
28	♖d4	♕b6
29	♗e4	g6
30	♖xd8!	1-0

There is no future for Black in 30...♖xd8 31 ♕xf7, 30...♕xd8 31 ♕e5+ f6 32 ♕f4 g5 33 ♕f5 or 30...gxf5 31 ♖xf8+ ♔g7 32 ♖axf7+ ♔g6 33 ♖xf5 ♔g7 34 ♖5f7#. Sosonko conducted the game in a highly impressive and very forcing manner. To find any worthwhile improvements on Black's play, it is probably necessary to start looking at move 12 or earlier!

Solution to Puzzle (posed after Game 18)

In the position with which you were presented, Black's king and e-pawns had no legal moves available. Therefore, to engineer a stalemate situation for Black, it is now only necessary to deprive his rook and bishop of any moves too. This can be arranged by placing black pawns on a3, a5, c3 and c5, but then one more pawn is also required on c4 to prevent the pawn on c5 from advancing.

I doubt if Black will be celebrating having three units more than his opponent, since his assorted collection of doubled and trebled pawns are all isolated, and must rank as one of the worst structures in history! The zero scope of his pieces is also unenviable, and, with his king about to be checkmated by force in six moves, we can safely say that Black is not safe here! It is true that White's pawns do not make a pretty picture either, but they do control many important squares, thereby denying Black's king any escape from the following sequence:

1 ♖h8 ♔d5 2 ♖h5! ♔e4 3 ♖h1 ♔d5 4 ♖d1+ ♔e4 5 ♖e1! ♔d5 6 e4#.

The rainy weather in Belgium helps me to feel quite at home (Scotland is not famous for sunshine)! It also brings to mind Columbo, the TV detective who is so attached to his raincoat. Did you ever see the episode about the two chess champions? Well, in case not, I'd better keep quiet. However, I have written my own little story to let you exercise your skills in logic, deduction, and chess.

The Red Rum Mystery

In this tale, the characters who are playing White and Black will be referred to as **W** and **B** respectively.

They have adjourned a game in the following position: *(D)*

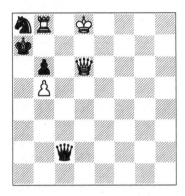

B

B is to move, but his king is looking very unsafe, and the knight is also severely lacking in scope and space to manoeuvre. **W**, with all his advantages in material and otherwise, is confident of winning. He tells **B** that he intends to celebrate the forthcoming victory by drinking a bottle labelled 'Red Rum'! **B** claims that things will be reversed (but not including the letters on the label, we must hope)! **B** does not seriously believe that he can win; only that he will draw easily. Here is their conversation just *before* resuming the game.

B: 'Not counting resignation, you will have only two legal possibilities in reply to my first move.'

W: 'I have already analysed that idea at home. I do not intend to blunder and let you drink the red rum.'

B: 'Naturally you will play the correct response. However, after my forced second move I intend to offer a draw.'

W: 'I thought you might say that, but when you see my following move I will accept your resignation.'

Can *you* solve this mystery by discovering the intended continuation? My solution awaits you after the next staggering game, but now we must return to a sober discussion of the four S's.

The following swift clash occurred in Belgium in a tournament sponsored by a company named *SWIFT*.

Game 20
B.Larsen – V.Korchnoi
Brussels 1987
Réti Opening

1	c4	♘f6
2	g3	c6

White's second move indicated a likely intention to fianchetto his king's bishop. Korchnoi's response to that is one of the most logical possible replies, designed to reduce the future scope of the enemy bishop on the h1-a8 diagonal. He wants to be able to maintain a pawn on the d5-square, so he makes the preparatory move ...c6. Of course, 2...e6 is a common and perfectly good move too, but one point in favour of Korchnoi's choice is that his queen's bishop will have lots of freedom on the c8-h3 diagonal once ...d5 has been played.

3 ♘f3

Changes in move-order can sometimes make critical tactical differences. For instance, 3 ♗g2 d5 4 b3?! allows 4...dxc4 5 bxc4 ♕d4!.

3 ... d5

4 b3 ♕b6!? (D)

W

One key aspect of this interesting idea is that after 5 ♗b2 dxc4, then 6 bxc4?? would leave White's bishop on b2 *en prise*. Black is about to reveal another more disguised detail.

5 ♗g2

5 d4 merits consideration. Although it leaves White rather exposed on the e1-a5 and b1-h7 diagonals, the move does gain some space.

5 ... e5!

Suddenly Korchnoi has a spatial advantage, made possible by the tactical point that if 6 ♘xe5?, then Black replies 6...♕d4.

6 0-0 e4

7 ♘e1

A sad, but almost forced retreat, in view of 7 ♘e5? ♕d4 and 7 ♘h4? g5.

7 ... h5!

Grandmaster Dr Colin McNab faced this seven years later at the 1994 Moscow Olympiad. Like Larsen, Colin also found that White's position is already both cramped and insecure. Black's very direct assault on the h-file is not subtle, but is nevertheless highly effective!

8 ♘c3

8 h4 might have slowed down Black's attack, but it would relinquish almost all control of the g4-square, since the move h3 could no longer be played. Also, 8...♗d6, threatening 9...♗xg3, shows up another drawback of the advance h2-h4.

8 ... h4

9 d4 hxg3

10 fxg3

Purely from a structural point of view, capturing towards the centre with 10 hxg3 is preferable, because it keeps White's pawns more compact. However, Larsen was probably, and quite naturally, afraid of Black's queen quickly finding her way to h2 and announcing 'Checkmate'.

10 ... ♕a5! (D)

W

11 ♕c2

11 ♗d2? e3! or 11 ♗b2 ♘g4, pouncing on the weaknesses at e3 and h2.

11 ... ♗b4
12 ♗b2 ♗e6!

12...♘g4 would be badly timed in this position due to 13 cxd5 cxd5 14 ♘xd5!, exploiting the unprotected situation of the bishop on c8.

13 cxd5 ♘xd5
14 ♘xd5

14 ♘xe4? ♘e3.

14 ... cxd5
15 a3 ♗d2!
16 ♕d1?

16 b4 ♗e3+ 17 ♔h1 ♕d8! 18 ♕c3 ♕g5 threatens ...♕xg3 or 19...♖xh2+! 20 ♔xh2 ♕h5+ 21 ♗h3 ♕xh3#. Maybe 16 ♔h1 is relatively best. For example, 16...♘c6? 17 b4 ♕c7 18 ♕xd2 ♕xg3 19 ♕f4! ♖xh2+ 20 ♔g1 even puts Black in trouble. However, 16...♗e3 is a big improvement: 17 ♕c3 (17 b4? ♕d8!) transposes to a line already given)

17...♕xc3 18 ♗xc3 ♘d7! 19 ♘c2 ♖c8! 20 ♘xe3 ♖xc3, when White is virtually lost because of his loose structure and congested army.

16 ... ♗e3+
17 ♔h1 ♕c7!

0-1

The final position underlines how helpless White's king is to defend against the threat of 18...♕xg3. His other pieces, even those very nearby, cannot come to his aid, because they are so lacking in scope and space in which to move.

'Red Rum' Mystery now solved!

Referring to the position which I left you considering before game 20, it is worth noting that it would be completely lost for Black even if only the two kings and b-pawns were on the board. Indeed, W is threatening ♖xa8+, since the reply ...♔xa8 can be answered by ♕c6+, winning quickly. 1...♕e4 loses in several ways, including 2 ♖xa8+ ♕xa8+ (2...♔xa8 3 ♕c6+) 3 ♔d7 ♕b7+ (3...♕h8 4 ♕c7+ ♔a8 5 ♕c8+ wins similarly for White) 4 ♕c7 ♔a8 5 ♕xb7+ ♔xb7 6 ♔d6 ♔a7 7 ♔c7 ♔a7 8 ♔c6 ♔a8 9 ♔xb6 ♔b8 10 ♔c6 ♔c8 11 b6 ♔b8 12 b7 ♔a7 13 ♔c7, followed by the promotion 14 b8♕.

When **B** declared that his intended first move would permit **W** to choose from only two *legal* replies, it can be deduced that the game continuation would start with **1...♕c7+!**. Naturally, **W** would not be so drunk on red rum as to read it backwards (murder), or to blunder with 2 ♔e8??. Therefore the game would proceed with **2 ♕xc7+ ♘xc7**. It does not seem unreasonable for **B** to offer a draw now, since he is threatening 3...♔xb8 or 3...♘xb5. His optimism is also based on the crucial fact that 3 ♔xc7 really *is* a draw: stalemate! However, apart from the bottle of red rum up his sleeve, **W** has also prepared the stunning **3 ♖a8+!!**. **B** can now resign, in view of 3...♘xa8 4 ♔c8 ♘c7 (only move) 5 ♔xc7 ♔a8 6 ♔xb6, eventually leading to promotion, as described earlier. The alternatives 3...♔xa8 4 ♔xc7 and 3...♔b7 4 ♖a7+! ♔xa7 5 ♔xc7 are also 'murder' for Black!

I do not believe that males play better chess than females, or vice-versa. Therefore it was not a deliberate decision to feature only two games so far in this book involving a woman or a girl (Hodgson-Zsu.Polgar, included in Game 17, and the brief encounter Fraser-Motwani, given during the introduction). The famous trio of Polgar sisters have all defeated numerous really strong opponents, thereby providing inspiration for others who might themselves hope to topple a few champions. Perhaps it is

more than a coincidence that the 34 letters in *Polgars into checkmating mode, as always* can be rearranged to give *Cool games sway a rattled champion's king*!

Sweden's Pia Cramling is another example of a highly talented lady player who regularly scores very successfully against players of both sexes on the international circuit. Having faced Pia twice myself, I know that her play combines all the elements of T.O.D.O. (I am mentioning that concept from Chapter two again to stress that the ideas we have considered in earlier sections are still useful now and in later parts of our H.O.T. chess journey, though at any particular stage emphasis will naturally be given to the main topic at that point). However, her brilliant attacking display against Levitina from the 1986 Women's Candidates event also contains lots of opportunities for discussing structure, space, scope and safety.

Game 21
P.Cramling – I.Levitina
Malmö 1986
Grünfeld Defence

1	d4	♘f6
2	c4	g6
3	♘c3	d5
4	cxd5	♘xd5
5	e4	♘xc3
6	bxc3	*(D)*

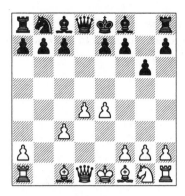

B

This position is frequently seen in practice, and so it has also become a subject of much theoretical debate. Its popularity can be explained at least partly by the fact that it offers interesting prospects for both sides. In a pure sense, Black has the better pawn structure, although White has already established an imposing central formation. Black will attempt to apply pressure to White's centre by means of ...♗g7 and ...c5. If those moves are later followed up by ...cxd4, then Black will have a queenside pawn majority of 2v1 when White recaptures with cxd4. Therefore, Black can often generate an outside passed pawn on the queenside. On the opposite wing, White may develop attacking possibilities, as Black's king is slightly vulnerable now that a knight is missing from the kingside.

I do not wish to over-simplify the complex interactions which tend to occur between the opposing armies of pieces in the Grünfeld Defence. However, I feel that a very concise and neat way in which to summarise the principal strengths and weaknesses of Black's position is: '+'*for Structure; '–'for Safety.*

6 ...   ♗g7
7 ♗c4

Fashions come and go. In 1995, I noticed 7 ♗b5+!? and 7 ♘f3 cropping up far more often than Cramling's choice. For instance, 7 ♘f3 c5 8 ♖b1 (it is be useful for White not to have a rook on the same diagonal as Black's fianchettoed bishop) **8...0-0 9 ♗e2** reaches a position that has occurred in countless games. Then the continuation 9...cxd4 10 cxd4 ♕a5+ 11 ♗d2 ♕xa2 has become a very fashionable and heavily analysed gambit. In H.Gretarsson-Dvoirys, Leeuwarden 1995, Dvoirys preferred to deviate with **9...b6!?**. The subsequent course of the game is highly instructive. You will see Black applying pressure to White's centre using a double fianchetto; then dissolving it with an elegant temporary sacrifice of a knight; and finally utilising a queenside pawn majority to create a passed b-pawn, which decides the outcome. The game proceeded **10 0-0 ♗b7 11 ♕d3 e6!?** (to prevent the central advance d4-d5) **12 ♗f4?!** (12 dxc5 ♕xd3 13 ♗xd3 ♘d7 gives Black superb piece play in return for his deficit of one insignificant pawn, White's structure being in such poor shape) **12...cxd4 13 cxd4 ♘c6 14 ♖fd1** (this would have been better timed on move 12) **14...♘xd4! 15 ♘xd4 e5 16 ♗e3 exd4 17 ♗xd4 ♗xd4 18 ♕xd4 ♕xd4 19 ♖xd4 ♖fd8 20 ♖bd1 ♖xd4 21 ♖xd4 ♔f8 22 f3 ♔e7 23 ♗c4 ♗c6 24 ♔f2 b5 25 ♗b3** (25 ♗d5 ♖d8 is unpleasant for White) **25...a5 26 a3 ♖a7 27 ♔e3 ♗d7 28 ♖d2 ♗e6 29 ♗xe6 ♔xe6 30 ♖d5 ♖b7 31 f4** (it is a worthwhile chess exercise to investigate the consequences of 31 ♔d2 ♖d7!, and you should find that Black will eventually win the pawn endgame resulting from the exchange of rooks, because at the correct moment he can use his queenside pawn majority to force White's king away from guarding his kingside pawns) **31...b4! 32 axb4 axb4 33 ♖d2 b3 34 ♖d2 ♖b4 35 g3 f6 36 ♔d2 g5! 37 fxg5** (37 ♔c3 ♖xe4 38 fxg5 fxg5 39 ♔xb3 ♔f5, intending ...♔g4-h3, is bleak for White) **37...fxg5 38 ♔c3 ♖b8 39 ♔d4** (39 ♖xb3 ♖xb3+ 40 ♔xb3 ♔e5 is also a hopelessly lost endgame for White) **39...g4 40 ♔e3 ♔e5 41 ♖b1** (41 ♔d3 h5 42 ♔e3 ♖f8! 43 ♖e2 ♖c8 44 ♖b2 ♖c3+ 45 ♔d2 ♖c2+ 46 ♖xc2 bxc2 47 ♔xc2 ♔xe4, followed by ...♔f3-g2, shows how an outside passed pawn can be used to divert the opponent's king, leaving pawns unprotected and ready for 'picking off') **41...♘2 42**

♔d3 h5 43 ♔c2 ♔xe4 44 ♖e1+ ♔f3 45 ♔b1 ♔g2 46 ♖e2+ ♔g1 47 ♖d2 ♖b5 *(D).*

W

White now **resigned**, since he is defenceless against the rook manoeuvre ...♖f5-f2, winning the kingside pawns. A logical, flowing game by the Russian grandmaster.

7	...	**0-0**
8	**♘e2**	**c5**
9	**0-0**	**♘c6**
10	**♗e3**	**♕c7**

10...♗g4 occurred in numerous Karpov-Kasparov clashes, White responding with 11 f3 ♘a5 12 ♗xf7+ ♖xf7 13 fxg4 ♖xf1+ 14 ♔xf1! (14 ♕xf1 ♘c4 15 ♗f2 ♘d2 is good for Black). Black then has some compensation for his sacrificed pawn, because he might use the c4-square as an outpost for his knight. However, it takes a brave person to gambit even a pawn against Karpov, whose excellent technique is well-known. Indeed,

Karpov showed that his extra g-pawn, despite the fact that it is doubled, has some value. For example, if White later advances e4-e5 to gain space or reduce the scope of the bishop on g7, and if, in turn, Black tries to activate that piece again by playing ...♗h6 (assuming the bishop is not simply *en prise* there), then White may seize more space with h4 and g5, shutting the bishop out again. Meanwhile the other half of the doubled duo remains on g2 to shelter White's king.

11	♖c1	♖d8
12	f4	

As a late extra, in March 1996 I spotted a game (played shortly before that in the Dutch inter-clubs league) in which IM Rudy Douven employed **12 ♘f4!?** against Erik Janssen. If 12...cxd4 13 cxd4 ♗xd4 (13...♘xd4?? 14 ♗xf7+), then 14 ♘d5! ♕e5 then:

a) 15 ♗xd4 is one possibility:

a1) 15...♘xd4? 16 f4!, intending 16...♕xe4? 17 ♖e1 or 16...♕g7 17 ♘xe7+, is good for White.

a2) 15...♕xd4! 16 ♕xd4 ♘xd4 17 ♘xe7+ ♔f8 is playable for Black.

b) Therefore White might prefer 15 ♗f4!?, with a dangerous initiative and tactical possibilities such as 15...♕xe4 16 ♖e1 ♕f5 17 ♕xd4! ♘xd4 18 ♘xe7+ ♔g7 (not 18...♔f8? 19 ♗h6+) 19 ♘xf5+ ♘xf5 (19...♗xf5 20 ♖e7 ♖d7? 21

♖xd7 ♗xd7 22 ♗e5+) 20 ♗e5+ and then:

b1) 20...f6 21 ♗a1 leaves Black's king very exposed along the 7th rank, and the unpleasant prospect of g4-g5 adds to his headaches.

b2) 20...♔f8 21 ♗f6 illustrates the power of White's bishop pair in an open position, giving more than enough compensation for a deficit of one pawn. For example, 21...♖e8 (21...♖d6 22 ♗b2 threatening ♗a3 is horrible for Black) 22 ♖xe8+ ♔xe8 23 g4 ♘h6 (23...♘e7 24 ♖e1 or 23...♘d6 24 ♖d1! ♘xc4 25 ♖d8#) 24 h3 leaves Black very tied up. If he plays ...♗e6, White can simply exchange bishops then infiltrate to the 7th rank with ♖c7, after which he will quickly recover at least one pawn.

Returning to the position after 12 ♘f4, Douven-Janssen actually continued **12...e6 13 d5** with some initiative for White. One of the points behind ♘f4 is that it supports the central push d4-d5. Also, 13...♘e5 14 ♕e2! ♘xc4 15 ♕xc4 e5 16 ♘d3 b6 17 f4 a5 18 ♕b3!, intending 18...♗a6 19 c4 or 18...c4 19 ♕xb6, was good for White in an earlier game Douven-Vanheste.

12	...	♗g4
13	f5	♘a5

13...cxd4 14 ♗xf7+! ♔xf7 15 ♕b3+ ♔e8 16 ♘xd4 (threatening 17 ♘e6 or 17 ♕g8+) 16...♗xd4 17 cxd4 gives White a ferocious attack for the sacrificed piece. Black's king and bishop are both in danger, and the threat of 18 d5 makes her situation even more difficult.

14 ♗d5?!   e6?!

This move looks very natural, but I like 14...gxf5! 15 h3 ♗h5 (15...♗xe2 16 ♕xe2 e6 17 exf5 exd5 18 f6, intending 19 ♕g4, is unclear) 16 ♖xf5 ♗g6, with an excellent position for Black.

15 fxe6   fxe6 *(D)*

W

16 ♘f4!   exd5

16...♗xd1 17 ♘xe6 is a highly confusing variation! For example, 17...♕d7 18 ♘xd8+ ♔h8 19 ♘f7+ ♔g8 20 ♘e5+ ♕xd5 21 exd5 should eventually result in a win for White. However, 17...♖xd5 18 ♘xc7 ♖d7 19 ♘xa8 ♗e2 20 ♖fe1 ♗d3 is much tougher to crack: White has an exchange and a pawn more, but all of her pieces lack scope, while those of her opponent are very actively placed. Note that if 16...♕xf4 17 ♖xf4 ♗xd1, White

has the *check* 18 ♗xe6+ before playing 19 ♖xd1.

17 ♕xg4   ♕d7

18 ♘e6 was threatened.

18 ♕e6+!   ♔h8

19 exd5   ♘c4

Not 19...♕xe6 20 ♘xe6 ♖xd5? 21 ♘c7.

20 ♗f2   cxd4

21 ♗xd4

Now 22 ♘xg6+! hxg6 23 ♖f8+! ♔h7 24 ♕xd7 ♖xd7 25 ♖xa8 is a threat.

21 ...   ♗xd4+

22 cxd4   b5

Black misses the lovely tactic which White now plays. However, 22...♕xe6 23 ♘xe6 ♖dc8 24 ♖f7 ♘d6 25 ♖xc8+ ♖xc8 26 ♖d7 is also hopeless for her (a player of Pia Cramling's calibre will not fall for 26...♘e4 27 ♖xb7?? ♖c1#).

23 ♘xg6+! *(D)* **1-0**

B

Black resigned in view of the variation 23...hxg6 24 ♖f8+ ♔g7

25 ♕f6+! ♔h6 26 ♕h4+ ♔g7 27 ♕h8#.

If chess is played with a warm spirit then it is a very healthy pursuit. Much spirit was being imbibed in a convivial atmosphere when I looked in at *Le Greenwich* for the first time (on 18 November 1995). It is a wonderful chess café situated in the heart of Brussels, and an ideal place for the adult population to engage in some casual chess encounters in a social setting. That is not to say the standard of play was mediocre. On the contrary, during an initial period of shyness when I decided to take a back seat to watch the goings-on, and subsequently in a good over-the-board tussle which I had with a Belgian man, I found that the quality of chess output was high. 'Practice makes perfect', as the saying goes, and it was evident that there was no shortage of male and female board partners at the café for anyone who is seeking to improve, or simply wanting 'friendly' games.

Here is the first of my friendly tussles in Brussels.

Game 22
P.Motwani – P.Dupont
Brussels 1995
Caro-Kann Defence

1 e4　　　c6
2 ♘e2!? *(D)*

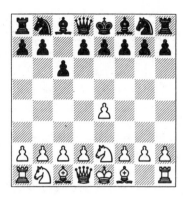

B

2 ...　　　d5
3 e5　　　♗f5

The super-grandmaster clash Short-Gulko, Horgen 1995, took a different path: **3...c5 4 d4 ♘c6 5 c3 ♗f5 6 dxc5!** e6 (6...♘xe5 is answered by 7 ♘d4!, exploiting the loose position of the bishop on f5, and threatening ♗b5+) **7 b4 a5 8 ♘d4 axb4 9 cxb4!** ♕c7 (9...♘xb4 10 ♗b5+ is horrible for Black) **10 ♗b5 ♗xb1 11 ♖xb1 ♕xe5+ 12 ♗e3** ♕c7 **13 0-0!** ♗e7 (13...♖xa2 14 ♖a1 ♖xa1 15 ♕xa1 leaves Black facing the terrible threat of 16 ♕a8+) **14 ♗xc6+ bxc6 15 b5! cxb5** (15...♗xc5 16 ♘xe6 fxe6 17 ♗xc5 is disastrous for Black, whose king position is very exposed) **16 ♘xb5 ♕c6 17 ♘d4 ♕c8** (17...♕xc5 18 ♘xe6 is even worse for Black than the actual game continuation) **18 ♕b3 ♘f6** (18...♗xc5?? 19 ♕b5+ ♔f8 20 ♖fc1 is totally bleak for Black) **19 ♕b5+ ♔f8** (the reply to either 19...♕d7 or 19...♘d7 would be 20 c6) **20 ♘c6 ♘e4** (20...♕d7 21 ♕b7 ♖e8 22 ♕xd7 ♘xd7 23 ♖b7 ♘f6 24 ♘xe7 ♖xe7 25 c6 ♖xb7 26 cxb7 ♔e7 27 ♖b1 ♘d7 28 ♗a7 ♘b8 29 ♗xb8 ♖xb8 30 a4 ♔d6 31 a5 ♔c7 32 a6 d4 33 a7 ♖xb7 34 ♖c1+ and 35 a8♕ is a long, but forcing variation illustrating the power of White's connected outside passed pawns on the a- and b-files) **21 ♘xe7 ♔xe7 22 ♕b2!? ♖d8** (22...f6 23 f3! ♘xc5 24 ♖fc1 ♖a5 25 ♕b4 results in a doubly painful pin on Black's knight) **23 ♕xg7 ♖xa2 24 ♖fc1 ♖g8 25 ♕e5 f6 26 ♕h5 ♖g7 27 c6** (intending 28 ♖b7+) **27...♔d6 28 c7! ♖a8** (or 28...♖xc7 29 ♖b6+ ♔e7 30 ♕xh7+ ♔d8 31 ♕g8+ ♔d7 32 ♕xe6+ wins shortly for Short) **29 ♗f4+ e5** (if 29...♔d7, then 30 ♖b8 wins) **30 ♗xe5+! fxe5 31 ♕h6+ and Black resigned** (due to 31...♖g6 32 ♖b6+ ♔d7 33 ♕xh7+). A very original and convincing game by Short.

4 ♘d4!?

A natural alternative is 4 ♘g3 ♗g6 5 h4 h6 6 d4 e6 7 h5 ♗g6 8 ♗d3 ♗xd3 9 ♕xd3. White is well placed to castle kingside and then attack with f4-f5; Black may concentrate on the other wing, perhaps starting with 9...c5.

4 ...   ♗g6

5 e6 *(D)*

A highly original position has arisen in the space of only five moves, but Black reacts well to the unfamiliar situation.

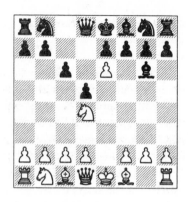

B

5 ...   ♕d6!

5...c5? allows 6 ♗b5+.

6 ♕e2   ♘a6

6...fxe6! deserves consideration. For example, 7 ♘xe6 ♗xc2 8 d4 (threatening 9 ♗f4) 8...♗d3!? 9 ♘xg7+ ♗xg7 10 ♕xd3 ♕b4+, winning White's d-pawn. Of course, 7 ♕xe6 is playable. In fact, Black must avoid 7...♕xe6+!? 8 ♘xe6, when he would have no good way of preventing 9 ♘c7+.

7 ♘c3   ♘c7

After 7...fxe6, 8 ♘xe6?! ♘b4 9 d3 ♘xc2+! 10 ♔d1 (or 10 ♕xc2 ♕xe6+) 10...♘xa1 11 ♗f4 ♕b4, intending 12 ♘c7+ ♔d8 13 ♘xa8? (13 ♘e6+ might offer some chances of a draw) 13...♕xf4, is very bad for White. However, 8 d3 gives plenty of positional compensation in return for the lost pawn. Indeed, after 8...e5 9 ♘f3 a pawn will be recovered, while if 8...♘c7 9 g3, then ♗f4 or ♗h3 is threatened.

8 exf7+   ♗xf7

9 ♘f3! **♛e6**
10 d4

10 ♘e5! is even stronger. White simply wants to play 11 d4, after which his knight will enjoy a secure outpost on e5. In that case, the e-pawn cannot advance beyond e6, with the result that Black will suffer from the structural weakness of a backward pawn. Furthermore, the scope of at least one of his bishops remains very limited. The attempt to introduce complications with 10...d4 is well answered by 11 ♘xf7 ♔xf7 (11...♛xe2+? 12 ♘xe2 ♔xf7 13 ♘xd4) 12 ♘e4, acquiring a fresh outpost, and threatening 13 ♘g5+.

10 ... **♗h5**

The trade of queens 10...♛xe2+ 11 ♗xe2 does not alleviate Black's difficulties: White can still follow up with ♘e5 or ♗f4, when the superiority of his structure and scope of his army is not in question.

11 ♗e3

I decided not to allow my pawn structure to be weakened through 11 ♛xe6 ♘xe6 12 ♗e3 ♗xf3 13 gxf3. It is true that, after the move chosen, Black could now force me to accept doubled f-pawns by playing 11...♛f6 followed soon by ...♗xf3. However, in the line 12 0-0-0 0-0-0 13 ♖g1 (intending 14 g4) 13...♗xf3 14 gxf3, White gains the possibility of ♗h3+, and having the queens still on the board increases his initiative in this case. In

the meantime Black has development problems, as 14...e6? loses material to 15 ♗g5.

11 ... **♘f6 (D)**

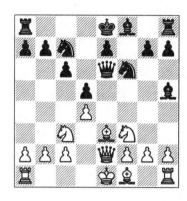

W

12 h3!

Preparing to gain space by advancing g2-g4, which will also break the pin which exists at present on White's king's knight.

12 ... **h6**
13 g4 **♗f7**
14 ♘e5 **♘d7**
15 f4

15 ♗f4! threatens ♘xf7 and then ♗xc7.

15 ... **♘xe5**
16 dxe5 **h5**
17 ♗g2 **hxg4**
18 hxg4 **♖xh1+**
19 ♗xh1 **♛h6?**

19...g5! should have been played to attempt to break up White's dangerous kingside pawn formation, which is cramping the black position badly.

20	0-0-0	e6
21	♗f3	♕h4 *(D)*

W

22 g5

Played to prevent ...♕e7 in reply to ♖h1. The immediate threat is 23 ♖h1 ♕g3 24 ♕f1, when Black cannot extricate his queen before 25 ♘e2 or 25 ♖h3 ensnare her, unless he incurs other huge losses of material (such as with 24...♗c5, almost equivalent to resignation).

| **22** | **...** | **d4?** |

However awful 22...♕h7 may have looked to Black, that move had to be tried, although after 23 ♖h1 ♕g8 the lady is a little short of breathing space!

23	♖xd4	♗c5
24	♖d1	♗xe3+
25	♕xe3	1-0

Apart from being a pawn down with a hopeless position, Black faced the unpalatable prospect of 26 ♖h1 ♕g3 27 ♗xc6+ bxc6 28 ♕xg3.

There cannot be very many people who have won tournaments ahead of Garry Kasparov. However, one such person is the Icelandic grandmaster Jon Arnason, who captured the 1977 World Cadet Championship in Cagnes-sur-Mer, France, leaving Kasparov in his wake. I remember feeling interested and inspired when I read about Jon's excellent performance. The following year, at age 16, I became the youngest-ever Scottish Champion, then a few months later I emulated Jon's fine example by winning the 1978 World Under-17 Championship (ahead of Nigel Short, Ivan Morović, Johan Hjartarson, Alon Greenfeld, and 35 other players) in the small Dutch town of Sas van Gent, situated not far from my current apartment in Belgium. Sometimes events in life have an amazing way of turning 'full circle'.

I never imagined that, 14 years after my first visit to Holland, I would return to Sas van Gent and have the honour of participating in the 1992 Professor Max Euwe Memorial Tournament. Professor Euwe, World Champion 1935-7, had presented me with my trophy in 1978, so it was particularly special for me to win a competition held as a tribute to him. People talk about being 'over the moon'. Well, five months earlier, in March 1992, the frozen landscape in Iceland made me feel as if I had made a lunar trip! The temperature and the welcome were considerably warmer when Jon Arnason and his wife Thorunn invited me to have a meal at their home. That was during a tournament in Hafnarfjördhur, a quiet little village whose name almost seems bigger than the place!

I consider the following game to be one of my best efforts in chess.

Game 23
P.Motwani – B.Jönsson
Hafnarfjördhur 1992
Vienna Game

1	e4	e5
2	♘c3	♘f6
3	g3 (D)	

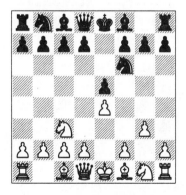

B

This is known as Smyslov's variation of the Vienna Game. Very few of my opponents have been well-prepared to meet it, often because they assumed the system was innocuous, and sometimes due to the fact that their 'home preparation' had focused on lines in the Ruy Lopez, Petroff Defence, and other openings which are more commonly seen in practice than the Vienna Game. 3 g3 has turned out to be one of the best point-scoring lines in my entire repertoire. I have never lost when playing it; in fact, my record with Smyslov's variation is close to 100%, including several grandmaster opponents.

3	...	d5

I could easily use the rest of this book to expand on my encounters with other third move alternatives, e.g. 3...♗e7/c5/b4; 3...♘c6; 3...g6; 3...b6; 3...d6; 3...c6. I will briefly summarise them by noting that, since White is about to play ♗g2, Black normally experiences difficulties in managing to achieve the freeing move ...d5, unless he plays 3...d5 or an early ...c6 then ...d5.

4	exd5	♘xd5
5	♗g2	♘xc3
6	bxc3	

White accepts a slightly inferior pawn structure, but obtains considerable activity and scope for his pieces. In particular, the fianchettoed bishop exerts pressure towards b7, and this can also be achieved by playing ♖b1, utilising the opened b-file.

6	...	♗d6

A more aggressive alternative for Black is 6...♗c5. The game

Motwani-Hebden, Scottish Weekend Open 1994 then continued 7 ♕h5!? ♘d7, and was eventually drawn after a tough fight. A tactical aspect of 6...♗c5 is that 7 ♘f3 can be strongly answered by 7...e4!, intending 8 ♘h4? g5 or 8 ♘d4 ♗xd4 9 cxd4 ♕xd4. White could consider 7 ♘e2.

7 ♘f3   0-0

7...e4?! 8 ♘d4 leaves the e-pawn vulnerable. For example, 8...0-0 9 0-0 (9 ♗xe4? ♖e8 10 d3 f5 costs White a piece) 9...f5 10 d3 exd3 11 cxd3 threatens 12 ♕b3+. 11 ♕xd3 is also strong, because although the white queenside structure remains ragged, he obtains active possibilities such as ♘b5, and 11...c6 12 ♖d1! keeps Black under persistent pressure.

8 0-0   ♘d7

In choosing the d7-square for his knight, Black retains the option of later playing ...c6 to limit the scope of White's bishop on the h1-a8 diagonal. Jon Arnason considers 8...♘c6, planning 9...e4, to be more natural.

9 ♖e1   c6

9...♖e8 10 d4 exd4 11 ♖xe8+ ♕xe8 12 cxd4 ♘f6 13 c4 c6 14 ♗g5 ♘e4 15 ♕d3!? ♘xg5 (not 15...♗f5? 16 ♖e1) 16 ♘xg5 g6 17 h4! (an attacking move which also gains space for White) 17...♗f5 18 ♕b3 h6 19 ♘f3 ♖b8 20 ♖e1 ♕d7 21 h5! g5 22 ♘e5 ♗xe5 23 ♖xe5 ♗g4 24 ♕e3! ♗xh5 25 d5 cxd5 26

♗xd5 ♗g6 27 ♕xa7 ♖c8 28 ♕b6 (threatening 29 ♕xg6+) 28...♔h7 29 ♕b4 ♖c7 30 ♔g2 f6 31 ♖e6 ♗f7 (31...♔g7 32 ♕b2 ♕d8 33 ♖b6! wins a pawn for White) 32 ♖xf6 ♗xd5+ 33 cxd5 ♕xd5+ 34 ♔h2 (with the threat 35 ♕b1+) 34...♔g7? (this was played in extreme time-trouble, but 34...♕xa2 35 ♕e4+ or 34...♕d3 35 ♕b6 does not help Black either) 35 ♕f8+ 1-0 was Motwani-Mannion, Richardson Cup Final 1993. One result of move 21 was that Black's king became more exposed, a factor that ultimately proved fatal. Note also that 23...♕xd4? would have left a bishop *en prise* (24 ♖xf5), so White had time to double on the e-file with 24 ♕e3. Thereafter, Black was under pressure in the centre, on both wings, and on the clock.

10 d4   cxd4
11 cxd4   ♘b6
12 ♕d3! *(D)*

B

White is ready to advance c2-c4, and 12...♗e6? is bad on account of 13 ♘g5.

12 ... h6

12...♕f6 13 c4 ♗f5 14 ♕b3 ♗c7 15 ♗b2 (15 c5, handing over the d5-square as an outpost for Black, is too risky on account of 15...♘d5 16 ♕xb7 ♖fb8 17 ♕a6 ♘b4) 15...♖ae8 16 d5 ♕d6 17 ♘d4 ♗d7 18 ♗a3 c5 19 ♘b5 ♗xb5 20 ♕xb5 was very unpleasant for Black in Finkel-Petek, European Under-20 Championship 1995.

13 c4 ♗e6 (D)

W

Black intends to answer 14 c5? by 14...♗xc5 15 dxc5?? ♕xd3, but White has prepared something much stronger.

14 ♖xe6!! fxe6

15 ♗xh6! ♖xf3

I had used 18 minutes on my clock so far, whereas Black, having thought for one hour on this last move alone, had now consumed a total of nearly 1½ hours on his clock. Despite being at a slight material deficit, White has a virtually winning position. The pawn-cover around Black's king has been shattered, leaving the monarch seriously exposed. This lack of safety is illustrated by the following variations:

a) 15...gxh6 16 ♕g6+ ♔h8 17 ♕xh6+ ♔g8 18 ♗h3! ♖xf3 19 ♗xe6+ ♖f7 20 ♕g6+ ♔h8 21 ♗xf7 (threatening 22 ♕h6#) 21...♕f8 22 ♖e1 (22 c5 also wins easily, but the rook move threatens ♖e4-h4) 22...♕g7 23 ♕xd6 ♕xf7 24 ♖e7 ♕f8 25 ♕e5+ ♔g8 26 ♕g5+ ♔h8 27 ♕h5+ ♔g8 28 ♕h7#.

b) 15...♕f6 16 ♗e3 (16 ♗g5 ♕f5 17 ♕xf5 ♖xf5 18 c5 is very strong too), intending 17 ♘g5 g6 18 ♘e4 ♕f5 19 c5.

c) 15...♗e7 16 ♕g6 ♗f6 17 ♘g5! ♖e8 18 ♖e1 ♕xd4 (18...♕d7 is met by 19 ♗h3 winning) 19 ♕f7+ ♔h8 20 ♖e4 ♕a1+ 21 ♗f1 ♖e7 22 ♗xg7+! ♗xg7 23 ♖h4+ ♗h6 24 ♖xh6#.

16 ♗xf3 ♕f6

17 ♗d2 ♖f8

18 ♗g2!

Not 18 ♔g2 ♘xc4! 19 ♕xc4? ♕xf3+.

18 ... ♕xf2+

19 ♔h1

Threatening 20 ♖f1.

19 ... c5

20 ♗e3 ♕f6

21 ♖e1!

21 ♖f1 ♕e7 is less convincing for White.

21 ...   cxd4

21...♕e7 22 dxc5 ♗xc5 23 ♗xc5 ♕xc5 24 ♖xe6 wins for White after either 24...♕xc4 25 ♕xc4 ♘xc4 26 ♗d5!, or 24...♘xc4 25 ♗d5 ♖f1+ 26 ♔g2! ♖f2+ 27 ♔h3, with the threats of capturing on c4, playing 28 ♖e8# or, giving numerous other deadly discovered checks.

22 ♗xd4   e5
23 ♗e3!

Renewing the threat of c4-c5 is much better than winning a pawn by 23 ♗xb6 axb6 24 ♗xb7. The resulting position with bishops of opposite colour would give Black some drawing chances, whereas in the game continuation White retains a decisive initiative which will reap greater material gains later. This is an example of the saying 'The threat is stronger than its execution' being put into practice.

23 ...   ♕e7 (D)

W

24 ♕d1!!

The dual threats are 25 ♗xb6 axb6 26 ♗d5+ ♔h8 27 ♕h5# and 25 c5 ♗xc5 26 ♗d5+! ♘xd5 27 ♕xd5+ winning Black's bishop.

24 ...   ♗b4

24...♗c5 loses to 25 ♗d5+!, and 24...g6 25 ♕g4 subjects Black to unbearable pressure.

25 c5

25 ♗xb6 also wins by force: 25...axb6 26 ♗d5+ or 25...♗xe1 26 ♗d5+ ♖f7 (26...♔h8 27 ♕h5#) 27 ♕xe1 axb6 28 ♕f2 ♔f8 29 ♕xf7+ ♕xf7 30 ♗xf7 ♔xf7 31 ♔g2, with an easily winning ♔+♙ endgame (White simply utilises his 2v1 kingside pawn majority to create a passed h-pawn, which he then uses to distract Black's monarch, allowing his own king to capture the e- and b-pawns).

25 ...	♗xe1
26 cxb6	e4
27 bxa7	♕b4
28 ♕d5+	♔h8
29 ♗xe4	♕a5

With his flag about to fall, Black saw that 30 ♕h5+ ♔g8 31 ♗h7+ ♔h8 32 ♗g6+ ♔g8 33 ♕h7# was threatened. He manages to stop that, but there is no way of coping with White's queenside threats.

30 ♕xa5   1-0

Black did not wish to face 30...♗xa5 31 ♗xb7.

Grandmaster Vassily Ivanchuk of the Ukraine is one of the most creative players in the world, but he also seems to have a tremendous ability to generate a dangerous initiative from virtually any opening he chooses. I noticed that, in 1995, he employed the Grünfeld Defence to quickly defeat the Ukrainian no. 2, Alexander Beliavsky. In their next meeting it was the Nimzo-Indian Defence which brought Ivanchuk another impressive victory.

Game 24
A.Beliavsky – V.Ivanchuk
Belgrade 1995
Nimzo-Indian Defence

1	d4	♘f6
2	c4	e6
3	g3	c5

The continuation 3...d5 4 ♘f3 ♝e7 5 ♝g2 0-0 6 0-0 dxc4 is a very common line of the Catalan system. Then the gambit variation 7 ♘a3 ♝xa3 8 bxa3 has occurred often, as has 7 ♘e5. The latter variation is designed to win a pawn back quickly, but White can also achieve that via 7 ♕c2, which has been the most popular choice in general. Then 7...b5? 8 a4 c6 9 axb5 cxb5 10 ♘g5 is extremely bad for Black, but 10...♘d5?? 11 ♕xh7# is worse! Of course, 7...a6 8 ♕xc4 b5 9 ♕c2 ♝b7 is more sensible.

4 ♘f3

4 d5 exd5 5 cxd5 d6 would result in yet another opening: the Modern Benoni.

| 4 | ... | cxd4 |
| 5 | ♘xd4 | ♝b4+ |

Ivanchuk chose to check at this cross-roads. Interesting options also arise from 5...♘c6 6 ♘c3. For example:

a) 6...♕b6 now with two main branches:

a1) This particular line is being included as an extra bonus, in view of the 'super-grandmaster' clash Anand-Leko, Wijk aan Zee 1996. The route taken was 7 ♘db5 ♘e5 8 ♝f4 ♘fg4 9 e3 a6 10 ♘c7+ ♕xc7 11 ♕xg4 d6. Black may have felt that 11...♕c6 12 ♝xe5 ♕xh1 was too risky with his queen temporarily out of play while at the same time lagging behind in development, but 11...♕xc4!? (with the tactical point 12 ♝xe5?? ♕xg4) 12 ♝xc4 ♘xg4 leaves Black a sound pawn up.

a2) 7 ♘b3 ♘e5 8 e4 ♝b4 9 ♕e2 d6 10 f4 ♘c6 11 ♝e3 (11 ♝g2 e5! 12 ♝e3 ♘d4! 13 ♕d3 ♘c2+! is excellent for Black) 11...♝xc3+ 12 bxc3 ♕c7 13 ♝g2 0-0 14 0-0 b6 produces a situation where White has more space, but Black's structure is superior. Which factor matters more is not easy to judge, but GM Eric Lobron played 15 g4 against superstar Vladimir Kramnik in a 1995 clash in Dortmund. The g3-g4 advance not only made further space gains for White, but also showed that Black's monarch is not completely safe, as Lobron created a kingside attack by following up with g5, ♖f3-h3 and ♕h5. He later lost, though his middle-game plan merits serious attention.

b) 6...♗c5!? 7 ♘b3 ♗b4 8 ♗g2 b6!? 9 0-0 ♗a6 10 ♘b5 ♖c8 11 ♗f4 d5 12 ♘3d4 ♘xd4 13 ♘xd4 (threatening 14 ♕a4+) 13...♕d7 14 cxd5 ♘xd5 gave Black superb scope and activity for his pieces in the game Rotshtein-Lazarev, Cannes 1995. However, 10 ♘d4!, intending 10...♖c8 11 ♘xc6 dxc6 12 ♕a4!, looks to me like a significant improvement for White.

6 ♘c3   0-0

Black could spoil his opponent's structure with 6...♗xc3+ 7 bxc3, but that capture is premature because the dangerous possibility of ♗a3 is given to White before Black's king has even castled.

7 ♗g2   d5 (D)

W

This position is well-known to theory. It is usually classified under the Nimzo-Indian Defence since it is often reached via the move order 1 d4 ♘f6 2 c4 e6 3 ♘c3 ♗b4 4 ♘f3 (for examples featuring 4 e3 or 4 ♕c2, see games 5 and 11 respectively) 4...0-0 5 g3 c5 6 ♗g2 cxd4 7 ♘xd4 d5.

8 cxd5

After 8 ♕b3 ♗xc3+, 9 ♕xc3 has often been played, although Black will gain tempi by harassing White's knight and queen with ...e5 and ...d4. The alternative 9 bxc3 leaves White with an inferior pawn structure, and he was fortunate to escape with a draw in the end in Kasparov-Suba, Dubai Olympiad 1986, since Black stood considerably better after 9...♘c6 10 cxd5 ♘a5 11 ♕c2 ♘xd5 12 ♕d3 ♕c7 13 0-0 ♗d7 (13...♕xc3? 14 ♕xc3 ♘xc3 15 ♗d2) 14 e4 ♘b6 15 f4 e5 16 fxe5 ♘ac4 17 g4 ♘xe5 18 ♕g3 ♘bc4 19 ♗f4 ♕c5 (19...♗xg4? 20 ♕xg4 ♘xg4 21 ♗xc7). Both of Black's knights then occupied excellent outposts, whereas White had the headaches of three isolated pawns and a fianchettoed bishop with little scope.

8 0-0 was played in the game Dannevig-Motwani, Gausdal Troll Masters 1992. The continuation was **8...dxc4 9 ♘c2** (9 ♕a4!? is a pet line of Oleg Romanishin, another Ukrainian grandmaster, and 9...♘a6 is probably Black's best response) **9...♗xc3 10 bxc3 ♕a5!** (this novelty was suggested by

Steffen Pedersen, a young Danish IM, during post-mortem analysis of the earlier game Dannevig-J.Grant, in which White soon recovered a pawn and kept Black under some pressure after 10...♕c7 11 ♘a3) **11 ♘a3 ♘c6** (11...♕xc3 12 ♖b1, threatening ♗b2 or ♘b5, allows White to develop a dangerous initiative) **12 ♘xc4· ♕xc3 13 ♕a4 ♗d7!** (13...♕b4? 14 ♗xc6 is a nightmare for Black, and 13...♕xa1 is also unnecessarily risky because of 14 ♗b2) **14 ♗b2** *(D)*.

B

14...♘d4! 15 ♗xc3 ♘xe2+ 16 ♔h1 ♗xa4 17 ♗e5 (intending 18 ♖fe1, embarrassing the knight on e2, but Black has seen further) **17...♖ac8 18 ♘d6 ♖c5 19 f4** (now Dannevig's second-rank defences around his king and his control over the e3-square have been seriously weakened, but 19 ♗xf6 gxf6 20 ♘xb7 ♖c2 should also win for Black) **19...♘g4 20 ♘xb7** (20

♖fe1? ♘f2#) **20...♖c2 21 ♗e4 f5! 22 ♗f3** (22 ♗g2 ♘e3 and 22 ♗xc2 ♗c6+ are just as hopeless for White) **22...♘xe5 23 fxe5 ♘d4** and **White resigned**, rather than face the unappetising prospect of 24 ♗g2 ♖xg2! 25 ♔xg2 ♗c6+.

8 ...   ♘xd5
9 ♕b3

9 ♗d2 is playable, but not very threatening.

9 ...   ♕a5
10 ♗d2   ♘c6
11 ♘c2?!

White takes a valuable tempo to make this retreat. Maybe he feared 11 ♘xc6 bxc6 12 0-0 ♗a6, but then he would have 13 ♘xd5! ♗xd2 14 ♘e7+ ♔h8 15 ♘xc6. Furthermore, 12...♖b8? would cost Black an exchange after 13 ♘xd5 cxd5 (but certainly not 13...♗xd2?? 14 ♘e7+ ♔h8 15 ♕xb8, and the price has gone up to a whole rook) 14 a3! ♗xd2 (14...♗d6? 15 ♕xb8! ♗xb8 16 ♗xa5 again leaves Black a rook down) 15 ♕xb8. The loss of time involved for White in making the move 11 ♘c2 is all that Ivanchuk needs to seize the initiative with Black.

11 ...   ♗xc3
12 bxc3

Beliavsky stands at least slightly worse after 12 ♗xc3 ♘xc3 13 ♕xc3 (13 bxc3 ♗d7! 14 ♕xb7? ♕xc3+) 13...♕xc3+ 14 bxc3 ♗d7, because he does not have enough activity to compensate for the two weak isolated pawns in his structure.

12 ...   ♕c7! *(D)*

W

Black threatens the manoeuvre ...♘a5-c4. This is all the more unpleasant for White since his queen will be harassed by the knight *en route* to the outpost at c4.

13 ♕a3

If 13 ♗xd5, then 13...♘a5 is possible, though I suspect that Ivanchuk intended 13...exd5. After 14 ♕xd5 ♗e6 15 ♕h5 ♘e5, White's queen is in an embarrassing situation: 16 0-0 ♗g4 17 ♕g5 ♗xe2 threatens ...♘f3+, and 16 ♗f4 allows 16...♕xc3+. Furthermore, 16 ♘d4 ♗g4 17 ♕h4 ♖fe8 18 f4 (18 0-0 ♗xe2! 19 ♘xe2? ♘f3+) 18...♘d3+ 19 ♔f1 ♗xe2+! 20 ♘xe2 ♕c6 21 ♖g1 ♕f3# demonstrates the force of Black's initiative, especially on the light squares, in the absence of White's light-squared bishop.

Some other general features of the position being considered after 13 ♗xd5 exd5 14 ♕xd5 are worth noting:

a) The presence of bishops of opposite colour is a factor which normally increases the drawing chances of the player who has a small material deficit. Therefore Black would be at little risk after sacrificing one pawn, especially because White's queenside pawn structure is badly damaged.

b) Having a bishop of opposite colour to that of the opponent tends to be a useful weapon to a player who has the initiative: his bishop can assist in attacking operations without ever being challenged by the enemy bishop.

c) In return for sacrificing his d-pawn, Black obtains use of an open d-file and gains at least one tempo by attacking White's queen while simultaneously developing a piece (14...♗e6). That gain of time is particularly valuable when the opponent's king has not yet castled into relative safety.

13 ...   ♘e5
14 ♗xd5

Beliavsky must have been very reluctant to part with his fianchettoed bishop, an important defender of the region into which White is about to castle. However, he naturally wishes to prevent Ivanchuk from playing ...♘c4. Therefore he captures on d5 in order to follow up with the move ♗f4, pinning the black knight.

14 ...	exd5
15 ♗f4	f6!

15...♗h3 16 ♘e3 ♖ad8 17 ♖d1 is less convincing for Black.

16 0-0	♕f7
17 ♘e3	♗h3
18 ♖fd1	g5!

Ivanchuk has an exceptionally keen eye for tactics. Here he exploits the lack of scope of his opponent's bishop to force an exchange on e5 which will result in the f-file being opened. Then he will have a clear avenue towards the weak f2 point. Suddenly White's king is looking very uncomfortable.

19 ♗xe5	fxe5
20 f3	e4! *(D)*

W

Full marks for courage and consistency. I say 'courage' as Black has exposed his own king by playing ...g5. However, having done that, Ivanchuk knows that he must proceed consistently with his plan of attacking the opponent's monarch. Some precise calculation leads him to the correct conclusion that it is not necessary to spend a valuable tempo to defend the pawn on d5.

21 ♕c5

Question: How should Black continue after 21 ♖xd5 exf3 22 ♖xg5+ ♔h8 23 exf3 ♕xf3 24 ♕e7? The answer will appear after the end of the game.

21 ...	exf3
22 exf3	

White could not permit a pawn to reach f2. For example, 22 ♕xd5? f2+ 23 ♔h1 ♕xd5+ and 24...f1♕+ would cost him too much material.

22 ... ♖ae8

Black's advantage is also clear after 22...♕xf3 23 ♕xd5+ ♕xd5 24 ♘xd5 ♖f3, due to White's shattered structure and the unhappy trapped position of his king.

23 ♖xd5

23 ♕xd5 ♖xe3? should lose for Black after 24 ♕xg5+ and 25 ♕xe3, but 23...♕xd5 24 ♘xd5 ♖xf3 is simple and strong.

23 ... h6!

Ivanchuk avoids a tricky trap: 23...♕xf3? 24 ♖xg5+ ♔h8 25 ♕d4+ ♖f6 26 ♖f5!!, winning for White after 26...♗xf5 27 ♕xf6+ ♔g8 28 ♘xf5 or 26...♕xe3+ 27 ♕xe3 ♖xe3 28 ♖xf6 or 26...♖xe3 27 ♕xf6+ ♔g8 28 ♕f8#.

24 ♖e5	♕xf3
25 ♕c4+	

No better is 25 罝xe8 豐f2+! (White can fight longer in the variation 25...罝xe8 26 豐d5+, although his position is still very bad after 26...豐xd5 27 ②xd5 罝e2) 26 當h1 奧g2+ 27 ②xg2 豐xc5, and Black wins easily.

25	...	當g7
26	罝xe8	罝xe8
27	豐d4+	當g6
28	豐d3+	罝e4
29	罝e1 (D)	

B

| 29 | ... | 當h5! |

0-1

White resigned since he was unable to prevent 30...罝xe3 in any satisfactory way. For example, 30 豐e2 罝xe3 31 豐xe3 豐g2# or 30 豐d2 罝xe3 31 罝xe3 豐f1#.

Answer to Question (posed at move 21): Black is threatened with 25 豐g7#, but he strikes first and delivers a forced mate in four moves as follows: 24...豐f2+ 25

當h1 奧g2+! 26 ②xg2 豐f1+ 27 罝xf1 罝xf1#.

That variation resulted from 24 豐e7 (see the note at move 21), but 24 豐c5! is a little tougher to crack. We have already seen that 24...罝ae8 25 豐d4+ 罝f6? loses to 26 罝f5!! (transposing to a line given earlier). Also, after 24 豐c5! 豐f2+! 25 當h1, 25...奧g2+?? is a blunder because of 26 ②xg2 豐f1+ 27 罝xf1 罝xf1+ 28 豐g1 (such long-range retreating moves are often overlooked). The correct path to victory for Black is 24 豐c5! 豐f2+! 25 當h1 罝ae8 26 豐d4+ 罝f6 27 罝f5 (see the final line given further on, where 27 罝e5 is considered) 27...奧g2+! 28 ②xg2 豐xd4 29 cxd4 罝xf5, when he has a decisive material advantage. That is also the case if White deviates with 26 罝e5, since Black has 26...奧g2+! 27 ②xg2 豐f1+ 28 罝xf1 罝xf1+ 29 豐g1 罝xg1+ 30 當xg1 罝xe5. Finally, if 27 罝e5, then 27...罝ef8 threatens 28...奧g2+! 29 ②xg2 豐xd4 30 cxd4 罝f1+ 31 罝xf1 罝xf1#. I love Ivanchuk's games, but sometimes I wish they were not so complicated (it causes too many headaches if one has to annotate them)!

A postcard in November 1995 from Erika Sziva, a friend who was competing in a tournament on the island of Crete, was one 'Greek gift' that I was happy to receive.

However, on the chess-board I always try to avoid having to accept such a fate ... even when the cards are stacked against me! The 'Greek gift' to which I am referring is the bishop sacrifice on h7. Its occurrences in international events are frequent, and normally mean that the situation in the game is looking black for Black (a corresponding sacrifice on h2 would indicate that the future is not bright for White).

Paul Fitzpatrick, an excellent teacher at St Saviour's High School in Dundee, Scotland, practically etched details of the Greek gift onto my mind when I was 12 years old. He used a variation of the Ruy Lopez to illustrate his point. **1 e4 e5 2 ♘f3 ♘c6 3 ♗b5 a6 4 ♗a4 ♘f6 5 0-0 ♗c5 6 c3 b5** 6...♘xe4 7 ♕e2!. **7 ♗c2 0-0?** 7...d6 8 d4 ♗b6 is better, enabling Black to maintain his central pawn on e5. **8 d4 exd4 9 cxd4 ♗b6 10 e5** White gains more space, time, and scope for his light-squared bishop while driving away a vital defender of Black's kingside. **10...♘d5** (D)

White now unleashes a devastating sacrifice. **11 ♗xh7+!** A typical finish to this Greek gift offer is **11...♔xh7 12 ♘g5+ ♔g8** 12...♔g6 13 ♕d3+ f5 14 exf6+ (this is a clearer route to victory for White than 14 ♕g3 f4) 14...♔xf6 15 ♕f3+ ♔g6 16 ♕e4+ ♔f6 (if 16...♖f5, then 17 g4) 17 ♘h7+ ♔f7 18 ♕xd5+ wins too. **13 ♕h5 ♖e8 14 ♕xf7+**

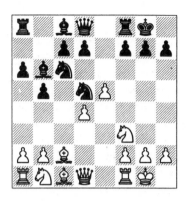

W

♔h8 15 ♕h5+ ♔g8 16 ♕h7+ ♔f8 17 ♕h8+ ♔e7 18 ♕xg7#.

Paul always stresses the importance of having the 'Trojan horse' ready to leap forward, with support, to the g5-square. All the key features of the Greek gift are present in the following encounter from the 1989 Lloyds Bank Masters event.

Game 25
M.Chandler – D.Agnos
London 1989
French Defence

1	e4	e6
2	d4	d5

The last French Defence in this book was back in Game 9, but there White chose 2 ♕e2.

| 3 | ♘c3 | ♘f6 |

This, the Classical Variation, is quite different in character to the Winawer Variation, 3...♗b4, of Game 8.

4 ♗g5   ♗e7

4...dxe4 5 ♘xe4 leaves Black without any pawn beyond his third rank, but offers plenty of scope for original play. An instructive example is provided by Hector-S.Agdestein, Reykjavik 1996, which went 5...♘bd7 6 ♘f3 ♗e7 7 ♘xf6+ ♘xf6 (I have found 7...♗xf6 to be a solid alternative) 8 ♗d3 c5 9 dxc5 ♕a5+ 10 c3 ♕xc5 11 ♕e2 ♗d7 12 ♘e5 ♗c6 13 0-0 ♘d7 14 ♗xe7 ♔xe7!? 15 ♘xc6+ bxc6 16 ♗e4 ♖ad8 17 ♕f3 g5! (advancing part of his kingside pawn majority to gain space and to worry White's monarch) 18 b4?! (certainly not 18 ♗xc6?? because of 18...♘e5, but the move played loosens White's queenside structure) 18...♕c4 19 ♕e3 h6 20 ♗c2 c5 21 f4 (21 ♗b3 ♕f4 is fine for Black) 21...cxb4! 22 fxg5 ♕xc3 23 ♕f4 ♖hf8 24 ♗b3 ♕c5+ 25 ♔h1 hxg5 with a decisive material advantage for Black. In that encounter, Grandmaster Simen Agdestein demonstrated that Black was secure on the central files and had active possibilities on both wings, with his moves 14-17 playing key roles. GM Jonny Hector clearly found it difficult to exploit Black's split queenside structure, and the king on e7 proved to be very safely sheltered by the neighbouring pawns.

I feel that, having seen the dynamic counterplay which Black generated, it is worth returning to

the position after 8 ♗d3 to take another look at that vital stage. *(D)*

B

Agdestein played the important freeing move 8...c5!. The following course of the game produced a situation in which White had a 3v2 pawn majority on the queenside, but Black was the one who retained a central pawn. That pawn on e6 provided vital shelter for his king. A further endorsement for Black's structure is the fact that Viktor Korchnoi and Jon Speelman are among the other top grandmasters who often play similar positions arising from the French Defence.

It is also instructive to see what can happen if Black does not play the key freeing move ...c5. For example, the game Jakirlić-Lücke, Bad Wörishofen 1996, deviated with **8...♘d5?! 9 ♗d2 ♗f6 10 ♕e2 0-0 11 0-0-0 a5 12 h4 ♘b4?** *(D)* Allowing a Greek gift sacrifice, but 12...h6 13 g4 or 13 ♕e4 also makes life extremely unpleasant for the black king.

W

13 ♗xh7+! ♚h8 After 13...♚xh7 14 ♘g5+ we have:

a) 14...♗xg5 15 hxg5+ ♚g6 (15...♚g8 16 ♕h5 f5 17 g6 seals Black's fate) 16 ♕h5+ ♚f5 17 ♖de1 (threatening either ♖e5# or g4#) 17...♕xd4 18 g6+ ♚f6 19 ♕g5#.

b) 14...♚g6 15 ♕e4+ ♚h5 16 g4+ ♚h6 17 ♕h7# or 17 ♘xf7#.

c) 14...♚g8 15 ♕h5 ♖e8 16 ♕xf7+ ♚h8 17 h5! and now:

c1) 17...♗xg5 18 h6 gxh6 19 ♖xh6+! ♗xh6 20 ♖h1 checkmates Black quickly.

c2) 17...♕d7 18 ♕g6 ♗xg5 (18...♚g8 meets with the same response 19 h6, threatening 20 h7+ ♚h8 21 ♘f7+ or 20 hxg7 ♗xg7 21 ♖h8+! ♚xh8 22 ♕h7#) 19 h6! ♗xd2+ (19...♗xh6 20 ♗xh6 ♚g8 21 ♗xg7! ♕xg7 22 ♕xe8+ ♕f8 23 ♖h8+) 20 ♖xd2 ♚g8 21 hxg7 ♕xg7 22 ♕xe8+.

c3) 17...♖e7! (relatively best) 18 ♕g6 (18 h6 ♖xf7 19 ♘xf7+ ♚g8 20 ♘xd8 should also win for White, but Black can resist for a while) 18...♗xg5 (or 18...♚g8 19 ♕h7+ ♚f8 20 ♕h8#) 19 ♗xg5 branching into:

c31) 19...♕e8 20 ♗xe7 ♕xe7 21 h6 ♚g8 22 hxg7 ♕xg7 23 ♕e8+ ♕f8 24 ♖h8+, a theme we also saw in variation 'c2'.

c32) 19...♗d7 20 h6 ♚g8 21 ♗xe7 (21 hxg7 ♖xg7) 21...♕xe7 22 hxg7 ♕xg7 23 ♕e4 leaves Black's king fatally exposed, the immediate threat being 24 ♖h3 and then ♖g3. White need only take care not to make a greedy ♕xb7 capture and lose his queen to ...♗c6.

That was a lot of analysis, but then the situation was different from most Greek gift examples because Black's pawn at g7 was initially protected, making it more difficult for White to totally destroy the enemy king's shelter. Note that Black could have played ...♘xa2+ in most variations, but it would not have helped the plight of the monarch on the opposite wing. We rejoin the game Jakirlic-Lücke at move 14. **14 ♗e4 ♘xa2+ 15 ♚b1 ♘b4 16 ♘g5 g6 17 h5! 1-0** The conclusion could have been 17...♗xg5 18 hxg6+ ♚g7 (18...♚g8 19 ♕h5) 19 ♖h7+ ♚f6 20 ♗xg5+ ♚xg5 21 ♕h5+ ♚f4 (21...♚f6 22 ♕h4#) 22 ♕f3+ ♚g5 23 ♖h5#. The clash Chandler-Agnos is waiting (probably impatiently!) for us to rejoin it at last.

> **5 e5**   **♘fd7**
> **6 ♗xe7**   **♕xe7**
> **7 f4**   **0-0**

7...c5 is risky for Black in view of 8 ♘b5!, with the dual threats of 9 ♘c7+ or 9 ♘d6+. However, a major alternative to castling on move seven is **7...a6**. Moldovan-Nicula, Romanian Team Championship 1995, continued **8 ♘f3 c5 9 ♕d2 ♘c6 10 dxc5** 10 0-0-0 c4!?, intending a queenside pawn storm with ...b5-b4, is a strategy that English IM Colin Crouch has employed successfully on several occasions with Black. **10...♘xc5** I would prefer 10...♕xc5 11 0-0-0 b5, with the idea ...♘b6 and ...b4. **11 ♗d3 b5** 11...♘xd3+ would favour White after either 12 ♕xd3 or 12 cxd3. It is true, in general, that the bishop is a slightly stronger piece than the knight, due to its longer-range capabilities, but here we have one of the exceptions. The point is that six of Black's seven remaining pawns are on light squares, and so the scope of his bishop on c8 is very limited. Exchanging on d3 would accentuate the superiority of White's knights in comparison to the knight and 'bad' bishop that Black would be left with. **12 0-0-0 b4 13 ♘e2 0-0** He wants to play ...a5 without allowing the knight on c6 to be pinned by ♗b5. **14 ♕e3 a5?** Tactics are more important

than purely positional considerations here, and, having castled, it was now vital for Black to play 14...♘xd3+ to eliminate the bishop that is pointing menacingly at h7 ... before it offers itself as a Greek gift. **15 ♗xh7+! 1-0** *(D)*

B

Black resigned on account of 15...♔xh7 16 ♘g5+ ♔g6 (16...♔g8 17 ♕h3 ♖d8 18 ♕h7+ ♔f8 19 ♕h8#) 17 f5+!! (17 ♕g3 or 17 ♕h3 also wins quickly) 17...exf5 18 ♘f4+ ♔xg5 19 ♕g3+ ♔h6 20 ♕h3+ ♔g5 21 g3, and anyone who finds a guaranteed way (excluding resignation) for Black to escape being checkmated by ♕h4# or ♕h5# on move 24 at the latest deserves a medal ... I wish *I* could find such a way!

> **8 ♘f3**   **c5**
> **9 ♕d2**   **♘c6**
> **10 0-0-0** **a6**

10...c4!? may look anti-positional because it places yet another of Black's pawns on a light square, and so further reduces the scope of his bishop. However, the move does have certain positive features. Black gains some space, and could follow up with ...♖b8 then ...b5-b4, storming White's castled position. As well as starting to threaten the safety of White's monarch, 10...c4 denies his bishop an active development on d3. One possible continuation is 11 f5 ♖b8 (11...♘b6, intending 12...exf5, also merits attention, especially since 12 f6 gxf6 involves White in making a rather speculative pawn sacrifice) 12 g4 b5 13 g5? b4 14 f6 (14 ♘e2 exf5) 14...bxc3, winning easily for Black after 15 fxe7 cxd2+ or 15 ♕xc3 ♕b4.

11	dxc5	♕xc5
12	♗d3	b5? *(D)*

White's next move introduced a significant theoretical novelty at the time of the game, and an elegant example of the Greek gift. How could Black have prevented it? 12...h6 invites an attack by g4-g5. 12...f5 13 exf6 ♘xf6 14 ♖he1 also looks pleasant for White, but may be relatively the best continuation for Black.

13	♗xh7+!!	♔xh7
14	♘g5+	♔g8

14...♔h6 15 ♕d3 g6 16 ♕h3+ ♔g7 17 ♕h7#.

15	♕d3	♖e8
16	♕h7+	♔f8
17	♕h5!	♘d8

W

The alternatives are no better:

a) 17...♖e7 18 ♕h8#.

b) 17...♕e3+ 18 ♔b1 ♕xf4 19 ♖hf1.

c) 17...g6 18 ♕h7 ♘d8 19 ♕h8+ ♔e7 20 ♕h4 ♔f8 (20...f6 21 ♕h7+ ♔f8 22 ♕h8+ ♔e7 23 ♕g7#) 21 ♖d3 b4 22 ♘h7+! ♔g7 23 ♖h3 bxc3 24 ♕h6+ ♔g8 25 ♘f6+ ♘xf6 26 ♕h8#.

d) 17...♔e7 18 ♕xf7+ ♔d8 19 ♘xe6+ ♖xe6 20 ♕xe6 ♘f6 21 ♕f7 ♖a7 22 ♕g6, with a winning position for White.

18	♘h7+!	♔g8

18...♔e7 19 ♕g5+ f6 20 ♕xg7+ ♘f7 21 exf6+ ♔d8 22 ♕xf7, and White is three pawns ahead with an overwhelming position.

19	♖d3!

The rook joins in the attack, with decisive effect. Sometimes a lot of courage is required from a player who sacrifices material. In this particular game, the fact that Black's pieces are so passively placed and with little scope can help White to have confidence that his earlier bishop sacrifice was completely sound. In fact, as most of Black's army is not performing any active function, White is, in effect, ahead on material. Still, he should make every move really count, and GM Murray Chandler has certainly done so.

19 ...   ♕e7

19...♘f8 20 ♘f6+! gxf6 21 ♖h3 ♘g6 22 ♕h7+ ♔f8 23 exf6 leaves Black defenceless against the threat of 24 ♕g7# or 24 ♕h8+ ♘xh8 25 ♖xh8#.

20 ♖h3

Threatening 21 ♘f6+ and 22 ♕h8#.

20 ...   f6 (D)

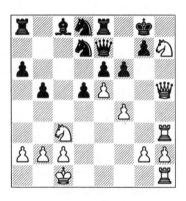

W

21 ♘xf6+!   ♘xf6

21...♔f8 22 ♘h7+ ♔g8 23 ♘g5 ♘f7 24 ♕h7+ ♔f8 25 ♕h8+ ♘xh8 26 ♖xh8# or 21...exf6 22 ♖g3+ ♔f8 (22...♕g7 23 ♕xe8+ ♘f8 24 ♖xg7+ wins very easily for White) 23 ♕h8+ ♔f7 24 ♖g7#.

22 exf6   1-0

Black resigned due to 22...♕f8 23 f7+! ♘xf7 24 ♕h7#.

The two youngest grandmasters among the top 20 rated players in the world (as at November 1995) are the 19-year-old Hungarians Judit Polgar and Zoltan Almasi. Polgar's progress has been meteoric, but Almasi is also a very fast-rising star. He dominated the 1995 Hungarian Championship, winning it with a score of 6½/9, and remaining undefeated. Almasi's clash against GM Csaba Horvath was a really tough fight.

Game 26
Z.Almasi – C.Horvath
Hungary 1995
Ruy Lopez

1	e4	e5
2	♘f3	♘c6
3	♗b5	♘f6
4	0-0	♗e7 *(D)*

4...♘xe4 was discussed in the notes of Game 12, the most common continuation then being 5 d4 ♘d6 6 ♗xc6 dxc6 7 dxe5 ♘f5 8 ♕xd8+ ♔xd8. Almasi himself employed that solid variation with Black against German grandmaster Stefan Kindermann, a very strong attacking player, at an event in Horgen earlier in the year. He outplayed his opponent *en route* to another impressive first place in a major tournament.

W

5 ≌e1

Defending the pawn on e4, and threatening to win Black's e-pawn after eliminating the knight on c6. I have seen players rated over 2400 forgetting in blitz games to protect adequately the pawn on e5, and automatically choosing something routine like 5...0-0?. There is hope for us all!

 5 ...   **d6**
 6 d4   **exd4**

6...♗d7 is another way to avoid loss of material, since if 7 ♗xc6 ♗xc6 8 dxe5 dxe5 9 ♕xd8+ ♖xd8 10 ♘xe5, Black has 10...♗xe4. 7 d5 and 7 ♘c3 are more promising responses to 6...♗d7, and Black will not find it easy to neutralise White's spatial advantage. It was Jon Arnason who first stressed to me that having a cramped position

is a kind of weakness, even if there are no structural weaknesses in one's position. After Jon's instructive lesson I rarely ended up in a situation with a lack of space.

 7 ♘xd4   **♗d7**
 8 ♗xc6   **bxc6**

8...♗xc6 9 ♘f5!? 0-0 10 ♗g5! ♖e8 11 ♘c3 ♗f8 12 ♕f3 threatens 13 ♘h6+! gxh6 14 ♗xf6 ♗e7 15 ♕g3+ ♔f8 16 ♕g7#.

 9 ♘c3   **0-0**
 10 ♕f3! *(D)*

B

I recall being shown this move by IM Craig Pritchett at a Scottish junior training session nearly 20 years ago. Craig also mentioned a possible follow-up idea of 11 e5, to continue after 11...dxe5 with 12 ♘xc6 ♗xc6 13 ♕xc6. Then Black no longer possesses a bishop pair, but White has preserved a structural advantage due to his opponent's isolated queenside pawns. In the actual game, Almasi chooses a different plan, preferring to avoid the exchanges that would result from playing e4-e5, and instead just keeping Black cramped.

| 10 | ... | ♖e8 |

10...♘g4? loses a pawn to 11 ♘xc6! ♗xc6 12 ♕xg4.

11	♗g5	h6
12	♗h4	♖b8
13	b3	♖b4
14	♖ad1!	♘h7

14...♗g4 15 ♕d3 ♗xd1? 16 ♘xc6 and 14...c5 15 ♘f5 ♗xf5 16 ♕xf5 ♕d7? 17 ♕xd7 ♘xd7 18 ♗xe7 ♖xe7 19 ♘d5 are terrible for Black.

15	♗xe7	♕xe7
16	a3	♖b6
17	♖e3!	

Any tactical ideas by Black based on ...d5 and ...♕xe1+ (if White were to open the e-file by exd5) have now been stopped.

17	...	♖a6
18	a4	♖b6
19	♕e2	♘f6
20	h3!	

This is a very useful prophylactic move. White rules out ...♘g4 for Black and at the same time provides his own king with a flight square at h2, in case of back-rank problems, which occur frequently in practical play. It is much easier for the player with more space to find constructive moves.

| 20 | ... | ♖b4 |

21 ♘f3, intending 22 e5, can now be met by 21...♘xe4 with the

threat of ...♘xc3. However, there is a drawback to Black's last move, and the alert Almasi pounces on it.

| 21 | ♕a6! | ♖b6 |
| 22 | ♕xa7 | ♕d8 *(D)* |

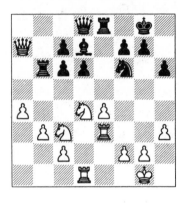

W

Black threatens ...♕c8 and then ...♖a6. White cannot extricate his queen by playing 23 ♕a5 because of 23...♖e5.

23 e5?!

This initiates a long and virtually forced sequence, but White's advantage is not completely clear at the end. I prefer the move-order 23 a5 ♖b8 24 ♕a6 (White gives himself more variations to calculate if he chooses 24 e5, because Black's reasonable options include 24...♖a8 or 24...♕c8 threatening ...♖a8) 24...♖a8 25 ♕c4 c5 26 ♘f3 ♖xa5 27 e5, when White has a superb position, almost free of risk.

| 23 | ... | dxe5 |

White wins after 23...♕c8? 24 exd6!, intending ♕xc7.

24 a5   exd4!

24...Іb4 and 24...Іb8 are both very easily refuted by 25 ⁇xc6 ⁇xc6 26 Іxd8, so Black correctly tries to complicate matters as much as possible.

25 Іxe8+   ⁇xe8
26 axb6   cxb6

If 26...dxc3?, then Black's material advantage will last no longer than a pint of beer in front of a thirsty Scotsman, in view of 27 b7 followed rapidly by b8⁇.

27 ⁇a4

Even if Almasi were to try a strong Scottish ale, it would be difficult to imagine him 'dropping' a rook by playing 27 Іxd4??, allowing the continuation 27...⁇e1+ 28 ⁇h2 ⁇e5+.

27 ...   ⁇e2
28 ⁇b8+!   ⁇h7
29 Іxd4   ⁇e1+
30 ⁇h2   ⁇xf2 *(D)*

W

31 ⁇e5!

Almasi centralises his queen, so that the full force of that piece radiates in many directions. Black's drawing chances would have been much greater after 31 ⁇f4 ⁇xc2 (31...⁇g4+? 32 hxg4 ⁇h4+ 33 ⁇g1 ⁇e1+ fails to draw because of 34 ⁇f1 ⁇e3+ 35 ⁇f2 ⁇c1+ 36 ⁇h2) 32 ⁇xb6 ⁇e6 33 b4 c5! 34 bxc5 ⁇xc5. On the last move of that variation, the alternative 34 Іd2 is easily answered by 34...⁇c3 (intending 35 b5? ⁇a5), whereas the more ambitious but unrealistic winning attempt 34 ⁇c7 backfires badly after 34...⁇xh3!! 35 ⁇xh3 ⁇f5+ and then 36 ⁇h2 cxd4 or 36 g4 ⁇f1+.

31 ...   ⁇d5!

31...⁇xc2 32 ⁇xb6 ⁇e6 33 b4 is unpleasant for Black. White's centralised queen makes it very difficult to play ...c6-c5 to swap the last pair of queenside pawns.

32 Іd3

This move performs several functions: it prevents Black from playing ...⁇e3, but also threatens Іf3 or Іg3.

32 ...   f6?

A more tenacious defence is 32...⁇xc2 33 Іg3 g6! (33...f6 34 ⁇d4 transposes to the actual game) 34 ⁇d4 b5 35 ⁇c5 ⁇f5 or 35 ⁇a7 ⁇e6 36 ⁇c5 ⁇f2! 37 Іf3 ⁇d4, maintaining a pin on the white knight. There is a logical reason which explains why ...g6 is better (in this case) than ...f6 to defend against a checkmate threat at g7 produced by White's queen and rook. The principal reason is that Black's light-squared bishop can protect a pawn at f7, but not at g7. 32...f6 actually exposes Black's g-pawn laterally along the 7th rank.

33 ♕d4

White's king is potentially vulnerable too, as is demonstrated by 33 ♕b2?? ♘f4 34 ♖g3 ♘e2, threatening ...♕g1# or ...♕xg3+.

33 ... ♕xc2
34 ♖g3 b5? *(D)*

W

35 ♕a7!

Now the point I explained in the notes to 32...f6 is revealed: if the f-pawn were on f7 instead of f6, then Black could defend it by 35...♗e6, securely maintaining a pawn on his second rank.

35 ... ♘e7

Horvath could have resigned, but was probably in time-trouble. 35...bxa4 36 ♕xd7 and 35...♕f5 36

♘c5 both cost him heavy amounts of material, due to the weakness of his g-pawn.

36	♕xd7	♘f5
37	♖f3	♘h4
38	♕d3+!	♕xd3
39	♖xd3	bxa4
40	bxa4	1-0

Black's pieces are too far from the a-file to have any hope of halting the imminent advance to promotion of White's outside passed pawn.

Well, we are rapidly approaching the final game of this chapter, and it will be action-packed with lots of ideas. So first let's get into gear by solving a puzzle.

White is Not OK!

B

Black is to move. What is his best continuation? Before we answer that question, consider some features of the position:

1) *Structure:* White has an isolated pawn on e4. Black's h-pawn is also isolated, but it keeps the enemy g- and h-pawns fixed, since the advance g4 can be met by the *en passant* capture ...hxg3.

2) *Scope:* Black's army of pieces is much more actively placed than his opponent's forces. The knight enjoys a superb outpost on e5, where it blockades White's isolated pawn. In contrast, the light-squared bishop cannot move at all at the moment, and in general its scope is severely limited by five of White's six remaining pawns being on light squares. White's rooks also have a purely passive role at present, but their defensive resources are not sufficient to cope with 1...♖dg8. Black could win at least the g-pawn after that move, since 2 ♖g1? ♘f3+ 3 gxf3 ♖xg1 is even worse for White.

3) *Safety:* The pin on the bishop on the d-file brings the safety of that piece, and White's king, into question. How can Black increase the pressure, and perhaps win material? If I am not certain about the answer, I sometimes find the strongest move by comparing several options and using a process of elimination to 'weed out' the weaker alternatives. For example, 1...♖dg8 nets a minimum of one pawn, as we have seen already, but it releases most of the pressure from the bishop. 1...♖g3 is a candidate

for consideration, but White is alive and kicking after the continuation 2 ♔e1 ♘xd3+ 3 ♖xd3 ♖dxd3 4 cxd3 ♖xd3 5 ♖f2 and then 5...♖e3+ 6 ♔d2 or 5...♖d7 6 ♖f4. However, examination of first-move possibilities with the pawns should lead to the discovery 1...c5!. In Molière-Motwani, Brussels 1995, the finish was 2 b3 b5 0-1. White's pieces are so cramped together (lack of *Space*) that he has no satisfactory way of preventing 3...c4, winning his poor bishop.

The following game won the Best Game prize at the Centenary Scottish Championships.

Game 27
P.Motwani – D.Bryson
St Andrews 1993
Scandinavian Defence

1	e4	d5
2	exd5	♘f6

One of the strongest players from Scandinavia, Danish grandmaster Curt Hansen, likes 2...♕xd5. Anand employed it too in game 14 of his 1995 World Championship match against Kasparov. He got a great position from the opening, but lost his way in later complications.

A truly stunning clash occurred between two much lesser known players at the 1995 Berlin Summer Open. The game Lochte-Schöngart transposed to **3 ♘c3 ♕a5 4 d4 ♘f6 5 ♘f3 c6 6 ♗c4** After 6 ♘e5 ♗f5, Michael Adams has played 7 ♗f4!?, intending 7...♘bd7 8 ♘c4 ♕d8 9 ♕e2! g6?? 10 ♘d6#. Anand preferred 6...♗e6!? 7 ♗d3 ♘bd7 8 f4 g6, with a solid position in the game already mentioned against Kasparov. **6...♘bd7?!** Black should first develop his light-squared bishop to avoid locking it in. **7 ♗d2** White's moves 5 to 7 were in fact played in a different order, but the order given here is the most common one. **7...♕c7 8 ♕e2 ♘b6** 8...g6? can be met by 9 ♘g5 e6 10 ♘xf7! ♔xf7 11 ♕xe6+ ♔g7 12 ♕f7# or 10 ♗xe6! fxe6 11 ♕xe6+ ♗e7 12 ♕f7+ ♔d8 13 ♘e6#. **9 ♗b3 ♗f5** 9...♗g4? 10 ♗xf7+! ♔xf7 11 ♘e5+ wins at least a pawn for White, and deprives Black of castling rights. **10 ♘e5! ♗g6** *(D)* 10...♘bd5 11 ♗xd5 cxd5 (alternatively 11...♘xd5 12 ♘xd5 cxd5 13 ♕b5+ ♗d7 14 ♕xd5 is also disastrous for Black) 12 ♘xd5! ♘xd5 13 ♕b5+ ♗d7 14 ♕xd5 transposes to the line given in brackets. Trying to shield the pawn on f7 by playing 10...e6 has the drawback of leaving the bishop on f5 rather short of safe squares after 11 g4 ♗g6 12 h4.

11 h4! White increases his spatial advantage with this aggressive move. Black is already in terrible danger, facing the threat of 12 h5. **11...♘fd7** 11...h5 can be answered by ♘xg6 sometime in the next few

W

moves, and Black's structure will be ruined when he recaptures with ...fxg6. At that stage, if ...e6 has been played, then the e-pawn will be *en prise* to ♗xe6 or ♕xe6. **12 ♗f4! ♘xe5 13 ♗xe5 ♕d7 14 0-0-0 h5** 14...e6? 15 h5 ♗f5 16 g4. **15 d5!** Black, lagging far behind in development and with his king unable to castle safely, will not survive White opening up the position. **15...♕f5** 15...0-0-0 16 dxc6 ♕xc6 17 ♘b5!, intending 18 ♘xa7#, is a quicker way for Black to capitulate. **16 dxc6 bxc6 17 ♘b5! cxb5 18 ♕xb5+ ♘d7 19 ♖xd7!! ♕xd7 20 ♗a4 ♗f5** 20...♕xb5 21 ♗xb5+ ♔d8 22 ♖d1+ ♔c8 23 ♗a6# and 20...0-0-0 21 ♕b8# are pretty points. **21 ♕b7! ♖d8** 21...♕xa4 22 ♕xa8+ ♔d7 23 ♖d1+ also wins quickly: 23...♔e6 24 ♕d5# or 23...♗d3 24 ♖xd3+. **22 ♗xd7+ ♗xd7** 22...♖xd7 23 ♕c8+ ♖d8 24 ♕xf5. **23 ♗c7 ♖c8 24 ♖d1 e6 25 ♖xd7! ♔xd7 26 ♗a5+ ♖c7** and **Black lost on time,** about to be mated by 27 ♕xc7+ ♔e8 28 ♕d8#.

3 ♘f3

3 d4, though obviously not bad, does allow Black the sharp possibility **3...♗g4!?**. *(D)*

W

Here is a game played on 24 February 1996 during the Cappelle la Grande tournament. It was no ordinary encounter... The roles of the pieces and pawns were performed by children from the little French town, who were dressed in beautiful costumes and standing on a huge board inlaid into the floor. Playing White were the lovely WGMs Alisa Maric and Almira Skripchenko facing GM Mark Hebden and IM Angus Dunnington in Black's shoes. Many local people turned up to see the spectacle live, hoping to witness an exciting time scramble: the time limit was 20 minutes per side for the entire game. As it turned out, the ladies'

and men's clocks registered consumed times of only 15 and 13 minutes respectively at the finish of the brief but brilliant clash, which began with some loud and dramatic music. After 3...♗g4, a critical test of the black opening is 4 f3, but our special feature continued instead with **4 ♘f3 ♕xd5 5 ♗e2 ♘c6 6 0-0 0-0-0** Black should avoid 6...♗xf3? 7 ♗xf3 ♕xd4?? 8 ♗xc6+, losing his queen. **7 c4 ♕f5 8 d5?!** 8 ♗e3 is better. **8...e6! 9 ♗d3 ♗xf3! 10 gxf3 ♕h3 11 dxc6 ♗d6 12 cxb7+ ♔b8 0-1** It was not worth going down either of the lines 13 f4 ♘g4 14 ♕xg4 ♕xg4+ 15 ♔h1 ♕f3+ or 13 ♖e1 ♗xh2+ 14 ♔h1 ♗g3+ 15 ♔g1 ♕h2+ 16 ♔f1 ♕xf2#.

	3 ...	♘xd5
	4 d4	♗g4
	5 c4	

5 h3 ♗h5 6 c4 ♘b6 7 c5 ♘6d7 8 ♕b3 *(D)*

B

8...♕c8? 8...♘c6? 9 g4! ♗g6 10 ♘c3 ♖b8 11 d5!, with the idea 11...♘xc5 12 ♕c4, gave White an overwhelming advantage in space after 11...♘ce5 12 ♘xe5 ♘xe5 13 f4 ♘d3+ (not 13...♘f3+? 14 ♔f2 ♘d4 15 ♕a4+) 14 ♗xd3 ♗xd3 15 ♗e3 ♕c8 16 0-0-0 ♗a6 17 ♖he1 ♔d8 18 f5 f6 19 ♗f4 ♕d7 20 d6 cxd6 21 cxd6 exd6 22 ♖e6 ♔c7 23 ♕b4 ♖d8 24 ♖exd6! ♗xd6 25 ♖xd6 1-0 in Motwani-Schaffarth, Luxembourg Open 1990. Black resigned because of 25...♕xd6 26 ♕c5+! or 25...♕e8 26 ♕c5+ ♔b8 27 ♖xd8#. Note that 8...b6! 9 ♕d5 ♗xf3 10 ♕xf3 c6, as in W.Watson-Adams, London (Watson, Farley and Williams) 1990, should be playable for Black: if the capture cxb6 occurs soon, then after ...axb6, he will have an open a-file and the outpost on d5 in front of White's isolated queen's pawn to compensate for his opponent's bishop pair. **9... ♗xf3 10 gxf3 ♘c6 11 ♗e3 g6 12 d5 ♘d8 13 0-0-0 ♗g7 14 h4! ♘f6 15 ♗h3** White obtained this active possibility and extra scope for his light-squared bishop in return for accepting a weakened kingside pawn structure at move 10. **15...e6 16 ♘e2! 0-0 17 ♘f4 ♖e8 18 ♖hg1 ♕d7 19 h5** White could win a pawn simply by 19 dxe6, but he decides to continue strengthening his position, and retain the capture on e6 as a threat. Remember the saying 'The threat

is stronger than its execution'. **19...♕e7** 19...gxh5? 20 ♗d4 ♕e7 21 ♖xg7+ (or 21 d6) 21...♔xg7 22 ♘xh5+ is hopeless for Black. **20 hxg6 fxg6** No better is 20...hxg6 21 dxe6 ♘xe6 22 ♗xe6 fxe6 23 ♖xg6, when Black's monarch is defenceless against the simple threat of ♖dg1, doubling rooks on the open g-file. **21 dxe6** Threatening 22 ♖d7! ♘xd7 23 exd7+ and 24 dxe8♕+. **21...♖f8** (D)

W

22 ♖xg6! hxg6 23 ♘xg6 ♕e8 24 e7+ ♖f7 25 exd8♕ ♖xd8 26 ♖xd8 ♕xd8 27 ♗e6 1-0, in view of 27...♕e8 28 ♘e5, was a previous Motwani-Bryson clash at Glasgow 1990.

5	**...**	**♘b6**
6	**c5**	

This is an ambitious, attacking advance which gains space for White. From a positional point of view, it may seem a dubious idea to give the opponent the d5-square.

However, the tactical justification is that 6...♘d5? 7 ♕b3 b6 (7...♗xf3 8 ♕xb7! is a key detail) 8 ♘e5! leaves Black without a satisfactory defence to the threats of 9 ♘xg4 and 9 ♗b5+.

| 6 | ... | ♘6d7 |
| 7 | ♗c4 | |

White threatens 8 ♗xf7+! ♚xf7 9 ♘g5+ and 10 ♕xg4 or even 8 ♘g5! ♗xd1 9 ♗xf7#. Those lines reveal a reason in favour of not chasing the bishop from g4 to h5 with an earlier h2-h3, since, on h5, the bishop would protect the weak f7 point.

7	...	e6
8	♘c3	♗e7
9	h3	♗h5
10	♗e3	0-0?!

Black underestimated the force of White's forthcoming kingside assault. Safer alternatives include 10...♘c6 or 10...c6.

     11 g4! *(D)*

B

| 11 | ... | ♗g6 |
| 12 | h4 | h5 |

12...h6 13 h5 ♗h7 14 ♖g1, intending 15 g5, also illustrates that, in this game, Black's monarch has not found safety through kingside castling.

| 13 | ♘g5 | ♘f6 |

13...hxg4 14 ♕xg4 ♘f6 15 ♕g2 leaves Black facing the dual threats of 16 ♕xb7 and 16 ♘xe6! fxe6 17 ♕xg6.

| 14 | gxh5 | ♗xh5 |
| 15 | ♗e2 | ♗xe2 |

If 15...g6, then 16 ♗xh5 ♘xh5 17 ♖g1, threatening 18 ♘xe6 fxe6 19 ♕xh5, is one of White's strong possibilities.

16	♕xe2	♘c6
17	0-0-0	♘b4
18	**d5!!** *(D)*	

B

There are several key variations underpinning this pawn sacrifice, but White's main idea is to clear the d4-square for use by his bishop, in order to eliminate the knight on f6. With that knight removed, ♕h5 followed by ♕h7# will be very difficult for Black to stop.

| 18 | ... | ♘bxd5 |
| 19 | ♘xd5 | exd5 |

19...♘xd5 20 ♕h5 ♘f6 is not immediately convincing for White. An improvement is 20 ♕c2 ♗xg5 (20...g6? 21 ♘xe6! fxe6 22 ♕xg6+ destroys all the pawn defences around Black's king, and leads to a quick victory for White) 21 hxg5 f5 22 g6 (22 gxf6 ♕xf6 leaves White without a clear win) 22...♘xe3 23 fxe3 ♕g5 24 ♖dg1 ♕xe3+ 25 ♔b1 ♕e4 26 ♕xe4 fxe4 27 ♖g4 ♖fe8 (27...♖f6? 28 ♖gh4! ♔f8 29 ♖h8+ ♔e7 30 ♖xa8 or 27...♖fd8 28 ♖gh4 ♔f8 29 ♖f4+ ♔e7? 30 ♖f7+ ♔e8 31 ♖h8#) 28 ♖gh4 ♔f8 29 ♖f4+ ♔g8 (29...♔e7? 30 ♖f7+ ♔d8 31 ♖d1+ ♔c8 32 ♖dd7 is hopeless for Black, in spite of his temporary material advantage) 30 ♖xe4 ♖ad8 31 ♖eh4 ♔f8 32 ♖f4+ ♔g8 33 ♖f7, threatening 34 ♖xc7 or 34 ♖h7. That long variation contains some nice rook manoeuvres which gain tempi for White. It also exemplifies the power of a rook on the 7th rank, and underlines the fact that two such rooks tend to prove fatal for the opponent.

However, returning to the position after 19...♘xd5, the strongest continuation for White is 20 ♕d3! ♗xg5 (20...♘f6 21 ♕c2 ♕c8 22 ♗d4 ♖d8 23 ♖hg1, threatening

♘xf7 and then ♕g6, is also terrible for Black) 21 hxg5 f5 (21...g6 22 ♕d4 f6 23 ♕h4 wins quickly for White) 22 g6 ♘xe3 23 ♕xe3 (preventing ...♕g5) 23...♕f6 24 ♖h8+! ♔xh8 25 ♕h3+ ♔g8 26 ♕h7#.

| 20 | ♗d4 | ♕d7 |

20...♖e8 is answered by 21 ♗xf6. Then 21...gxf6 22 ♘e6! fxe6 23 ♖hg1+ ♔f8 24 ♕xe6 and 25 ♖g8# is a forcing line, while 21...♗xf6 22 ♕h5 ♕d7 23 ♕h7+ transposes to the actual game continuation.

The fact that White is one pawn down with an untidy kingside structure is of negligible importance. It actually helps him not to have a g-pawn, since the opened g-file can be used for attacking purposes against the insecure castled position of Black's king. A typical variation is 20...♘h7 21 ♘xh7 ♔xh7 22 ♕h5+ ♔g8 23 ♗xg7! ♔xg7 24 ♖hg1+ ♔f6 25 ♖de1! followed by ♕g5#, ♕f3# or ♕e5# on the next move. It is worth noting that virtually all of White's pieces are assisting in the attack, whereas Black is, in effect, down on material, as his rook on a8 has no time or scope to participate in the game.

| 21 | ♕c2 | ♖fe8 |

21...g6 22 ♖dg1, threatening 23 ♘xf7 or 23 h5, is also bleak for Black.

22	♗xf6!	♗xf6
23	♕h7+	♔f8
24	♕h8+	♔e7
25	♖he1+	♔d8

26 ♘xf7+! *(D)* **1-0**

B

Black resigned on account of 26...♕xf7 27 ♖xd5+! ♕xd5 28 ♕xe8#. Bryson showed great tenacity and strength of character by recovering quickly from that loss, and succeeding in achieving his third IM norm with a score of 6/9 in the tournament.

Well, as I write now, Christmas 1995 is snowballing rapidly towards us. It is almost time for me to wrap up this chapter, and begin the coming New Year with a new phase of our H.O.T. chess adventure. Before that happens, there is enough space and scope in this section to provide a little message and a problem to keep things ticking over. I can safely say that they have been structured to be solved without a huge tree of analysis, but, when you are ready, the answers can be checked further on.

Get the Message

In the coded message, !, ?, and * represent three different letters which must be found to decode the statement.

!?y !o ge! !hi* ?igh! & *ha?pen you? *kill*.

Checking the Captures

Black to play and win in the following position.

B

4 C.H.A.M.P.

I have looked in mirrors more in the last year than ever before! That may sound vain, but without doing so I could not have passed my driving test. Before we move up to fourth gear in this chapter, let us briefly reflect on what is behind us.

The initial phase of our H.O.T. journey was designed to help us to face chess more calmly. *F.A.C.E.* indicated a way of approaching each game and opponent without fear, but rather with an aim to enjoy the occasion. The importance of consistently following a plan was also stressed, and we have witnessed numerous examples of effective planning in the games of the first three chapters. Less successful cases very frequently occur due to a neglect of 'allegro', in which a player does not develop his army of pieces with enough speed or efficiency. The *four S's*, namely safety, scope, space, and structure, are other features which, as we have seen, can greatly influence the course of a game. *T.O.D.O.* provided an idea for improving qualities which can make a person a more complete player, and much better equipped to tackle the many different styles of opponent that exist.

What other qualities can one improve in order to become an even more all-round player? Whether you are already a champion or not, **C.H.A.M.P.** will help to answer the question. The five elements making up C.H.A.M.P. are: *Calculation, Harmony, Alertness, Memory, Preparation.*

Chess players cannot avoid *calculation*. Consider the next hypothetical but very plausible position.

Just a Dead Draw?

W

White is to move. What ideas come to mind? I will return with my assessment and calculations soon, but for the moment the position is all yours!

The coded message I left you with at the end of Chapter 3 is like an exact, forced line of calculation. It can be decoded simply by considering various possibilities until the only answer that makes sense is found. The solution is that **!**, **?**, and ***** represent **t**, **r**, and **s** respectively, so that the message reads **Try to get this right & sharpen your skills.**

Of course, the analogy linking the coded message to a chess calculation only applies up to a point. For instance, no chess clock was ticking while the code was being cracked, but time limitations normally play a part during competitive play. However, if the time is used efficiently (which is an area where I certainly need to improve), then it is quite possible to arrive at a good, constructive move at each stage without habitually getting into time-trouble.

In practice, in a chess struggle there may be several reasonable options for the next move, instead of only one correct answer existing (as in the case of the code). It can be nice to have choices, but ways of choosing between them are needed. Consider, for example, the position at the close of the previous chapter. It was reached in the game Lautier-Motwani, Novi Sad Olympiad 1990. Black had a choice of 31 legal possibilities for his next move. A computer might rapidly

analyse all of them, but we humans could, in an economical manner, quickly reject from our calculations any moves which give away material without compensation or which have no constructive idea behind them. In fact, it is very natural to look directly for ways of winning material. Black has four possible **captures**, three of which put his queen *en prise*, but the fourth option, **1...♗xg3!**, wins a pawn. The concluding moves of the game were **2 ♗xg3 ♕c3+ 3 ♔d1 3 ♕c2 ♕xg3** leaves White with a deficit of one pawn instead of two, but, with his queen in a passive, defensive position on c2, the situation is still hopeless. **3...♕xb3+ 4 ♔d2 ♕xg3 5 ♕d7 ♕f4+ 6 ♔d3 ♕f1+ 7 ♔c3 ♕e1+ 0-1.** 8 ♔d3 g3 9 ♕c6+ ♔b8 10 ♕e8+ allows 10...♕xe8. So White resigned instead, two pawns down and without any realistic prospects of drawing by perpetual check.

There is a helpful chess phrase, 'Never miss a check; it might be mate'. I can recall occasions not so long ago when I managed to miss possibilities which would have immediately checkmated my opponent, or would have prevented him from doing the same to me. A lack of *alertness* was responsible for those aberrations. Alertness may be impaired by a variety of factors, including tiredness, time-trouble (in some cases), and the wrong kind of drinks! On the other hand, alertness can be improved by cultivating the habit of asking oneself questions like 'Am I overlooking something?' or 'Am I missing any important **checks or captures** for myself or my opponent?', before reaching out a hand to play the next move. *'Count to ten'* is another excellent piece of advice which my mother taught me many years ago, and I have found it to be very useful, not only in chess, but in life generally. The idea is that, by making oneself pause for a few moments (long enough to count up to ten), a little extra care and thought goes into the move or action which one is about to do. Consequently, the results should be better.

One of my favourite opening traps arises from Owen's Defence after the moves **1 e4 b6 2 d4 ♗b7 3 ♗d3 f5?!** This move puts Black's king in great danger, but 3...e6 is a safer way to play the opening, which top grandmasters such as Tony Miles and Edwin Kengis have frequently employed with success. **4 exf5! ♗xg2 5 ♕h5+** Never miss a check! **5...g6 6 fxg6** *(D)*

6...♗g7 is the 'recommended' move, but I cannot imagine myself playing such a risky line. However, **6...♘f6?** is even worse! An alert player with White would consider 'checks and captures' and score a quick win with **7 gxh7+! ♘xh5 8 ♗g6#.**

B

Did you feel the potential *harmony* between White's pieces in the position I left you to consider at the start of the discussion regarding 'calculation'? White's king and bishop are already co-operating well together, and we could note that the check 1 ♗c6+ leaves Black with only two possibilities: either 1...♔b8 or resigning! The latter possibility may seem far-fetched, but what if White's knight could take away the ...♔b8 option? The knight would need to be on a6, c6 or d7. Since the first two squares should be reserved for the king and bishop respectively, d7 must be vacated for the knight. A logical corollary is that **1 d8♕+!** should be considered. Black can just manage to draw, through the sequence 1...♗xd8! 2 ♘d7 ♘e5! 3 ♘xe5 ♔b8!, when his monarch escapes from the a8 corner, and White's material advantage is not sufficient to *force* a win. That was the case anyway from our initial position being analysed, so 1 d8♕+ is still the best attempt to win. However, Black must be alert to avoid the pitfall **1...♘xd8?**. He might be dreaming of 2...♘e6 and 3...♘c5#, but in the meantime **2 ♘d7** would complete the harmony in White's army, leaving Black powerless to prevent mate within three more moves (2...♗h2 3 ♗c4 ♗g1 4 ♗d5+ ♘b7 5 ♗xb7# being a typical finish).

The word 'finish' reminds me of the fact that players often experience difficulties in bringing a game to its most natural conclusion (especially winning a 'won position' – actually converting a large advantage into a full point). Tenacity is one quality which matters, as we have already seen earlier in this book. However, I have also found some words of the great Scottish athlete and missionary, Eric Liddell (whose story was a major ingredient in the film *Chariots of Fire*), to be very helpful. In 1924, he said: 'Where does the strength come from to see the race to its end? It comes from within'. I believe he was speaking about the Kingdom of God within each of us. Liddell certainly had a high degree of inner harmony, and his achievements (sporting and otherwise) were magnificent. His example is a very fine one for us to emulate, and not only in our chess. That does not mean that he never experienced difficulties, but his inner harmony helped him to cope with them in a good way.

On the chess-board, harmony between pieces will not, in general, be sufficient alone to force a finish. Nevertheless, when harmony is present amazing things can be accomplished. Consider the following position.

Not a black and white situation

B

Black is to play, and, not surprisingly, he could win quickly with 1...c2. However, after **1...b2?** it is White who wins! The 'queening square' b1 is a light square, which allows the bishop to prevent successful promotion with **2 ♗f5!**, since 2...b1♕ 3 e5+ ♔xe5 4 ♗xb1 ♔d4 5 ♘f7 ♔e3 (5...♔c4 6 ♗c2 ♔b4 7 ♘e5 ♔a3 8 ♘d3 followed by a king march to capture the pawn also wins for White) 6 ♘e5 ♔d2 7 ♘c4+ ♔c1 8 ♗e4 c2 9 ♘e3 ♔d2 10 ♘xc2 or 2...c2 3 e5+ ♔xe5 4 ♗xc2 ♔d4 5 ♘f7 ♔c3 6 ♗e4 ♔d2 (6...♔b3 7 ♗b1! ♔c3 8 ♘e5 ♔d2 9 ♘d3, again followed by a king march to the queenside, wins for White) 7 ♘e5 ♔c1 8 ♘d3+ ♔c2 (8...♔b1 9 ♘b4+ ♔a1 10 ♘c2+ ♔a2 11 ♗d5+ ♔b1 12 ♘a3+ ♔a1 13 ♗e4 ♔a2 14 ♘b1 is similar) 9 ♘c5+ ♔c1 10 ♘b3+ will simply require White to be able to force mate with ♔+♘+♗ v ♔. A likely conclusion is **2...♔e5 3 ♘g6+ ♔f6 4 ♘h4 ♔e5 5 ♔g5!**, completing the beautiful harmony between White's pieces. After **5...b1♕ 6 ♘f3+ ♔d6 7 e5+** and **8 ♗xb1**, Black should resign. This would also be true after 5...♔d4 6 ♘f3+ ♔e3 7 e5 ♔xf3 8 e6 followed rapidly by e7-e8♕. That lovely example combined accurate calculation with harmony, but, of course, if Black is alert to the dangers of 1...b2?, then he will choose 1...c2 and win.

The ability to recall relevant details of information is an asset to chess players, particularly when there is so much data available in many forms nowadays. I have been told that I have a good *memory*. My parents, brother and two sisters are all medical doctors who know a great deal about the documented theory regarding the subject of 'memory', but, as they would say,

the best way to improve your memory is to use it as much as possible. For example, as I am typing this book, several new sentences may suddenly come to mind. I could write them out on paper then key them into the computer afterwards. I prefer to try to type the words from memory.

Doing calculations by mental arithmetic, instead of automatically going for a calculator, uses short-term memory to keep numbers clearly in mind until the answer is reached. This enhances one's ability to perform sequences of operations mentally. It then becomes easier to follow a chess calculation through to an end point. Also, a lot of fun can come from a friend giving you a calculation to do mentally (as quickly as possible) while he or she checks your answer on a calculator. If the friend starts to tease you about being too slow getting the answers, reverse the roles so that you now have the calculator! Similar games involving chess puzzles could be arranged, for instance with one person being presented with a position to analyse while the other person studies something else from the book containing the solution. While you are with that friend, why not demonstrate a game you saw or played some time ago? Exercise your memory by trying to show the game without looking at the scoresheet, or whatever other record of the moves you hold ... except the one in your memory!

Memory Failure

W

Unfortunately for me, I was Black in this position against the talented attacking player Gary Quillan in the 1988 NatWest British Speed Chess Championships. Just *before* the game ended **1 ♗g4! 1-0**, I remembered the final position! It arose from a Vienna Game, which I sometimes employ as White myself, and I had previously analysed the entire game at home. It would have been nice if I had been more alert in the real encounter with Gary, but at least I now have a memory of it! If I could sing on my wedding day, then showing you all the moves of the miniature should not embarrass me. They were: **1 e4 e5 2 ♘c3 ♘f6 3 f4 d5 4 fxe5 ♘xe4 5 d3 ♘xc3 5...♕h4+?! 6 g3 ♘xg3**

7 ♘f3 ♕h5 8 ♘xd5! is generally reckoned to be better for White. **6 bxc3 d4 7 ♘f3 ♘c6** There are several opportunities in this game for Black to make the capture ...dxc3, but it would cost him a valuable tempo. Therefore White is happy to offer the gambit. **8 ♗e2 ♗e7 9 0-0 0-0 10 ♕e1 f6 11 ♕g3** I have successfully tried 11 exf6 ♗xf6 12 c4 as White, although Black's position is very sound at this stage. **11...fxe5 12 ♗h6 ♗f6 13 ♘g5 ♘e7!** After 13...♔h8? 14 ♗xg7+! ♗xg7 15 ♖xf8+ ♕xf8 (of course not 15...♔xf8?? 16 ♘f7#) 16 ♖f1 ♕e8 (16...♗f5 17 ♗h5!? or 17 ♗g4 ♘e7 18 ♗xf5 ♘xf5 19 ♕h3 is horrible for Black), there are two main branches:

a) 17 ♘f7+ ♔g8 18 ♘h6+ ♔h8 19 ♘f7+, and White clearly has at least a draw. He can try to win with 19 ♗h5!?, in view of 19...♕xh5? 20 ♖f8+! ♗xf8 21 ♕g8# or 19...♕e7? 20 ♖f7! ♗xh6 21 ♖xe7 ♘xe7 22 ♕xe5+. However, 19...♕e6! 20 ♘f7+ (21 ♖f8+ ♗xf8 22 ♘f7+ ♕xf7 23 ♗xf7 ♗g7 gives Black ♖+♗+♘ for his queen, or ♖+2♗ in the case of 22 ♗f7 ♗g7! 23 ♗xe6 ♗xe6) 20...♔g8 21 ♘g5 ♕h6 is not clear, since in many variations Black has the defensive resource ...♘d8 to protect the key f7-square.

b) 17 ♕h4! h6 (17...♕g6? loses to 18 ♗h5) 18 ♘f7+ ♔h7 19 ♕e4+ ♔g8 20 ♕g6 (20 ♗h5!? threatens ♘xh6+ or ♗g6-h7+) 20...♕e6 21

♘xh6+ ♔h8 22 ♖f8+ ♗xf8 23
♘f7+ ♕xf7 24 ♕xf7 ♗g7 25 ♕e8+
♔h7 26 ♗f3, intending 27 ♗e4+
♔h6 28 ♕g6#.

Some people dislike long notes
such as that one, but I feel that careful study of the tactics within the
analysis can really improve skills
in calculation and increase alertness for actual play.

14 ♘e6 *(D)* 14 ♖xf6 ♖xf6 15
♘e6 ♘f5! wins for Black.

B

14...♗xe6? 14...♘f5! 15 ♖xf5
♗xe6 or 15 ♘xd8 ♘xg3 are much
better for Black. **15 ♖xf6 ♘g6**
15...♘f5 16 ♖xf5 ♖xf5 17 ♕xg7#.
**16 ♖xe6 gxh6 17 ♖xg6+! hxg6 18
♕xg6+ ♔h8 19 ♕xh6+ ♔g8 20
♗g4! 1-0** Black resigned, having
no satisfactory answer to 21 ♗e6+.

Blitz Addicts

Three sentences from here, I am
going to give you a problem to
solve. As a challenge, prepare
yourself to try to get the answer in-
side ten seconds. I took almost exactly ten seconds to get it right, but
you can do a 'Linford Christie' and
smash that time. 'If two people
could play blitz chess non-stop for
one week, with five minutes per
player per game, what is the minimum number of games they could
finish in that period?'

Grandmasters Valentin Arbakov and Ognjen Cvitan made a val-
iant attempt (not to solve the
problem, but to become the people
in it!). At the 1996 Cappelle la
Grande Open, those two blitzchess
addicts entertained lots of onlook-
ers with their (almost) non-stop
lightning encounters. It certainly
seemed like they finished hundreds
of games, although 1008 is a tall
order.

Quick problems such as that one
are nevertheless good exercises for
keeping the mind alert by combining rapid calculation, a little use of
memory, and a small dose of logic
too. My thought processes *en route*
to the answer went something like
this: 'Each game lasts not more
than ten minutes, so the players can
finish at least 6 games per hour or
6x24 =144 per day or 144x7 =1008
per week'. Incidentally, because
there are a large number of games
and in practice many of them last
less than ten minutes, the time
'saved' allows for resetting the

pieces and clock between games, plus short breaks for sleeping, eating and going to the toilet. Hence it was not unreasonable to ignore such factors in the calculation. Besides, Arbakov and Cvitan played as if they did not want to ever stop!

Preparation can take many forms, including theoretical, mental, physical and spiritual. In my opinion, all of these areas are important, and they have all been mentioned, directly or otherwise, already in this book. For two of my twenty opponents in a 'Charity Simultaneous Exhibition', perhaps only the theoretical input mattered. That hardly makes them sound human, but then they were not. They were computers! It is time to see C.H.A.M.P. in action.

Game 28
P.Motwani – Fritz 3
Glasgow 1995
English Opening

1	c4	♘f6
2	♘c3	c5
3	e4!?	*(D)*

3 ♘f3 ♘c6 4 e4!? is also unusual and interesting. The encounter Ivanchuk-Vaganian at the 1993 World Team Championships went 4...e5 5 g3 d6 (White, being half a move ahead of Black, can retain some initiative in the 'symmetrical' continuation 5...g6 6 ♗g2 ♗g7 7

0-0 0-0 8 ♘h4 ♘h5 by playing 9 ♘f5!?) 6 ♗g2 ♗e7 7 d3 0-0 8 0-0 a6 9 ♘e1 ♘d4 10 ♘c2 b5 11 ♘e3! (completing an instructive manoeuvre) 11...bxc4 12 dxc4 ♖e8 13 f4, and Ivanchuk enjoyed the freer position (1-0 in 35 moves). I find Ivanchuk's games fascinating, and I got the idea to play 3 e4!? partly from thinking about his game with Vaganian. However, notice that I have not blocked my f-pawn with ♘f3. A favourite motto of mine is 'f for forward'!

B

3	...	e5
4	f4	

The computer had paid nothing towards the funds being raised for charity through the simultaneous display, which maybe explains my very direct attempt to beat it and not let the silicon chip on my shoulder escape scot-free! The game has already taken a highly original path, but now, or on the next move, d3! would have been a simpler and sounder course for White.

    4 ...   **exf4**

    5 e5   **♘g8**

5...♕e7 is strongly met by 6 ♕e2, and White will gain a tempo by harassing Black's queen with ♘d5 soon.

    6 ♘f3

It is worth noting that White is actually two tempi ahead compared with the King's Gambit Accepted 1 e4 e5 2 f4 exf4 3 ♘f3. However, the pawn which has advanced to e5 can become a target for Black to attack.

    6 ...   **♘c6**

6...d6 7 exd6 ♘c6! is strong, intending 8 d4 cxd4 9 ♘b5 ♗xd6 or 9 ♘xd4 ♕h4+.

    7 d4   **cxd4**

After 7...♘xd4, the simple capture 8 ♗xf4 gives White excellent piece play, a significant lead in development, and a strong bind stifling Black's development, all in return for a pawn. Steinitz once stated 'A pawn ahead is worth a little trouble', but not that much! White needs no alternative to 8 ♗xf4, but 8 ♘xd4 ♕h4+ 9 ♔e2 (9 ♔d2 cxd4 10 ♘d5 is also good) 9...cxd4 10 ♕xd4 f3+ 11 ♔d3 ♕xd4+ 12 ♔xd4 fxg2 13 ♗xg2 ♘e7 14 ♘b5 ♔d8 15 ♗g5 h6 16 ♘d6! is a variation showing great harmony between White's pieces, including the king playing an active part in the endgame.

    8 ♘b5 (D)

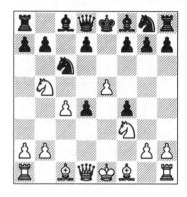

B

How was I feeling at this stage, being material down against the machine? Well, to be honest, it had come as a bit of a shock to find that, besides eighteen human opponents, I had to face two computers in this 'simul'. My sneaky friend John Henderson forgot to mention he would be bringing an unusual pair of guests along! I was surprised (but not complaining) when Novag Scorpio decided to capture a 'poisoned' b-pawn early on. To save its queen it was forced to sacrifice a piece, but soon had to bite (or should I say 'byte'!?) the dust. I had to pluck up more courage to sacrifice two pawns against Fritz 3, especially since John had not been slow to mention at the start of the game that his pet was running on a 90 MHz Pentium processor.

During this game, in spite of the material deficit, I thought that I had a very good position after 8 ♘b5. For the computer to develop its kingside pieces quickly, it seemed to me that it would need to play ...♗b4+ followed by ...♘ge7. I assessed that, when the dark-squared bishops get exchanged after ♗d2, White will land a devastating knight check on d6. That is basically the way the game proceeds. Yet I now wonder why Fritz 3 did not play 8...d6. To me, 9 ♗xf4 dxe5 10 ♘xe5 ♗b4+ 11 ♔f2 ♘xe5 12 ♗xe5 initially looked strong for White. That was until I discovered 12...♘f6!, threatening 13...♘g4+. Let us consider some 13th move options for White:

a) 13 ♕xd4? ♗c5! 14 ♕xc5 (14 ♘c7+ loses to the reply 14...♕xc7) 14...♘e4+ wins for Black.

b) 13 ♕a4 0-0 14 ♕xb4 ♘g4+ 15 ♔g1 ♘xe5 keeps Black a pawn up with a better position.

c) 13 ♘c7+ ♔f8 14 h3 (14 ♘xa8? ♘g4+ 15 ♔g1 ♘xe5 leaves White's knight trapped in a corner, while his king is also boxed in and facing threats such as ...d3 then a deadly check on the g1-a7 diagonal) 14...♕e7! 15 ♕e2 (15 ♗h2? ♕e3#) 15...d3, and once again the tactics work in Black's favour.

The freeing move 8...d6, challenging the pawn on e5 that currently gives White a spatial plus, can be compared to the liberating move 8...c5 in the Hector-Agdestein clash, embedded within the

notes to Black's fourth move in Game 25.

8	...	♕a5+?
9	♗d2	♗b4
10	♗d3	

White need not hurry to give the check on d6. Remember the adage 'The threat is stronger than its execution'.

10	...	♗xd2+
11	♕xd2	♕xd2+
12	♔xd2	♖b8
13	♖ae1	♘ge7
14	♘d6+	*(D)*

B

All the elements in C.H.A.M.P. are relevant here.

Calculation: I have listed and explained many calculations already in this game, and my computer opponent may still have been calculating millions of lines at this stage. However, I felt that the game had now entered a phase in which simple logic was more appropriate than feverish computation. Indeed, much more than several years ago, I now find many of my moves through general considerations of the position (such as the four S's). In the position after 14 ♘d6+, the lack of scope of Black's pieces was sufficient alone to convince me that calculating power would not help Fritz to free its army locked behind pawns. That is not to say that I had now completely stopped calculating, but there is no point in expending energy on unnecessary calculations. It was Grandmaster Mihai Suba who emphasised to me that a player should conserve as much energy as possible for whenever it is really needed.

Harmony: It has already been observed that Black's army can scarcely move. In contrast, White's position is very harmonious, and his pieces are about to combine in an attack against the enemy monarch.

Alertness: As is often the case when Black has not castled, the pawn on f7 is defended only by his king. If White is alert to that fact, then it is not difficult to arrive at the idea of attacking f7 using knights on d6 and g5, with a rook joining in on the f-file.

Memory: In this game, I recalled the 'Ivanchuk e4' idea early on. Then (short-term) memory was needed to calculate numerous lines correctly until suitable endpoints. At the stage after 14 ♘d6+, I was

now using my memory mainly to draw on experiences of similar past situations, which told me quickly that Black's position was almost hopeless.

Preparation:

a) **Theoretical**: This part has been quite successful, although, as was noted earlier, 4 d3! is sounder than the adventurous 4 f4.

b) **Physical**: The big lunch before the game was not the best preparation! My excuse is that my wife Jenny and I had been invited for the meal, and I did demonstrate some self-discipline by declining the offer of wine! Seriously though, I normally only eat lightly before a game; otherwise I feel sleepy during play. Fresh air clears any mental cobwebs, so I like to go for a stroll prior to playing. On this occasion I had not had time to do so, but I was getting plenty of physical exercise walking between all the tables of my many opponents!

c) **Mental**: After some initial trepidation, I managed to remain calm and enjoy this game. Actually, before any game, I always remind myself to approach it in that peaceful manner, but sometimes I have to tell myself again during play.

d) **Spiritual**: During my customary pre-game stroll, I like to say a quiet prayer. I never pray that I will win; only that I will have the strength to do the best I can. Since one can make a prayer out of any good work, I concentrated on giving a good 'simul', without letting the fact that I had missed my usual walk worry me.

| 14 | ... | ♔f8 |
| 15 | ♘g5 | f6 |

White wins after the continuation 15...♘d8 16 ♖hf1 h6 17 ♘gxf7! ♘xf7 18 ♖xf4.

16 exf6

Simple chess. 16 ♘xh7+ and 16 ♘gf7 are also very strong.

16	...	gxf6
17	♘h3	f3
18	♖hf1!	♘e5 *(D)*

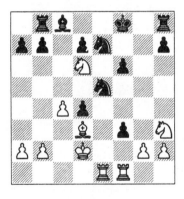

W

19	♖xe5!!	fxe5
20	♖xf3+	♔g8
21	♖f7!	

This is more logical than playing to win back an exchange immediately with 21 ♘f7, since the knight on d6 is worth more than a rook in this situation. With the knight firmly entrenched on its outpost, Black's queenside is rendered virtually immobile.

| 21 | ... | ♘c6 |

21...♘g6 is also answered by 22 ♘g5, intending 23 ♘ge4 and 24 ♘f6#.

| 22 | ♘g5 | ♘d8 |
| 23 | ♖e7 | |

23 ♗xh7+ ♖xh7 24 ♖xh7 ♘e6 25 ♖h5 is another route which is adequate to lead White to victory. The fact that the kingside pawns are connected passed pawns, and, in particular, that Black's queenside pieces are merely spectators, makes White's advantage overwhelming.

| 23 | ... | ♘c6 |

23...♔f8 24 ♖e8+ ♔g7 25 ♘f5+ ♔f6 26 ♖xh8 ♔xg5 27 ♖xd8 is equally bleak for Black.

| 24 | ♗xh7+ | ♖xh7 |

24...♔f8 25 ♖f7#.

| 25 | ♖xh7 | b5 |

A desperate lunge.

26 ♘f5

I was spoilt for choices of ways to win. The move chosen threatens ♖f7, ♘h6+ and ♖h7# in consecutive moves.

26	...	d5
27	♖g7+	♔f8
28	♖f7+	♔e8
29	♘g7+	

'The knights are fair drawing in' was John Henderson's comment!

29	...	♔d8
30	cxd5	♘e7
31	d6	♘d5

32	♘5e6+	♗xe6
33	♘xe6+	♔e8
34	♖h7	

This is even easier than 34 ♖f8+. The main threat is 35 d7#, and 34...♘f6 allows 35 ♖e7#.

| 34 | ... | ♖d8 |
| 35 | ♘c7+ | |

The most elegant finish.

| 35 | ... | ♘xc7 |
| 36 | dxc7 | **1-0** |

Fritz's resignation took the form of J.H. pulling out the computer's plug. This was not premature, in view of 36...♖c8 37 ♖h8+ ♔d7 38 ♖xc8 ♔xc8 39 h4, and White will promote a pawn.

The promotion referred to in the last note naturally meant promotion to a queen, although numerous instances of 'under-promotion' to a rook, bishop, or a knight exist in composed chess studies and in examples from practical play. I can recall one case of under-promotion from my personal experience. I thought I was going to draw the game, until my ingenious opponent played g8♘ and announced 'check', since my king was on e7. The knight accomplished something which could not have been done by a bishop, rook or queen (you can assume that the check was not a discovered check). A queen can move like a bishop or a rook, but the mysterious L-shape manoeuvre of the knight is beyond her

capabilities. This explains why a queen and knight that combine their powers can complement each other very harmoniously, and often produce an attractive piece of combinative play in the process. Consider the following hypothetical but plausible situation, with Black to move.

Material matters less

B

Despite being a rook down, Black wins beautifully with **1...♕c3+! 2 ♔d1** 2 ♔b1 ♕c2+ 3 ♔a1 ♕c1#. **2...♘f3!** Threatening 3...♕d2#. **3 ♔e2** 3 ♖d6 ♕a1+ or 3 ♕e1 ♕d3+ 4 ♔c1 ♘xe1 5 ♘xe1 ♕e3+ are also hopeless for White. **3...♘d4+ 4 ♔f2** 4 ♔d1 ♕c2+ 5 ♔e1 ♕e2#. **4...♕f3+ 5 ♔g1 ♘e2+ 6 ♔h2 ♕g3#**.

To keep us alert, here is another position, but this time from a real encounter and with a different theme to the solution.

Saved by giving it all away

W

White is to play. Can you manage to salvage a draw? The correct continuation appears after the following game.

Game 29
A.Sokolov – I.Donev
Bern 1995
Petroff Defence

1	e4	e5
2	♘f3	♘f6
3	♘xe5	

In the first round of this 7-round event, the game A.Sokolov-Beimfohr had gone 3 ♘c3 ♘c6 4 ♗c4 ♗c5 4...♘xe4!, intending 5 ♘xe4 d5, is very comfortable for Black. Did that possibility somehow get erased from Sokolov's memory? Perhaps he would have played the gambit 5 0-0, and may even have had a prepared follow-up idea in

mind. However, after 5...♘xc3 6 dxc3 ♗e7 (6...d6? 7 ♘g5) 7 ♕d5 0-0 8 ♘xe5 ♘xe5 9 ♕xe5 ♗f6, Black has returned the pawn in order to castle safely, and should have little to fear. **5 d3 d6 6 ♗g5 h6 7 ♗xf6 ♕xf6 8 ♘d5 ♕d8 9 c3 a6 10 d4 ♗a7 11 dxe5 dxe5** 11...♘xe5!? 12 ♘xe5 dxe5 13 ♕h5 0-0! 14 0-0-0 (14 ♕xe5 ♖e8 is risky for White with his king not yet castled) 14...c6 15 ♘f4 ♕g5 16 ♕xg5 hxg5 took most of the sting out of White's opening in the game T.Wall-Parker, Edinburgh 1995. **12 ♕e2 ♗c5 13 0-0-0 ♗d6** The manoeuvre ...♗c5-d6 was designed to block the d-file to avoid discovered attacks against Black's queen. For example, ♘b6 would have simultaneously attacked the rook on a8 and the queen on d8 (by the rook on d1) if some measures had not been taken to prevent it. However, the dark-squared bishop has moved four times already, and Black is lagging behind in development. **14 ♖d2!** The simple but strong idea is ♖hd1 then ♘xc7. **14...b5 15 ♗b3 ♗e6?!** 15...♘a5 is better. **16 ♖hd1** White has obtained a complete and harmonious development. **16...♕b8 17 ♘h4! ♘a5** (D)

18 ♘xc7+!! White is very alert. He has calculated correctly, and seizes the chance to sacrifice a piece in order to prise open the defences around Black's uncastled

W

B

monarch. **18...♗xc7 19 ♗xe6 fxe6
20 ♕h5+ ♔f8 21 ♖d7 1-0**

3 ... d6

3...♘xe4? 4 ♕e2 is a well-known
trap which Black should avoid. A
pitfall with a similar theme arose in
Zapata-Anand, Biel 1988. After
3...d6 4 ♘f3 ♘xe4 5 ♘c3 ♗f5?? A
rare lack of alertness on the part of
the Indian grandmaster. **6 ♕e2 1-0**
Black resigned in view of 6...d5 7
d3 or 6...♕e7 7 ♘d5 ♕d8 8 d3.

4 ♘f3 ♘xe4
5 d4 ♗e7
6 ♗d3 ♘f6

Black chooses a solid but rather
passive line. 6...d5 7 0-0 ♘c6 8 c4
♘b4 9 ♗e2 0-0 10 ♘c3 ♗e6 11
♘e5, transposing to Milos-Zarnicki,
Pan-American Team Championship 1995, is a popular alternative.

7 h3! 0-0
8 c4 *(D)*

I like White's last two moves
very much. By playing the prophylactic h2-h3, he restricted the scope

of Black's light-squared bishop
(since it cannot develop to g4 without becoming *en prise*). Also, after
kingside castling, White's king
will have a useful flight square on
h2 in case of any problems on the
back rank later. c2-c4 is an aggressive advance which gains some
space.

8 ... d5
9 ♘c3 dxc4
10 ♗xc4 ♘bd7
11 0-0 ♘b6
12 ♗b3

I am reminded of the saying
'Great minds think alike' here, because the position after Andrei
Sokolov's last move has also been
reached by Grandmaster Ivan Sokolov, but from a Queen's Gambit
Accepted! The game I.Sokolov-
Hübner, Wijk aan Zee 1996 opened
**1 d4 d5 2 c4 dxc4 3 e3 e5 4 ♗xc4
exd4 5 exd4 ♘f6 6 ♘f3 ♗e7 7 0-0
0-0 8 h3 ♘bd7 9 ♘c3 ♘b6 10
♗b3.** The concluding moves were:

10...c6 11 ♘e5 ♘bd5 12 ♖e1 ♗e6 13 ♗g5 ♖e8 14 ♖c1 ♘d7 15 ♗xe7 ♖xe7 16 ♘e4! f6 17 ♘d3 ♘f8 18 ♕f3 ♕c7 19 ♘g3! Eyeing the f5-square, but also threatening 20 ♖xe6! ♘xe6 21 ♗xd5, utilising the fact that some of the force emanating from White's rook on the c-file is directed towards Black's queen. 19...♖d8 20 ♘c5 ♗f7 21 ♖xe7 ♕xe7 22 ♘f5 ♕c7 23 ♕g3! ♕xg3 24 fxg3 b6 25 ♘b7! A bold venture further into the heart of Black's camp, but Sokolov has calculated that the brave knight will be safe. 25...♖d7 26 ♘fd6 *(D)*

B

The harmony in White's army is so great that Black is now faced with unavoidable loss of material. For example, 26...♖c7 27 ♘xf7 ♔xf7 28 ♗xd5+ cxd5 29 ♖xc7+. 26...♗e6 27 ♖xc6 ♘e7 28 ♖c3 h5?? Black cracks under the enduring pressure to which he has been subjected. 29 ♗a4 1-0

In theoretical preparation, it is good to be alert to possibilities of transpositions between different openings. The quick defeat of a top grandmaster which we have just witnessed, and the course of the game of which we are about to resume our analysis, suggest that the chances in the position after 10 ♗b3 (or 12 ♗b3 in the case of the main game) are clearly in White's favour, as Black made no glaring errors until very near the finish (by which stage he was lost anyway). White's greater freedom for manoeuvring outweighed any negative factors associated with his IQP on d4. Besides, the isolated pawn is not a serious weakness if the opponent cannot generate any pressure against it.

12	...	♘fd5
13	♘e4	c6
14	♘c5	

Control of the e5- and c5-squares is one of the positive aspects of White having an IQP on d4.

14	...	♗f6
15	♖e1	♕c7

Black protects his b-pawn so that his light-squared bishop can move from c8.

16	♕d3	♗d7
17	♗g5	♖ae8

When one has a slightly cramped position, it is natural to want to exchange pieces. However, the continuation 17...♗xg5?! 18 ♘xg5 ♘f6? 19 ♖e7 costs Black material, and 18...g6 19 ♕e4 (intending ♕h4) would soon force him to weaken his kingside pawn formation further.

18	♗xf6	♖xe1+
19	♖xe1	♘xf6
20	♖e7 *(D)*	

B

20	...	♕d6
21	♕e2	♘c8
22	♖e5	♕c7

22...b6 23 ♘e4 ♘xe4 24 ♕xe4 keeps White in command of the game and leaves Black facing the unpleasant possibility of 25 ♘g5 ♕h6 26 ♘xf7 ♖xf7 27 ♖e8+! ♗xe8 28 ♕xe8#.

23	♘g5	h6
24	♘ge4	♘xe4
25	♕xe4	♘d6
26	♕h4	♖e8
27	♕f4!	

Sokolov plays very alertly. He immediately exploits the fact that Black's last move left the f7-point weakened, and would undoubtedly have calculated the threat 28 ♗xf7+! ♘xf7 29 ♖xe8+ ♗xe8 30 ♕xc7. His army, although not so great in numbers after several earlier exchanges of pieces, is nevertheless still menacing.

| 27 | ... | ♗c8 *(D)* |

| 28 | ♘e4!! | |

I would not be surprised if Sokolov had this winning idea prepared in his mind before playing his 27th move. The harmony between White's forces is such that no satisfactory continuation can be found for the opponent. For example, 28...♖xe5 29 ♕xe5 ♘b5 30 ♕e8+ ♔h7 31 ♗xf7 (threatening 32 ♕g8# or 32 ♗g6#) and 28...♗e6 29 ♖xe6! fxe6 30 ♘xd6 ♖d8 31 ♗xe6+ ♔h7 (31...♔h8? 32 ♘f7+) 32 ♕e4+ are completely hopeless for Black.

28	...	♖f8
29	♘xd6	♕xd6
30	♗xf7+!	♔h8

Black loses his queen after 30...♖xf7 31 ♖e8+.

31 ♖e8!! ♛b4

White also wins after 31...♛xf4 32 ♖xf8+ ♚h7 33 ♗g8+ (or 33 ♗g6+) and 34 ♖xf4.

32 a3 1-0

Black's queen can no longer find a safe square from which to protect the rook on f8. An emphatic win by Grandmaster Andrei Sokolov, especially because his international master opponent did not make any moves that could be classed as obvious blunders.

The position which I left you analysing before the last game, occurred in the game Fercec-Cvitan from the 1995 Croatian Championship. Grandmaster Ognjen Cvitan, who is normally very alert, had just moved his bishop from e4 to capture a pawn on g2. Until that error, he was well on course to victory, effectively having a bishop plus three pawns to outweigh his opponent's rook. Of course, Black's idea in capturing on g2 was that 1 ♛xg2? loses quickly to 1...♛d1+ and 2...♛xb3. However, he must have failed to calculate the surprising 1 ♖g3!!. The game concluded 1...♛xg3 2 ♛h6+! ♚g8 Capturing the queen immediately results in stalemate. 3 ♛h8+ ♚f7 4 ♛e8+ ♚xe8, and White was probably quicker 'on the draw' than Clint Eastwood!

Twins

The next position is simpler, but, being a 'Gemini' myself, I thought it would be nice to provide a twin, of a kind, which follows soon afterwards.

W

White is to play. 1 c6+? ♚d8 2 ♚xa8 ♚c8 allows Black to stalemate White. A case which shows that, although it is good to 'never miss a check', you do not have to actually play it! Instead, White should *change the move-order*: **1 ♚xa8 ♚c8 2 c6 ♚d8 3 ♚b7** and **4 a8♛** wins very easily.

Grandmaster David Bronstein once stated 'The most powerful weapon in chess is the next move'. Here *(D)* we have a curious situation in which neither player wants to have the next move! However, Bronstein's statement becomes highly significant if we alter the

position by giving White a knight on e1 and Black a bishop on g4.

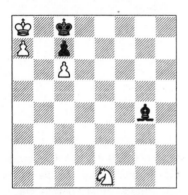

If it is Black to play, he wins beautifully with **1...♝d1!**, intending 2...♝a4 and 3...♝xc6#. Here are White's options:

a) **2 ♘c2 ♝h5!!** (2...♝f3? 3 ♘b4 ♝e4 4 ♘d5! only leads to a draw) **3 ♘b4 ♝e8** followed by **4...♝xc6#**.

b) **2 ♘d3 ♝a4 3 ♘b4 ♝b5** and **4...♝xc6#**.

c) **2 ♘f3 ♝b3!** (2...♝a4? 3 ♘d4 ♝d1 4 ♘f5 ♝f3 5 ♘e7+ ♚d8 6 ♚b7 wins for White) **3 ♘d4 ♝d5** and **4...♝xc6#**.

d) **2 ♘g2 ♝f3** and **3...♝xc6#**.

Notice that 1...♝e2? only draws after 2 ♘d3!! ♝h5 (2...♝f3 3 ♘b4 ♝e4 4 ♘d5! transposes to a drawing variation given earlier) 3 ♘e5 ♝e8 (3...♝d1? 4 ♘g6!, intending ♘e7+, wins for White) 4 ♘d7 ♝f7 5 ♘c5 ♝d5 6 ♘b7! ♝xc6 stalemate.

If it is initially *White* to move in the position being considered, then **1 ♘d3!** is the only way to draw (1 ♘c2 ♝h5! or 1 ♘f3 ♝e6! both win for Black). The variations given show that the outcome was very finely balanced, and could tip either way. Therefore, alertness and precise calculation were needed from both White and Black. We should naturally try to avoid errors in strategy, but the last example was a powerful illustration of the fact that tactical mistakes (that is, errors in calculation) can mean 'sudden death', and so it is even more important to prepare ourselves well by frequently solving practical problems and puzzles that will keep us sharp.

The first position on the next page arose after 12 moves of a game Motwani-Borwell.

Black is OK, but not in this line

Can you identify the opening and moves which led to that position, and also find the continuation

W

B

which caused Black to resign after three more moves by White? The solution appears after the next game.

Game 30
C.McNab – P.Marusenko
Dutch Defence
Hastings 1991/2

1 ♘f3

Johan van Mil, a strong Dutch international master and friend of mine, once remarked that he feels safer playing the Dutch Defence as Black when White opens with 1 ♘f3 rather than 1 d4. The point is that White has certain ultra-aggressive options after **1 d4 f5** which are not appropriate after 1 ♘f3 f5. Let us consider such an example, leaving White's king's knight on g1: **2 ♘c3 ♘f6 3 g4!?** *(D)*

When the Dutch Defence begins 1 d4 f5, it is, up to a point, like a *mirror image* of the Sicilian Defence *1 e4 c5*. Michael Fallone, the

1963 Scottish Champion, had good results in the international chess arena with the 'Wing Gambit' *2 b4* against the Sicilian, although its popularity was not increased by the game Shirazi-Peters, US Championship 1984, which ended abruptly after *2...cxb4 3 a3 d5!* (responding to the opponent's operations on the wing with a reaction in the centre) *4 exd5 ♕xd5 5 axb4??* (5 ♘f3 is much better) *5...♕e5+ 0-1.* 3 g4!? is a kind of delayed wing gambit against the Dutch Defence. **3...fxg4** 3...♘xg4 4 e4 also gives White good attacking prospects. It looks safer to decline this particular gambit by playing 3...e6 or 3...d5 (or to accept it, but return the surplus material quickly, as discussed in the next note). However, if ♘f3 had already been played, then ...fxg4 would be attacking that knight. **4 h3 d6** This is where the 'mirror image' concept breaks down. In the Shirazi-Peters game, Black was able to react with ...d5, since the central pawn was protected by his queen. The 'mirror' move for Black in the Dutch Defence would be ...e5, but unfortunately it is not protected by the king! Therefore dxe5 would simply refute that idea. How would the Ukrainian grandmaster Vladimir Malaniuk, a renowned expert on the Dutch Defence, handle White's gambit? Well, it is significant that Malaniuk chose to return Black's surplus pawn in his encounter with GM Pavel Tregubov at the 1996 Linares Open. 4...g3 5 fxg3 d5 6 ♘f3 e6 7 ♗g2 ♗d6! transposes to that game. **5 hxg4 ♗xg4 6 ♕d3!** (*D*)

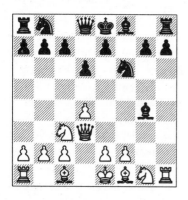

B

White's queen now has her eyes bearing down on h7, while at the same time creating the possibility of ♕b5+ and also unpinning the pawn on e2. A wonderfully economical move! **6...♘c6 7 ♗g5 ♕d7 8 f3! ♘b4 9 ♕d2 ♗e6** 9...♗h5?

loses material to 10 a3 ♘c6 11 ♗xf6 exf6 12 ♖xh5. **10 ♗xf6!?** The point of this voluntary capture is to allow White to follow up with d4-d5. **10...exf6 11 d5! ♗f7 12 e4** White has achieved a strong and harmonious position very easily, at the cost of one pawn. **12...g6?** Black was probably anticipating 13 ♗h3, to which he could have responded with 13...♕e7 then ...♗g7 or ...h5 and ...♗h6. However, he must have failed to calculate the consequences of White's bishop developing in a different direction. **13 a3!** White is tactically alert, and seizes his chance to win material. The point is that 13...♘a6 14 ♗b5 c6 15 dxc6 bxc6 16 ♗xa6 leaves Black a piece down, so ... **1-0** Kerkmeester-Brink, Dutch Inter-Clubs Championship 1995. Note that one does not have to prepare and memorise lots of variations to adopt Hans Kerkmeester's enterprising gambit approach to the opening. His play involved very straightforward, natural, attacking moves, which were perhaps not subtle, yet difficult to deal with, and highly effective! The saying 'Fortune favours the brave' comes to mind. Just because White's chosen line was not a 'main' line does not necessarily mean it is inferior. On the contrary, his refreshing, original play brought rewards quickly. We shall see that the same is true in the case of Grandmaster Colin

McNab as we return to the main game now.

| 1 | ... | d6 |

1...f5 2 d4 ♘f6 would be my preferred move order as Black, but not 2...g6, which is risky because of 3 h4! ♘f6 4 h5 ♘xh5 5 ♖xh5 gxh5 6 e4 fxe4? 7 ♘e5 with the winning threat of 8 ♕xh5#.

| 2 | d4 | f5 |
| 3 | ♘c3!? | |

3 g3 ♘f6 4 ♗g2 is a much more common, but not necessarily better, continuation.

| 3 | ... | ♘f6 |
| 4 | ♗g5 | ♘e4?! *(D)* |

Black may have been worried about White playing e4 soon. For instance, 4...e6 5 e4 and 4...g6 5 h4!? ♗g7 6 ♗xf6 ♗xf6 (6...exf6 7 h5) 7 e4 are pleasant for White. 4...d5 was the correct way to prevent e2-e4. Although Black would be moving his d-pawn for the second time early in the opening, and making the e5-square an outpost for White's pieces, his bold decision would be justified by the fact that White too must use a tempo, to move the knight from c3, if he wants to be able to play c2-c4.

5	♘xe4	fxe4
6	♘d2	d5
7	e3	♗f5
8	c4	c6
9	f3!	

Black's central pawn chain is now under fire at its base and head.

| 9 | ... | exf3 |

W

10	♕xf3	♕d7
11	♗e2	e6
12	0-0	♗b4
13	♘b3	

c5 and then a3 is now a threat.

| 13 | ... | ♗d6 |
| 14 | ♕h5+! | ♗g6 |

Black's dark-square weaknesses are horrible after 14...g6 15 ♕h6 ♗f8 16 ♕h4.

| 15 | ♕h3 | |

16 ♗g4 is a powerful threat.

15	...	♗f5
16	♗h5+!	g6
17	♖xf5!	exf5
18	♗xg6+	hxg6

18...♔f8 19 ♗h6+ ♔g8 20 ♗xf5 ♕d8 21 ♗e6# is another way for Black to go.

| 19 | ♕xh8+ | |

White is a pawn ahead with an overwhelming position. In fact, he will either checkmate Black or win more material. For example:

a) 19...♔f7 20 ♕h7+ ♔f8 (alternatively 20...♔e8 21 ♕xg6+) 21

♗h6+! ♔e8 22 ♕g8+ ♔e7 23 ♗g5#.

b) 19...♗f8 20 ♘c5 ♕f7 (if 20...♕c7, then 21 ♕xf8+! ♔xf8 22 ♘e6+ and 23 ♘xc7 or 20...♕c8 21 ♕g8 threatening 22 ♕xg6#) 21 ♕e5+ ♗e7 22 ♘xb7 ♘d7 23 ♘d6+ ♔f8 24 ♕h8+ ♕g8 25 ♗h6#.

So very soon the game ended ... **1-0**.

Colin McNab's pieces combined with each other in great harmony to force that quick win. Of course, Colin was alert to the tactical possibilities which existed, and calculated them with typical precision to produce a neat miniature. He also has an excellent memory, but, by preparing a repertoire consisting mainly of systems which he likes and understands thoroughly, he actually does not have to rely on his memory too much. His chosen systems are not, in general, very heavily analysed in opening books, but what is important is that they suit his style.

The position I gave you to consider before the last game arose from the **Sveshnikov Variation of the Sicilian Defence** after the moves **1 e4 c5 2 ♘f3 ♘c6 3 d4 cxd4 4 ♘xd4 ♘f6 5 ♘c3 e5 6 ♘db5 d6 7 ♘d5 ♘xd5 8 exd5 ♘e7** (8...♘b8 is more popular) **9 c3 ♘g6?!** (9...a6? 10 ♕a4! is even worse for Black, but 9...♘f5 is better than 9...♘g6?!, which, in spite of looking so plausible, is actually

very difficult for Black because of the continuation in the game) **10 ♕a4! ♗d7 11 ♕c4!** (11 ♕b4 ♕b8 12 ♕c4 ♔d8 is perhaps not quite as bad for Black as what happens in the game) **11...♖c8?** (as this natural looking move loses virtually by force, with the benefit of hindsight, Black should have played 11...♗xb5 12 ♕xb5+ ♕d7) **12 ♕b4 ♗xb5** (Black's pawns on a7 and d6 were both *en prise*, ...♕b8 was no longer possible, and 12...♕b6 would have lost to 13 ♗e3). White now calculated a forced win, and finished the game as follows: **13 ♗xb5+ ♔e7 14 ♗g5+! f6 15 ♕g4! 1-0**. White alertly pounced on the weakness at e6 forced by the check on move 14. His queen and bishop pair were very harmoniously placed, and Black resigned because he had no satisfactory way of preventing 16 ♕e6#. For example, 15...♕c7 16 ♕e6+ ♔d8 17 ♕e8#. I had studied the idea of 9 c3 and 10 ♕a4 more than ten years before that game. I just had to use my memory a little to recall my preparation, although I discovered the ♗g5+ and ♕g4 combination during the game itself.

Surprise Tactics

It is Black to play and win in the following position, which occurred after 9 moves in Marchyllie-Motwani, Cappelle la Grande 1992.

B

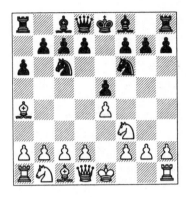

W

Can you identify the opening and moves that led to that position, and also find the continuation which wins material for Black by force? The solution appears after the next encounter, a daring game for which Grandmaster Glenn Flear won the Brilliancy Prize at the 1989 Guernsey Chess Festival.

Game 31
R.Britton – G.Flear
Guernsey 1989
Ruy Lopez

1	e4	e5
2	♘f3	♘c6
3	♗b5	a6
4	♗a4	♘f6 *(D)*
5	d3	

Another way to deviate from the main lines arising after 5 0-0 and to avoid the Open Variation 5...♘xe4 (see Game 12), if White wants to do so, is **5 ♕e2**, the Worrall Attack. However, in that case, there is

plenty of scope for Black to inject some originality into the game too. The encounter Tiviakov-I.Sokolov, Groningen 1995, went **5...♗e7 6 c3 6 ♗xc6 dxc6 7 ♘xe5 ♕d4** causes Black no headaches. **6...0-0!? 7 d4** 7 ♗xc6 dxc6 8 ♘xe5 ♖e8 (intending ...♗d6) 9 d4 c5! gives Black excellent compensation for his sacrificed pawn. When Tiviakov and Sokolov faced each other a few weeks later at Wijk aan Zee 1996, the continuation was 7 0-0 b5 8 ♗b3 d5! (this can be compared to the Marshall Attack) 9 d3 ♖e8 10 ♖e1 h6 11 ♘bd2 ♗e6 12 ♘f1 ♗c5 13 ♘g3 a5, and a complicated struggle was in progress. Black won in 41 moves, but only after serious errors from both players. **7...exd4! 8 e5 ♖e8! 9 0-0** *(D)* 9 cxd4 ♗b4+ 10 ♘c3 d6, intending ...♗g4, subjects White's pawn centre to great pressure.

9...dxc3!! 10 exf6 10 ♘xc3 ♗b4 is similar to the previous note, but

B

here White would already be a pawn down. Also, Black has at least a draw after the continuation 10 ♗xc6 dxc6 11 exf6 ♗xf6 12 ♕c2 ♗f5! 13 ♕b3 ♗e6 14 ♕c2 (14 ♕a3? ♗c4) 14...♗f5. **10...♗xf6 11 ♕c2 ♘b4!** 12 ♕b3 ♘d3 Renewing the threat of ...cxb2. **13 ♘xc3 ♘xc1 14 ♖axc1 b5** Recovering all the sacrificed material. **15 ♗xb5 axb5 16 ♘xb5 ♖b8**, and Black had a very harmonious position, with open lines and diagonals for his pairs of rooks and bishops (0-1 in 48 moves). Either at the board or in pre-game preparation, Grandmaster Ivan Sokolov showed tremendous tactical alertness in finding a well-calculated and highly convincing sequence stretching from moves 6-16.

5 ...   **♗c5**

The game A.Martin-Motwani, British Club Team Championship 1995, diverged with **5...b5 6 ♗b3 ♗c5 7 c3 d6 8 ♘bd2** 8 d4 ♗b6

leaves White a tempo behind compared with an established line of the Arkhangelsk variation, because he has used two moves, instead of only one, to get a pawn on d4. In fact, that is basically what happened (but via a different move order) in 'Ferret'-Shirov, a clash involving computer versus human, played on 14 March 1996 via the Internet. To give a very brief summary of the game, the computer inappropriately closes the centre and queenside, thereby allowing Shirov a free hand on the kingside: 8 d4 ♗b6 9 0-0 0-0 10 d5 ♘e7 11 ♘bd2 ♘g6 12 a4 ♗g4 13 a5? ♗a7 14 ♗c2 ♘h4 15 h3 ♗h5 16 ♗d3 (16 g4 ♘xg4!) 16...♘g6!? 17 ♖e1 ♘f4 18 ♗f1 ♕d7 19 ♘b3 g5! 20 ♗xf4 gxf4 21 ♕d3 ♔h8 22 ♖e2 ♖g8 23 ♔h2 ♖g6 24 ♘bd2 ♖ag8 25 b3 ♘g4+!! 26 hxg4 (26 ♔g1 ♘xf2! 27 ♖xf2 ♕xh3) 26...♗xg4 27 ♔h1 ♖h6+ 28 ♘h2 ♖g5 29 ♘f3 ♖gh5 30 g3 ♗xf3+ 31 ♕xf3 ♖xh2+ 32 ♔g1 fxg3 33 ♗g2 ♖xg2+ 34 ♕xg2 gxf2+ 35 ♖xf2 (35 ♔f1 ♖g6) 35...♖g6 0-1. We return now to the Martin-Motwani game. **8...0-0 9 ♘f1** A well-known manoeuvre in the Ruy Lopez: the knight is heading for e3 or g3, where it will be nearer to the kingside. However, the drawback of White's plan is that it is slow. Therefore Black is fully justified in now using a tempo to move his d-pawn for the second time in order to react strongly in the centre. **9...d5! 10 ♕e2 dxe4 11 dxe4 ♘g4 12 ♘e3 ♘a5! 13 0-0** 13 ♗c2 ♗xe3 14 ♗xe3 ♘xe3 15 ♕xe3 ♘c4 is very pleasant for Black, and reveals a key point of his 12th move. **13...♘xb3 14 axb3 ♗e6! 15 ♘xg4** 15 b4? ♗xe3 16 ♗xe3 ♗c4 costs White an exchange. **15...♗xg4 16 h3 ½-½** 16...♗h5? 17 g4! ♗g6 18 ♘xe5 is good for White, but 16...♗xf3 gives a level position with few pieces remaining. So Andrew and I agreed a draw then had a chat on the telephone ... since the match was being played using that wonderful invention of Alexander Graham Bell!

6 0-0

6 ♗xc6 dxc6 7 ♘xe5? runs into 7...♕d4.

6 ... d6

7 ♘c3?!

Britton soon discovers that it would be better to have a pawn on c3 to prevent Black from playing ...♘d4.

7 ... b5

8 ♗b3 ♗g4

A strong threat after this pinning move is 9...♘d4.

9 h3 ♗h5

10 g4

It is difficult to suggest reasonable alternatives to this advance, which is needed to remove the uncomfortable pin on White's king's knight. White also hopes to render Black's light-squared bishop almost inactive. The problem with

this strategy is that Black has not castled kingside, and so he is able to react dangerously with ...h5 shortly, having the support of his king's rook behind it.

10 ... ♗g6

10...♘xg4? is refuted most convincingly by 11 ♗d5! ♕d7 12 ♗xc6 ♕xc6 13 hxg4 ♗xg4 14 ♘xe5!: 14...♗xd1 15 ♘xc6 or 14...dxe5 15 ♕xg4.

11 ♘d5 *(D)*

B

11 ... h5!

12 ♗g5 hxg4

13 ♗xf6

13 hxg4? ♕d7! is very unpleasant for White.

13 ... gxf6

14 hxg4

White hopes that his king's position will prove to be secure in spite of its shaky appearance. The fact that he has left Black with a pawn to protect on f6 prevents 14...♕d7. However, Glenn Flear has prepared a daring sacrifice initiated by that doubled pawn.

14 ...   f5!

A brave, but also very logical sacrifice, since White's king will become exposed on the g-file. Besides, Black had to attack quickly, before the lack of scope of his light-squared bishop became the dominant, negative, feature of his position.

15 exf5 (D)

B

15 ...   ♗xf5
16 gxf5   ♔d7

Introducing the deadly threat of 17...♕g8+.

17 ♖e1   ♖h3!

17...♕g8+ 18 ♔f1 ♖h1+ 19 ♔e2 ♕g2 (threatening ...♕xf2#) is a plausible alternative. I analysed the resulting position for a long time, and found that it was not nearly as easy as I had expected for White to deaden Black's attack, e.g. 20 ♘f6+ ♔e7 21 ♘e4 ♖h3 and now:

a) 22 f6+ ♔d7 23 ♘xc5+ dxc5 24 ♗d5 ♖xf3! 25 ♗xf3 ♘d4+ 26 ♔e3 ♕g5+ 27 ♔e4 ♕f5+ and then 28 ♔e3 ♕f4# or 28 ♔d5 e4#.

b) 22 ♘fg5? ♕g4+ 23 ♔d2 ♕f4+ 24 ♔e2 (24 ♔c3 ♗d4#) 24...♘d4+ 25 ♔f1 ♖h1+ 26 ♔g2 ♕h2#.

c) 22 ♘g1 ♗xf2!? (D) (the line 22...♕g4+ 23 ♔f1 ♕xg1+ 24 ♔xg1 ♖g8+ 25 ♔f1 ♘d4 only just fails to work for Black because of 26 ♘g3).

W

This sacrifice blasts open the shelter on the second rank with the force of a falling tree. It branches into:

c1) 23 ♘xf2 ♘d4+ 24 ♔d2 ♕xf2+ (24...♕g5+ 25 ♔c3 is really wild, but mild compared with the forthcoming variation 'c2'!) 25 ♔c1 ♖h2 with an enduring attack.

c2) 23 ♘xh3 ♘d4+ 24 ♔d2 ♗e3+!? (the 'obvious' 24...♗xe1+ is clearly not bad in view of 25

♔xe1 ♘f3+ or 24 ♔c1 ♕xh3 {24...♗h4 25 f6+!? ♔d7? 26 ♗d5! threatening ♘c5+} 25 f6+ ♔d7 26 ♕xe1 ♖g8, with dangerous threats such as ...♖g1, but I felt that the beautiful variations after 24...♗e3+ should not be hidden even if they are almost too fantastic) 25 ♔c3 (25 ♔xe3? ♘xf5#) 25...♖b8! with incredible possibilities including:

c21) 26 ♕h5 ♗d2+! 27 ♘xd2 b4+ 28 ♔c4 ♕c6#..

c22) 26 a3 b4+ 27 axb4 ♘b5+ 28 ♔c4 d5+ 29 ♔xd5 ♖d8+ 30 ♔c6 (30 ♔c4 ♘d6+ and then 31 ♔c3 ♗d4# or 31 ♘xd6 ♕c6#) 30...♖d6+! 31 ♔b7 ♖b6+ 32 ♔a8 ♕g8#.

c23) 26 ♖xe3 b4+ 27 ♔c4 ♖b5! 28 ♘f4 c6! 29 ♘xd6 ♕d5+! 30 ♘xd5 cxd5# *(D)*.

W

That must be the most complicated variation in this book, and I hope you will forgive me for not being one hundred per cent sure

about its soundness (since, for example, f6+ could affect matters if White wanted to throw in that check at some moment). Still, it was worth finding, even just to see the beautiful harmony between Black's (few) remaining pieces at the end. I think that the final position, and the calculations leading up to it, will stay indelibly imprinted within my memory!

Needless to say, White has other options after 19...♕g2, but, as we have seen, he cannot afford not to stay alert.

18 ♔f1   ♕h8
19 ♘e3

19 ♔e2 ♖xf3! (not 19...♕h5?? 20 ♘f6+) 20 ♔xf3 ♘d4+ 21 ♔e4 (21 ♔g2 ♖g8+ 22 ♔f1 ♕h1#) 21...♕h4+ 22 f4 ♖e8 gives Black a decisive attack. 19 c3 looks better, but after 19...♖g8 it is still far from easy for White to survive the pressure, before he can even begin to think about safely consolidating his extra material. For example:

a) 20 ♘e3 ♗xe3 21 fxe3 (21 ♖xe3 ♖h1+) 21...♖h1+ 22 ♔f2 ♖h2+! 23 ♘xh2 (23 ♔f1 ♕h3#) 23...♕xh2+ 24 ♔f3 ♕g2#.

b) 20 a4 ♗xf2! 21 ♔xf2 ♖h2+ 22 ♘xh2 (22 ♔e3 ♕h6+ 23 ♔e4 ♖g4+ mates in two more moves) 22...♕xh2+ 23 ♔e3 *(D)*

23...♘d4!? (a fascinating alternative to 23...♖g3+ 24 ♕f3) 24 cxd4 (24 ♘f6+ ♔d8 25 ♘xg8 ♕f4#) 24...♕h6+!! and now:

B

b1) 25 ♔e2 ♖g2+ 26 ♔f3 ♕h3+ 27 ♔e4 ♕h4+ 28 ♔f3 ♖f2+ 29 ♔e3 exd4#.

b2) 25 ♔f2 ♕h4+! 26 ♔e3 (26 ♔f1 ♕h3+ 27 ♔f2 ♖g2+ 28 ♔f1 ♕h1#) 26...♕g5+! 27 ♔e4 (27 ♔f2 ♕g2+) 27...♕g2+ 28 ♕f3 ♖g4+ 29 ♔e3 exd4#.

b3) 25 ♔f3 ♕h3+ 26 ♔e4 ♕g2+ 27 ♕f3 ♖g4+ 28 ♔e3 exd4#.

b4) 25 ♔e4 ♕h4+ 26 ♘f4 (other moves lose in a similar manner to the lines given already) 26...♕xf4+ 27 ♔d5 ♕xd4#.

Notice the recurring ...exd4# finish, which is why I wanted to sacrifice the knight with 23...♘d4 in variation 'b'.

c) 20 ♔e2 ♖xf3 21 ♔xf3 ♕h5+ 22 ♔e4 ♕h4+ 23 f4 ♖g3 (stops d4 and ♔d3, while the threats include 24...♘e7) is a very tempting line for Black because of 24 ♖h1? ♕xf4+! 25 ♘xf4 ♖e3+ 26 ♔d5 ♘e7#. However, objectivity and alertness are needed to see that 24

♕h5!! refutes Black's attack. Thus, after 20 ♔e2, I prefer 20...♗xf2! to eliminate the key pawn which was shielding White's king along the second rank. Then 21 ♔xf2 ♖h2+ leads to virtually the same lines as in variation 'b', the only difference being that White's a-pawn is still on a2. The critical move is 21 ♖f1!, declining to take Black's bishop, but 21...♗a7 22 ♔d2 ♖gg3!? is still very tricky, as 23 ♕e2? ♖xf3! 24 ♖xf3 ♖h2 shows.

19   ...   ♘d4!

20 ♘xd4

20 ♘g1 looks so passive that, at first, I thought 20...♖g8 (threatening 21...♖xg1+ 22 ♔xg1 ♖h1+ 23 ♔g2 ♕h3#) would win simply for Black. However, 21 ♗d5! is not easy to refute. For example:-

a) 21...♖h1 22 ♗xh1 ♕xh1 23 ♘g4 threatens 24 ♘f6+.

b) 21...♖xe3 22 ♖xe3 ♕h2 23 ♘h3! (23 ♖g3? ♖xg3 24 fxg3 ♘xf5 25 ♕f3 ♕xg1+ 26 ♔e2 ♘d4+ wins) 23...♘xf5 24 ♕f3!? ♘xe3+ 25 fxe3 is not convincing for Black.

So, after 20 ♘g1, I turned to look at 20...♖h1 (threatening 21...♕h3+ 22 ♘g2 ♕h2). This is Black's correct path. For instance, 21 ♗d5 ♕h3+ 22 ♗g2 ♖g8!! *(D)*.

Capturing the queen allows the reply ...♖xg1# with either of the black rooks, yet White must deal with the threat of ...♕h2. There is no satisfactory solution for White, but a likely continuation is 23 c3

W

♕h2 (23...♖xg2 24 ♘xg2 ♘f3 25 ♔e2 ♕xg2 is also sufficient to win) 24 cxd4 ♖xg1+ 25 ♔e2 ♖1xg2 26 ♘xg2 ♖xg2 27 ♖f1 ♗xd4, with an overwhelming position for Black.

Note that 20 ♗d5 would simply transpose to the same line, after 20...♖h1+ 21 ♘g1 ♕h3+ 22 ♗g2 ♖g8.

20 ...   exd4

A key point of Black's 19th move is revealed: the e-file has opened, and White's monarch will not be permitted to escape.

21 ♘g2

After 21 ♘g4, 21...♖h1+ 22 ♔e2 (22 ♔g2? ♕h3#) 22...♖e8+? allows 23 ♗e6+! fxe6 24 ♖xh1, winning for White. However, 21...♕h4! keeps Black's attack hot after 22 ♗d5 ♖g8:

a) 23 ♗f3 ♖xg4! 24 ♗xg4 ♖h1+ 25 ♔e2 (25 ♔g2 ♖h2+ 26 ♔f3 ♖xf2+ 27 ♔e4 ♕e7+ 28 ♔d5 c6#) 25...♕xg4+ 26 ♔d2 ♕f4+ 27 ♔e2 ♖h2 28 ♖f1 ♕e3#.

b) 23 ♗g2 ♖xg4 24 ♗xh3 ♕xh3+ 25 ♔e2 ♖g2 26 ♕d2 (or 26 ♔d2 ♕h6+ 27 ♔e2 ♕e3+) 26...♕g4+ 27 ♔f1 ♖g1#.

c) 23 f3 ♖h1+ 24 ♔e2 ♖h2+! 25 ♘xh2 (if 25 ♔f1, 25...♕h3+) 25...♕xh2+ 26 ♔f1 ♖g1#.

21 ...   ♖e8!

21...♖h1+ 22 ♔e2 ♖e8+ 23 ♗e6+! fxe6 24 ♖xh1 was a trap which Black alertly avoided.

22 f3?! (D)

22 ♖xe8 ♖h1+ 23 ♔e2 ♕h5+! (note again the pitfall 23...♕xe8+? 24 ♗e6+!) would have won the white queen, and eventually the game, for Black, although this was White's best way to fight on.

B

22 ...   ♖g8!

0-1

An elegant finish. Some people might have played 22...♖h1+, intending 23 ♔f2 ♖exe1 24 ♘xe1 ♕h4+ 25 ♔e2 ♕h2+ 26 ♘g2 ♕xg2#, but White could put up tougher resistance with 24 ♕xe1 ♖xe1 25 ♖xe1. Instead, after the text-move, White is defenceless against the combined attacking power of Black's heavy pieces. Both players would have calculated the following line, which once again demonstrates the harmony in Black's army: 23 ♔f2 ♖xg2+! 24 ♔xg2 ♖h2+ 25 ♔g1 (25 ♔g3 ♕h4#) 25...♖h1+ 26 ♔f2 ♕h2#.

The position I gave you to consider before the last game arose from the **French Defence** after the moves **1 e4 e6 2 d4 d5 3 e5 c5 4 c3 ♘c6 5 ♘f3 ♗d7 6 dxc5 ♗xc5 7 ♗d3 f6 8 ♗f4?** 8 b4 ♗b6 9 b5! ♘xe5 9 ♘xe5 fxe5 10 ♕h5+ is nice for White. Black could diverge from that line with 8...fxe5!?, intending 9 bxc5 e4. White, too, can play tricks with 9 b5, planning 9...e4 10 bxc6 bxc6 11 ♘e5 exd3 (11...♕f6 12 ♘g4) 12 ♕h5+, but 12...g6 13 ♘xg6 ♘f6 14 ♕h4 ♖g8 gives Black a fine position. **8...fxe5 9 ♘xe5.**

Black now won material with **9...♕f6! 10 ♘xd7 ♗xf2+! 11 ♔xf2 ♕xf4+ 12 ♕f3 ♕xf3+ 13 gxf3 ♔xd7.** The remaining moves were **14 ♖g1 g6 15 ♘d2 ♘f6 16 ♖ad1 ♖hf8 17 c4 ♘e5 18 ♘b3 ♖ac8 19 cxd5 ♘xd3+ 20 ♖xd3 ♖c2+ 21 ♔g3 ♘h5+ 22 ♔g4 ♖c4+ 23 ♔g5 23 ♖d4 ♖xd4+ 24 ♘xd4 ♖f4+ and 25...♖xd4** also wins for Black.

23...♘f4 24 dxe6+ ♔e8! 25 ♖g4 *(D)*

B

White was facing dual threats of 25...♘xd3 and 25...♘h3+, but, even after the text-move, Black still has a forced winning sequence. It was prepared at move 18. The necessary calculations were made more possible because of the great harmony existing between the black pieces, a fact which tends to lead in a natural way to combinative conclusions if one stays alert.

25...♖f5+ 26 ♔h6 There are only two 'branches' here. Therefore it was not so difficult several moves ago to visualise the winning lines in both cases. Memory would have been needed to a greater extent to calculate the possibilities if White had more ways of continuing. However, the only other option here is 26 ♔h4, which loses to 26...♖h5+ 27 ♔g3 ♖h3+ 28 ♔f2 ♘xd3+. **26...♖h5+ 27 ♔g7 ♖c7+**

0-1, in view of 28 ♖d7 ♘xe6+ 29 ♔f6 ♔xd7.

The Mystery Moves

The players who have White and Black in this puzzle will be referred to as **W** and **B** respectively. **W** opens with her favourite first move. **B** replies by moving the only pawn which would allow **W** to check him on her second move. **W** makes a capture instead. **B** then moves a knight. For her third move, **W** defends the attacked pawn with a pawn. **B** captures the pawn which his opponent has just moved. However, **B** resigns without waiting to see the next move by **W**.

Can you discover all the moves made by both players, and explain why Black resigned? The solution appears after the following game.

The next encounter is between Yasser Seirawan (before he became a grandmaster) and Michael Wiedenkeller, who is now a Swedish international master. It was played in the 1979 World Junior Championship in Wiedenkeller's home country. Myself and others who saw Seirawan win the tournament so impressively had little doubt that he would go on to become a top GM. His chess is as hot as he once said (on TV) that he felt! During the commentary to a game against Anatoly Karpov, Seirawan remarked that he was feeling too hot, and on his next appearance would shed his stylish suit and play in his underwear!

Game 32
Y.Seirawan – M.Wiedenkeller
Skien 1979
Queen's Gambit Declined

1	c4	♘f6
2	♘c3	e6
3	♘f3	d5

For discussions of 3...b6 for Black, and of the earlier white option 3 e4, see Game 14.

4	cxd5	exd5
5	d4	♗e7 (D)

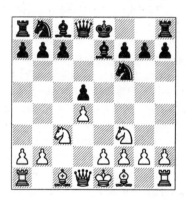

W

The fact that White exchanged his c-pawn on move four, instead of maintaining the tension with 4 d4, means that Black no longer has to watch out for the possibility of White playing c4-c5. Thus I would have opted for 5...c6, intending to develop the dark-squared bishop more actively to d6 without being harassed by ♘b5. 5...c6 is also useful if Black wants to play ...♗f5, because a subsequent ♕b3 by White is then easily answered by ...♕b6.

I am reminded of a statement by Grandmaster Mihai Suba: 'Black's information is always greater by one move'. In other words, because any move by Black is always preceded by a White move, Black can respond according to what White does, whereas White must show his hand first. If Black can maintain a *flexible* position, then he will have plenty of options available to himself. That makes it more difficult for White, in choosing his own move, to predict which move Black will respond with.

In the position after White's fifth move, 5...c6 is slightly more flexible than 5...♗e7. The reason is that the c-pawn is normally well placed on c6 in the Queen's Gambit Declined to give extra support to the pawn on d5, whereas there is a choice of at least three squares (e7, d6, b4) to which Black's dark-squared bishop may be usefully deployed. If one, as far as possible, begins by playing the moves which are (almost) certainly going to be needed, and reserves options with other pieces and pawns whose future roles are not yet so clear, then one will have a more flexible position.

That was a long note to the move 5...♗e7, especially since it can hardly be described as an error, but I know from personal experience, and observations of other players' games, that it is worth stressing the benefits of flexibility.

6	♗f4	0-0
7	e3	b6
8	♗e2	♘h5?!

This does not seem to be a consistent way to follow up 7...b6. The alternatives 8...♗b7 or 8...c5 are more natural.

9 ♗e5!

Instead of immediately moving the bishop to g3, White first induces Black into weakening his king's position.

| 9 | ... | f6 |

If 9...♘c6, then 10 h3 (intending ♗h2) sets a tricky trap for Black: 10...♘xe5? 11 dxe5!, with the dual threats of 12 g4 and 12 ♘xd5.

| 10 | ♗g3 | ♘xg3 |
| 11 | hxg3 | |

Black must now be alert to avoid a trap which Seirawan probably prepared in his calculations when he played 9 ♗e5. The point is that ...f6 left Black particularly vulnerable on the a2 to g8 diagonal, and so 12 ♕c2 g6 13 ♘xd5! ♕xd5? 14 ♗c4 is threatened.

| 11 | ... | ♗e6 |
| 12 | ♗d3! | |

White moves his bishop for the second time, but there is a direct threat which is already extremely difficult to deal with. So this is a well-spent tempo.

12 ... g6? *(D)*

Black overlooks White's stunning reply, but 12...f5 or 12...h6 were also very unpleasant for him, in view of 13 ♘e5 or 13 ♘h4 respectively, with ♕h5 threatened soon afterwards.

W

13 ♖xh7!! f5

13...♔xh7 14 ♘g5+! fxg5 (or 14...♔g8 15 ♘xe6) 15 ♕h5+ ♔g7 16 ♕xg6+ ♔h8 17 ♕h7#. A lovely variation, showing the harmony between White's pieces in the attack.

14 ♖h1

14 ♖h2, to be followed soon by ♖dh1 after 0-0-0, does not disguise White's intentions, but is nevertheless a strong, economical and logical move.

14 ... ♘d7

15 ♕d2 ♗f6

16 0-0-0

White was right not to expect to win instantly. It would be very easy to lose objectivity, and probably the game too, by playing the rash sacrifice 16 e4?, which is comfortably dealt with by 16...fxe4 17 ♕h6 ♕e7 18 ♕xg6+ ♕g7. White could reach an endgame in which he would be a piece down yet have three extra pawns, but it is hardly the best way to proceed from the nearly winning position he has achieved by move 15.

16 ... ♕e7

17 ♖h2 ♔g7

18 ♕c2 c5

An understandable reaction to White's last move. Black does not wish to defend passively, so he seeks counterplay on the c-file, especially since his opponent's king and queen are both located there. However, the pawn on d5 can no longer be supported by ...c6, and a calm yet powerful response from Seirawan soon exposes its vulnerability.

19 ♗b5!

Black should not be allowed to lock in White's bishop behind the pawns by ...c4.

19 ... ♖ac8

20 ♖dh1 ♖h8

21 ♖xh8 ♖xh8

22 ♖xh8 ♔xh8 *(D)*

23 ♕a4!

White is co-ordinating his forces very harmoniously, and, in spite of the reduced material left on the

W

board, Black's position is under considerable pressure.

| 23 | ... | ♘f8 |
| 24 | ♗c6 | ♛h7 |

Wiedenkeller desperately strives for activity. 24...♛d6 25 ♗b7 would have left him facing the threats of 26 ♛xa7 or infiltration of White's queen to the back rank by 26 ♛e8.

25	♗xd5	♛h1+
26	♔d2	♛xg2
27	♔e2	

I saw this and numerous other Seirawan encounters 'live', and I remember thinking that he generally made his king play an active role in the struggle, particularly in the endgame phase. Since he did not neglect the monarch's safety, he was absolutely correct in his approach.

| 27 | ... | cxd4 |
| 28 | exd4 | ♗d7 |

Black would lose even more quickly after 28...a5? 29 ♗xe6 ♘xe6 30 ♛e8+.

29	♛xa7	f4
30	♛b8	♔g7
31	♛xf4	♗h3
32	♘d2	♛h2
33	♘ce4	♗f5

33...♗xd4 34 ♛f7+ is equally hopeless for Black.

34	♘xf6	♔xf6
35	♛e5+	♔g5
36	♘f3+	1-0

White handled that game in a simple but highly convincing manner, showing that good, strong moves do not necessarily have to be very complicated.

Mystery Moves Found!

The moves were **1 c4 d5 2 cxd5 ♘f6 3 e4 ♘xe4?? 1-0**, on account of 4 ♛a4+ winning the knight on e4.

Explanation: If **W** was able to check **B** on move two, then she must have opened by advancing her c- or e-pawn, to free White's queen or light-squared bishop sufficiently to deliver the check. However, if **W** had moved the e-pawn, then **B** could have allowed checks on b5 or h5 by moving his d- or f-pawns respectively. We were told that **B** moved the *only* pawn which would allow a check. Therefore **W** must have advanced her c-pawn instead, and **B** must have moved his d-pawn in response (to allow ♛a4+). Did those pawns advance one square or two? Well, since **W**

continued with a *capture*, the first moves could only have been 1 c4 d5, to allow 2 cxd5. We know that, on move three, **W** defends her attacked pawn (on d5) with a pawn move, which can only be 3 e4. At that stage, we also know that **B** captures White's e-pawn. So **B's** knight move on move two must have been 2...♘f6, followed by 3...♘xe4.

That puzzle could be solved by logical deduction, but what about the quality of the actual moves? When I composed that puzzle, I was reminded of two other opening traps:-

a) 1 e4 c5 2 ♘f3 d6 3 c3 ♘f6 4 ♗e2 ♘xe4?? 5 ♕a4+.

b) 1 d4 ♘f6 2 ♗g5 c6 3 e3?? ♕a5+.

It would do us no harm to store them well in the memory, because, incredibly, there have been numerous instances of players, including masters, falling into both traps! A little extra care and alertness can stop the list of victims from growing further! Incidentally, after 1 c4, the defence 1...♘f6 2 ♘c3 d5 is playable, but, as the puzzle demonstrated, 1...d5 is not to be recommended.

Opening Lines

The next position was reached after White's 11th move in Slingerland-Bosboom, Holland 1995.

B

Can you identify the opening and moves which led to that position, and also find the extremely powerful continuation that Black now played? The answers appear after the next attacking game.

Game 33
M.Adams – D.Bisby
Hastings 1995
Pirc Defence

1	e4	d6
2	d4	♘f6
3	♘c3	g6
4	♗e3	c6
5	♕d2	♘bd7
6	♘f3 (D)	
6	...	b5

This queenside expansion is often played by Black in the Pirc Defence. However, if the advance is made too early, then the pawn on b5 can become a target for White to attack by means of a2-a4, as Michael Adams soon demonstrates.

B

A more compact option for Black is **6...♕c7**. One feature of this queen move is that if White plays 7 ♗h6, then Black can response with ...♗xh6 without losing a tempo (which would be wasted if he had previously played ...♗g7 and then moved the same piece again). The game Motwani-McNab from the Dundee '800' grandmaster tournament in 1991 (a 10-player all-play-all event, organised by Castlehill Chess Club to celebrate Dundee's 800th birthday, with a required score of 7/9 for a GM norm), continued **7 a4 ♗g7 8 ♗c4 0-0 9 0-0 b6 10 ♖fe1 ♗b7 11 e5!? dxe5 12 dxe5 ♘xe5 13 ♘xe5 ♕xe5 14 ♗xb6 ♕d6 15 ♕xd6 exd6 16 ♗c7 d5 ½-½.** I included that game as Grandmaster Colin McNab is truly an expert on the Pirc Defence, and his ideas in it are well worth studying. Colin and I have had many much tougher tussles together, but that particular encounter occurred in the last round of the tournament, which had already been a tough and tiring competition (won by Grandmaster Glenn Flear on 6½/9, one point ahead of GM Mihai Suba and myself in joint runner-up position). To borrow an expression from Clint Eastwood, there must have been a hundred reasons why we should not have agreed a draw, but right then neither of us could think of one!

Sincerely though, Colin and I both very much appreciate all the efforts which so many people made for us. Happily, we became Scotland's first two grandmasters in 1992.

7 ♗d3

White develops his last minor piece, and defends his e-pawn because of the threat of ...b4.

7 ... e5

7...♗g7 was played in Motwani-Neuschmied, Vienna 1991. That game continued **8 ♗h6**, which is more aggressive than 8 0-0 0-0 9 ♖fe1 e5 10 dxe5 dxe5 11 a4! b4 12 ♘e2 ♕a5 13 ♗h6, though in Mainka-Lorscheid, Binz 1995, Black lost quickly with 13...♘c5? 14 ♗xg7 ♔xg7 15 ♘xe5 ♘cxe4 16 ♗xe4 ♘xe4 17 ♕d4 (maybe Black miscalculated and overlooked this move) 17...♕d5 18 ♘xc6+ ♕xd4 19 ♘exd4 1-0. Returning to Motwani-Neuschmied, the game proceeded with **8...0-0 9 ♗xg7 ♔xg7 10 e5!** In many other situations, such an attack in the centre can be answered on the flank by ...b4, intending ...bxc3 to harass White's queen. However, here White is threatening to capture on f6 *with check*. **10...♘e8** 10...dxe5 11 dxe5 ♘g4 12 ♕g5 is also strong for White. **11 h4!** With a knight no longer on f6, Black's kingside is poorly defended. So it is logical for White to begin attacking operations in that sector of the board. **11...h5 12 g4! hxg4** *(D)*

W

13 h5! It was not necessary for White to make a lot of calculations before embarking on this sacrificial line. The lack of harmony between Black's pieces is a strong indicator that White's attack will be irresistible even with a deficit of one piece. **13...♖h8** 13...gxf3 14 hxg6, threatening 15 ♕h6+, is hopeless for Black. **14 0-0-0 ♘c7** 14...gxf3 15 hxg6 ♘c7 16 gxf7 leaves Black's king bare, while

14...gxh5 15 ♕g5+ ♔f8 16 ♖xh5 ♖g8 17 ♕h6+ ♘g7 18 ♗h7 ♖h8 19 ♖g5 is also bleak for him. **15 hxg6 f6** 15...fxg6 is met by 16 ♕g5. **16 exd6 exd6 17 ♖de1 ♖h3** I had the variation 17...gxf3 18 ♖xh8 ♕xh8 (18...♔xh8 19 ♕h6+ ♔g8 20 ♕h7+ ♔f8 21 ♕f7#) 19 ♖e7+ and then 19...♔g8 20 ♖h7 or 19...♔f8 20 g7+ prepared in my mind when I opened the h-file at move 15. When the e-file opened on the following move, 17 ♖de1 was a natural way to seize control of it, although White had to be alert to the tactics involved. **18 ♖xh3 gxh3 19 ♘e4 ♕f8 20 ♘g3 1-0** White's army exhibits great harmony, and Black is defenceless against the numerous threats which arise naturally from it. 20...♘b6 21 ♘h5+ ♔g8 22 g7 ♕f7 23 ♕h6 is one variation which persuaded Black to resign.

8	dxe5	dxe5
9	h3	

This prophylactic move is not strictly necessary, but White rules out any ideas which his opponent might have had of playing ...♘g4.

9	...	a6?!

9...♗b7 looks better, intending in general to counter a2-a4 by ...b4 rather than with the passive ...a6.

10	a4!	♗b7
11	0-0	♕e7?

It is clear that Black is not at ease with his position, but this move loses virtually by force. Black was already lagging dangerously behind in development, and the queen move does not help his situation. However, the manner in which White now refutes Black's play is very forceful.

12 axb5   cxb5 *(D)*

W

13 ♘xb5!!   axb5
14 ♖xa8+   ♗xa8
15 ♖a1   ♕d8

Or 15...♗c6 16 ♗xb5! and now:

a) 16...♗xb5 17 ♖a8+ ♕d8 18 ♖xd8+ ♔xd8 19 ♕a5+ is hopeless for Black.

b) 16...♗xe4 is answered simply and strongly by 17 ♘g5.

c) 16...♘xe4 17 ♕d3 ♕e6 (or 17...♘ec5 18 ♕c4 ♗xf3 19 gxf3 ♕d8 20 ♗xc5) 18 ♖a6 ♘ec5 19 ♗xc5 ♘xc5 20 ♖a8+ ♔e7 21 ♕d8#.

16 ♗xb5   ♗e7

This developing move comes too late to save Black.

17 ♘xe5   ♗xe4

18 ♘xd7   ♘xd7
19 ♖a7   ♗f5
20 ♗xd7+

It is surprising that White gives up the piece that was pinning the black knight, but Adams has alertly spotted a fairly forcing variation. Still, 20 c4 is straightforward yet very strong. The threats would then include the further advance c5-c6 or 21 ♕d5 ♗e6 22 ♗xd7+ ♗xd7 23 ♖a8 ♗c8 24 ♕c6+.

20 ...   ♗xd7 *(D)*

W

21 ♗b6   ♕c8
22 ♕d4

This move not only protects White's bishop in the ensuing sequence, but, by making Black play ...f6, it also induces a weakness at e6 in Black's camp. It becomes clear shortly that Black's reduction in control of the e6-square is fatal.

22 ...   f6?!

22...0-0 loses immediately to 23 ♕xd7 while 22...♖f8 23 ♕d5! leads to some pretty finishes. For example:

a) 23...♗c6 24 ♖xe7+! ♔xe7 25 ♗c5+ ♔f6 (25...♔e8 26 ♕d6) 26 ♕d4+ ♔g5 27 ♕e3+ ♔h5 (27...♔f6 28 ♗d4+ ♔f5 29 g4#) 29 g4+ ♔h4 30 ♕h6#.

b) 23...♗e6 24 ♖xe7+! ♔xe7 25 ♗c5+ ♔f6 26 ♕d4+ ♔g5 27 ♗e7+ f6 (27...♔h6 28 ♕h4+ ♔g7 29 ♗f6+ ♔g8 30 ♕h6 and 31 ♕g7#) 28 ♕e3+ ♔h5 29 ♗xf8 ♕xf8 30 ♕xe6 with an easy win.

22...♖g8 is Black's most tenacious defence. I do not see a line against it as clear as the variations that have just been given, which is another reason why I felt White's 20th move was unnecessarily hasty. Nevertheless, he is not in trouble, since, at the very least, 23 ♖c7 is possible.

| 23 | ♖c7 | ♕d8 *(D)* |

W

| 24 | ♖c3! | ♕a8 |
| 25 | ♖e3 | |

The threats on the next move include ♕xf6, ♕d6, ♗c5 and ♕c5.

| 25 | ... | ♕c6 |
| 26 | ♕c5! | **1-0** |

I believe that Adams visualised the final position at least six moves earlier. His last move is elegant yet vital, and must have been prepared in his calculations, since 26 ♗c5? is answered by 26...♗e6. White has few pieces remaining at the finish, but they still co-ordinate beautifully to ensure that he will end up at least two pawns ahead after, e.g., 26...♕xc5 27 ♗xc5 followed soon by ♖xe7. Note that 27...♗e6 is answered simply by 28 ♖xe6, which illustrates a deep point of White's 22nd move!

The position that I left you considering, before the last game, arose from the **Paulsen Variation of the Sicilian Defence** after the moves **1 e4 c5 2 ♘f3 e6 3 d4 cxd4 4 ♘xd4 a6 5 ♗d3 ♘f6 6 ♘c3** (6 e5? runs into 6...♕a5+) **6...♕c7 7 a4 b6 8 0-0 ♗b7 9 ♕e2 h5! 10 h3 ♗c5 11 ♘b3?**. 11 ♗e3 was necessary, as the text-move gets refuted in stunning fashion by **11...♘g4!! 12 hxg4** (12 g3? loses instantly to 12...♕xg3+) **12...hxg4 13 e5** *(D)*

13...♗f3!! (13...♕d8? fails to 14 ♕xg4) **14 gxf3 ♕d8! 0-1**. The conclusion could have been 15 ♔g2 ♕h4 16 ♖g1 ♕h3#. Dutch international master Manuel Bosboom showed great tactical alertness in

B

W

his calculations. I would not be surprised if he had prepared his final move as early as 9...h5. The whole combination flowed beautifully, and has remained bright in my memory ever since I first saw that game.

A Knight to Remember

The inspiration for this puzzle came from a game of my friend Stephen Mannion, a Scottish international master. At Perth in 1989, Stephen reached a position, as White against Ian Mackay that is similar to the following one.

You are possibly wondering if there is an error in the diagram, because at the moment White is a piece down. We will soon change that! There are five unoccupied squares on the c-file. You may place a **white knight** on one of those squares. Your puzzle is then to find out how White, to move, wins.

Have a good night, then check your solution against the one given after the next encounter.

When I sat down to play Grandmaster Michael Adams at the 1994 Moscow Olympiad, I hoped at least to make it a closer fight than the last time I had faced 'Mickey' (as he is affectionately known). On that previous occasion, Mickey pulverised my Sicilian Defence. However, I knew that that need have no bearing on the course of the game we were about to play. So, as usual, I aimed to play without fear, and to enjoy the game, while trying to make the best use I could of whatever strength I have been given. This time the result was a very happy one for me and my Scottish team-mates, and, true to his pleasant and generous nature, Mickey was the first to offer congratulations. He also showed great character, as he has often done, by going on to achieve an excellent 71% final score in the Olympiad, without suffering any further defeats. Mickey seems to put a motto of one of his favourite actors into practice. I am referring to the saying 'I'll be back'!

Game 34
P.Motwani – M.Adams
Moscow Olympiad 1994
Přibyl Pirc

1	e4	d6
2	d4	♘f6
3	♘c3	c6

Mickey has a wide opening repertoire, therefore it was difficult during pre-game preparation for me to predict what his choice would be. So I decided to get plenty of rest, and approach the game in an alert and focused state of mind, but without stress.

Incidentally, I have seen 3...c6 being given different name tags, including 'Czech Pirc', but the most popular name for it seems to be 'Přibyl Pirc', attributing the title to the Czech international master Jan Přibyl, whose games in the system did much to increase its popularity.

4	f4	♕a5 *(D)*
5	e5	

5 ♗d3 e5 is more common. Let us see two examples:-

a) Zso.Polgar-Adams, 'Young Hungary v. Young England' match,

W

1989, went **6 dxe5** By making this capture (which is actually very popular), White helps Black to gain freedom for his dark-squared bishop. Keeping the tension in the centre with 6 ♘f3, as Grandmaster Joe Gallagher does in game 'b', seems more logical to me. **6...dxe5 7 ♘f3 ♗g4 8 fxe5 ♘fd7 9 e6** 9 ♗f4 is generally regarded as a more challenging test of Black's position. **9...♗xe6 10 ♘g5 ♘c5 11 0-0 ♘bd7 12 ♕h5 g6 13 ♕f3 0-0-0! 14 ♘xf7?** Zsofia Polgar has a rare lapse of alertness here. Unfortunately her miscalculation (wherever it occurred in the following sequence) loses by force. **14...♗xf7 15 ♕xf7 ♘xd3 16 cxd3** *(D)*.

16...♗c5+ 17 d4 ♗xd4+ 18 ♔h1 ♖hf8 19 ♕c4 ♗xc3! 20 ♖xf8 20 bxc3 ♕xc3! 21 ♕xc3 ♖xf1# illustrates the weakness of White's first rank, and exploits the fact that the queen on c4 is overworked trying to protect it and the c3-square.

B

20...♘xf8 0-1 After 21 bxc3 ♖d1+, checkmate follows on the next move.

b) The game Gallagher-Laske, Baden, Switzerland 1995, deviated from the last game with **6 ♘f3 ♗g4 7 ♗e3 ♘bd7 8 ♕d2 ♗e7 9 ♕f2!? ♗h5 10 h3 exf4 11 ♗xf4 ♗g6 12 ♗d2** This move, which creates the possibility of uncovering an attack against the black queen, was itself made possible by White's interesting ninth move. **12...♕b6 13 0-0-0 ♘e5** Black utilises the fact that White's d-pawn is pinned to force an exchange of one pair of minor pieces. The idea is good in one sense because it helps to relieve the slightly cramped nature of Black's position. However, the negative aspect of it is that Black will have to move his queen several times more in the forthcoming tactics. **14 ♘xe5 dxe5 15 ♗e3 ♕a5 16 dxe5 ♕xe5 17 ♗d4 ♕g5+ 18 ♔b1 0-0 19 e5 ♘h5 20**

♘e2! 'Solid domination is the ultimate concept in chess' is a statement of Mihai Suba. Here White's knight dominates the black counterpart, by denying it safe access to the f4- and g3-squares, so that 21 g4 is now threatened. **20...c5 21 ♗c3** This calm but strong move maintains the protection of the e-pawn, and therefore also renews the threat of g2-g4 since Black's knight cannot escape safely to f6. **21...♗xd3 22 ♖xd3 g6 23 ♖d7** The biggest threat now is 24 h4, to deflect Black's queen from defending the bishop on e7. **23...♖ae8 24 g4 ♘g7 25 ♕f3!** Joe Gallagher aims to win more than Black's b-pawn: he is alert to the fact that his opponent's queen is precariously short of safe squares. His calculations would have included 25...b5? 26 h4 (White's queen on f3 protects the pawn on g4 to allow this advance of the h-pawn) 26...♕h6 27 ♗d2, winning quickly. **25...h5 26 ♘g3** The harmony in White's army is now overwhelming. **26...b5 27 ♘e4** Now 27...♕h4 would lose to 28 ♗e1. **27...♕h6** (D)

28 ♖xe7! A neat finish. I think that White probably prepared this at least two moves ago. **28...♖xe7 29 g5 1-0** Black resigned in view of 29...♕h8 30 ♘f6#.

We resume our H.O.T. journey in Moscow now!

| 5 | ... | ♘e4 |
| 6 | ♕f3 | ♘xc3 |

W

7	&d2	&f5
8	&d3! *(D)*	

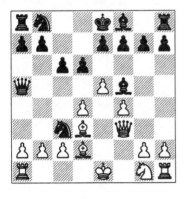

B

'It's basically a very good move' was Adams' comment in our post-mortem discussion of the game. Actually, he already knew about this rare but strong move, and considered it to be a serious test of the soundness of Black's system.

Memory played a role in my case, because I recalled seeing 8 &d3 in Kengis-Hausner during the 1990 Luxembourg Open. This way of handling the opening certainly poses Black more problems than the tame 8 &xc3, after which 8...&d5 is fine.

8	...	&xd3
9	cxd3	&d5
10	bxc3	

This is the real point of the approach that Grandmaster Edwin Kengis adopted four years before me. A white rook will have a good future on the b-file.

10	...	dxe5
11	fxe5	

Capturing on e5 with the other pawn would have brought an end to White's doubled d-pawns, but the move chosen provides fresh possibilities on the f-file.

11	...	&xf3
12	&xf3	e6
13	&e2	

My friend Peter Walsh, who is one of the funniest people I know, comes to mind here. Many years ago he was a pupil of the great Nancy Elder (who won the Scottish Ladies Championship on numerous occasions), and she used to wisely advise him 'Get your king tucked away safely, Peter'. Nancy was referring, in general, to the benefits of castling, but here she would have agreed that White's king is safely and ideally placed near the centre in the middlegame without queens on the board.

13	...	&d7

14 ♖hb1   b6

14...0-0-0? loses quickly after 15 ♘g5.

15 a4   ♗e7

15...a5 would leave the b-pawn very weak, inviting White to manoeuvre his knight to c4 via d2.

16 a5   b5

16...0-0 17 c4 is also uncomfortable for Black, whose position is rather cramped in spite of the fact that three pairs of pieces were exchanged earlier.

17 c4   a6 *(D)*

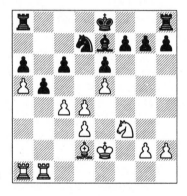

W

18 ♖c1!   0-0

18...♘b8 19 cxb5 axb5 is an attempt to stop White's rooks from infiltrating Black's camp along the c-file. However, not surprisingly, such passive defence fails to hold after 20 a6! ♖a7 21 ♗e3 ♔d7 22 d5 ♖xa6 23 dxc6+!:

a) 23...♖xc6 24 ♖a7+ ♔e8 (or 24...♔d8 25 ♖xc6 ♘xc6 26 ♖a8+) 25 ♖b7 ♖xc1 26 ♖xb8+.

b) 23...♔c7 (23...♔c8 24 c7 ♖xa1 25 cxb8♕+ ♔xb8 26 ♖xa1) 24 ♘d4! ♖xa1 25 ♘xb5+ ♔c8 26 ♖xa1 ♘xc6 27 ♖a8+ ♘b8 28 ♖a7 ♖e8 (28...♘c6? 29 ♖c7+, 28...♗d8 29 ♘d6#) 29 ♖c7+ ♔d8 30 ♗b6 ♘d7 31 ♗a5 demonstrates the coordination between White's pieces, and also shows again that calculations tend to flow logically and beautifully when such harmony exists.

19 cxb5   cxb5

20 ♖c7   ♖fd8

21 ♖ac1   ♔f8 *(D)*

21...b4 22 ♖b7 ♖ab8 23 ♖cc7 b3 24 ♗c3 also leaves White in control of the game.

W

22 d5!!

White's pieces are ideally positioned to support this sacrificial breakthrough.

22 ...   exd5

23 e6!   ♘f6

23...fxe6 is answered by 24 ♘d4! and now:

a) 24...♔f7 25 ♘c6 wins at least an exchange, while still leaving Black virtually tied up.

b) 24...♗d6 25 ♘xe6+ ♔e7 26 ♘xd8 ♗xc7 27 ♗g5+! ♘f6 28 ♖xc7+ ♔xd8 29 ♖xg7 also wins for White.

24 ♘g5　　h6

24...♗d6 25 exf7! ♗xc7 26 ♖xc7 ♖d6 27 ♗b4 ♖d8 28 ♘e6#. I had calculated this and the other variations given since move 18 when I played 18 ♖c1. Whether that is practical or not depends on the player concerned, but, in my case, doing such calculations keeps me alert. However, after 24...h6 I had originally intended to play 25 ♘xf7, but it would have been a mistake to do so without at least pausing to consider whether any stronger continuations could be found. I must also admit that I was a little nervous at this stage in the game, partly because Michael kept reeling out the most tenacious defensive moves so quickly, and partly because he is such a strong player! I thank God for giving me the courage to change my mind and offer a new sacrifice.

25 ♖xe7!　　hxg5 *(D)*

25...♔xe7 26 ♗b4+ (26 ♖c7+ ♘d7! is less clear for White) 26...♔e8 27 ♖c7! fxe6 (27...hxg5? 28 exf7#) 28 ♖e7+ (28 ♘xe6? ♖d7) 28...♔f8 29 ♘xe6+ ♔g8 30 ♖xg7+ ♔h8 31 ♖g6 wins for White.

26 ♗b4?

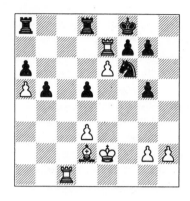

W

This move does not spoil White's winning position, but the '?' is because a much more powerful continuation could have been played. If I had been more alert and in less time-trouble I might have found a line that I discovered later: 26 ♖cc7 ♘e8 27 ♗b4!! ♘xc7 28 exf7!! ♖e8 (28...♘e8 29 ♖d7+ ♘d6 30 ♗xd6#) 29 ♖xe8+ ♔xf7 30 ♖e7+ and 31 ♖xc7.

26 ...　　♖e8
27 ♖xe8+

Note that after 27 ♖b7+ ♔g8 it is desirable but unfortunately illegal to play 28 exf7+!

27 ...　　♔xe8
28 ♖c7　　fxe6
29 ♖e7+

White is still winning, but 29 ♖xg7 is simpler and more precise. For example, 29...g4 30 ♗e7 ♘h5 31 ♖g8+ ♔xe7 32 ♖xa8.

29 ...　　♔d8
30 ♖xg7　　♘e8
31 ♖xg5

The situation has been clarified a lot. Since Black's passed b-pawn is immobilised and his pieces are much less actively placed than White's forces, the position remains desperate for Black. The connected passed pawns on the kingside make White's advantage even more decisive.

| 31 | ... | ♖a7 |
| 32 | ♖g6 | ♖h7 |

Black gets no counterplay after 32...♔d7 33 h4.

33	♖xe6	♖xh2
34	♔f3	♖h4
35	♗e1!	

More convincing than 35 ♗e7+ ♔d7.

| 35 | ... | ♖h1 |
| 36 | ♗g3 | ♖d1? |

This accelerates the end, although after 36...♘c7 37 ♖d6+ ♔c8 38 ♖c6 Black's position is also hopeless.

| 37 | ♗h4+ | ♔d7 |
| 38 | ♖e7+ | ♔c6 |

38...♔d8 39 ♖e1+ wins Black's rook.

| 39 | ♖xe8 | b4 |

Black could also resign after 39...♖xd3+ 40 ♔e2 ♖a3 41 ♖e6+ ♔b7 42 ♖b6+ ♔a7 43 ♗f2.

| 40 | ♔e2 | 1-0 |

The Scottish team captain, Jonathan Grant, was delighted, although he would have been less tense beforehand if I could have left myself with more than 13 seconds to spare on the white side of the digital clock! Still, Jonathan's happiness and excitement must have been mild compared with the feeling on New Year's Day 1996, when he and his gorgeous Georgian fiancée, Ketevan Arakhamia, announced the great news of their engagement. Lots of congratulations to a wonderful couple.

Late news: Jonathan and Keti married on 24 February 1996. The same day, I met GM Tony Miles in Cappelle la Grande, and he told me that it was, to the day, almost exactly twenty years since he became England's first grandmaster. To celebrate both those wonderful occasions, let us see two great endings, the first being one of Tony's favourite puzzles.

White is OK after all!

W

It is White to play and draw. He achieves that with 1 ♔c1 ♗a2 2 ♔d2!!. White must be alert to avoid the trap 2 ♔b2? ♗b3!!, when he loses after 3 cxb3+ ♔d3 4 e4 ♔xe4 5 ♔c2 ♔e3 6 ♔c1 ♔d3 7 ♔b2 ♔d2 8 ♔b1 ♔c3 9 ♔a2 ♔c2 10 ♔a1 ♔xb3 11 ♔b1 ♔c3 12 ♔c1 b3 13 ♔b1 b2 14 ♔a2 ♔c2 15 ♔a3 b1♕ 16 ♔a4 ♕b6 17 ♔a3 ♕b3#. However, after 2 ♔d2 Black can make no progress. For example:

a) 2...♔d5 3 c3 b3 4 ♔c1 ♔e4 5 ♔b2 (5 c4 ♔d3 6 ♔b2 is also a draw, but not 6 c5? ♔c3 7 c6 b2+) 5...♔xe3 6 c4 ♔d4 7 c5 ♔xc5 8 ♔a1 ♔c4 9 ♔b2 ♔d3 10 ♔a1 ♗b1 (what else?) 11 ♔xb1 ♔c3 12 ♔c1 b2+ (if Black could stand still and ask White to move instead, then he would win exactly as in the variation ending with 17...♕b3#) 13 ♔b1 ♔b3 stalemate.

b) 2...♗b3 3 cxb3+ ♔xb3 4 e4 ♔a2 5 e5 b3 6 e6 b2 7 e7 b1♕ 8 e8♕ draws.

Ice Cool

The second ending which I have chosen here was won by Icelandic grandmaster (elect) Throstur Thorhallsson against Armenian GM Ashot Anastasian at Cappelle la Grande 1996.

It is White to play, and Throstur alertly avoided the trap 1 b6? ♖c4+! 2 ♖xc4 stalemate. Instead, he played the better winning attempt **1 ♖c6**, and was rewarded after **1...♖a7? 2 ♖b6! ♖a5** No better is 2...♖h7 3 ♖a6+ ♖a7 4 b6 ♖xa6 5

W

b7+ ♔a7 6 b8♕# or 2...♖a4 3 ♖b8+ ♔a7 4 b6+ ♔a6 5 ♖a8+, again winning for White. **3 ♖b7! 1-0**, since 3...♖a4 4 ♖b8+ wins as in the line just given. However, I can find no forced win for White after 1...♖a1, when a vital factor is that Black's rook retains more freedom than in the game continuation. For instance, 2 ♖b6 ♖c1+ or 2 b6 ♖b1 3 ♖c5 ♖b5! 4 ♖c4 ♖c5+! 5 ♖xc5 stalemate.

Solution to puzzle (posed before game 34)

The best available square on the c-file for White's knight is **c7**. He can then proceed with **1 ♘e8+!!**, which wins by force as the following lines show:

a) 1...♕xe8 2 ♕f6+ ♔g8 3 ♖h2 and 4 ♖h8#.

b) 1...♖xe8 2 ♕xf7+ ♔h6 3 ♖h2+ ♔g5 4 ♖h5+! and then 4...gxh5 5 ♕xh5# or 4...♔xg4 5 ♕f3#.

c) 1...♔g8 2 ♘f6+ ♔g7 3 ♖h2 ♕d4+ 4 ♔h1 ♖h8 5 ♘e8+! and then 6 ♕xf7#.

The Heroic Rook

The inspiration for this puzzle came from a game of my friend Craig Pritchett, a Scottish IM. At the 1988 Rilton Cup tournament in Sweden, Craig reached a position, as White against J.Hall, which is similar to the following one.

W

Your puzzle is to find the winning continuation for White, without peeping at the solution given after the next tussle!

Game 35
J.de Roda – P.Motwani
Sas van Gent 1996
Queen's Indian Defence

	1	d4	♘f6
	2	c4	e6

	3	♘f3	b6
	4	a3 *(D)*	

B

This prophylactic move, known as the Petrosian System, aims to stop ...♗b4+, and was a favourite of Garry Kasparov. In the past I had always answered it with the immediate fianchetto 4...♗b7, but in this game I adopted a fresh approach consistent with my theoretical preparation around that period.

	4	...	♗a6
	5	♕c2	♗b7
	6	♘c3	c5

The point of Black's fourth and fifth moves becomes clear. By luring White's queen away from the d1-square, Black has caused a reduction in White's control on the d-file. So there is a threat to win a pawn by 7...♗xf3 8 gxf3 cxd4.

	7	e4	cxd4
	8	♘xd4	♗c5

8...♘c6 is a highly fashionable alternative. White should respond with **9 ♘xc6**, since 9 ♗e3?! ♘g4! 10 ♘xc6 ♘xe3 is very pleasant for Black. Let us consider some possibilities after **9...♗xc6**:

a) 10 e5?! ♘g4 11 ♗f4 ♗c5, and Black has seized the initiative.

b) The game at the 1987 North London Open between James Cavendish and Tony Miles, England's first-ever grandmaster, continued **10 ♗e2 ♕b8! 11 0-0 ♗c5 12 ♔h1 h5! 13 f4 ♘g4 14 ♗f3 ♕d8!** Threatening 15...♘xh2! 16 ♔xh2 ♕h4#. **15 g3 h4!!** *(D)*

W

16 ♗xg4 hxg3 17 h3 f5! Black has conducted the kingside attack with great energy. His bishops are directed powerfully towards the enemy monarch (a fact which has been utilised in the last move), and once the bishop on g4 has been eliminated, White's remaining battered defences will quickly be overwhelmed by Black's queen

and king's rook. Note that White's extra piece is of almost no significance, since most of the members of his army are located on the queenside, far away from the scene of the main action. **18 ♗xf5** 18 ♗f3 ♖xh3+ 19 ♔g2 ♖h2+ 20 ♔xg3 ♕h4#. **18...exf5 19 ♕g2 ♕h4 20 ♘d5 ♕g4! 21 ♘e3 ♖xh3+ 22 ♔g1 ♗xe4 23 b4 ♗xg2 24 bxc5 ♗e4 25 ♘xg4 ♖h1#**. An impressive display by Tony Miles, who only used 7 minutes on his clock (compared with 70 minutes by White) for the entire game.

c) 10 ♗f4! (to prevent ...♕b8) 10...♗c5 (10...♘h5 11 ♗e3 ♗d6?? 12 ♕d1! 1-0 showed a rare lapse of alertness from one of the strongest ever players in Christiansen-Karpov, Wijk aan Zee 1993) 11 ♗e2 0-0 12 0-0-0!? ♘e8 (12...♗xf2? 13 e5 ♘e8 14 ♗d3! ♗c5 15 ♗xh7+ ♔h8 16 ♗e4 is very strong for White) 13 ♗g3 e5!? 14 ♔b1 ♕e7 15 ♖he1 ♗d4 gave Black a reasonable position in Timman-Tiviakov, Wijk aan Zee 1996.

9 ♘b3

9 ♗e3?! ♘g4! echoes an idea given early in the last note.

9 ...　　　♘c6
10 ♗g5　　♗e7

I considered that it was worth using one tempo to neutralise the pin on my king's knight.

11 ♗e2 *(D)*

The first of the eight games in the 1995 match between top Dutch grandmasters Jeroen Piket and Jan Timman took a different path: **11 ♖d1 0-0 12 ♗e2 ♕b8!? 13 ♗h4** 13 0-0?! ♘g4! 14 ♗xg4 ♗xg5 15 ♖xd7? ♘e5 wins for Black, while 13 ♗xf6 ♗xf6 14 ♖xd7 ♘e5 gives him tremendous activity as compensation for the sacrificed pawn. In the latter variation, Black can soon follow up with ...♖c8, co-ordinating that rook in harmony with the knight to exert great pressure against the c-pawn. **13...♘e5 14 ♗g3 ♖c8 15 0-0 a6** Preparing a possible ...b5 advance to prise open the c-file more, so Piket decides to get his queen out of the line of fire of Timman's rook on c8. **16 ♕b1 d6 17 ♖d4 ♘c6 18 ♖d2 ♘e5 19 ♖d4 ♘c6 20 ♖d2 ♘e5 ½-½**. A few weeks after including this game in the book, I was chatting to Wouter Janssens, a Dutch correspondent, about Jan Timman's games in general. Wouter kept saying 'Look out for the Timman knight moves!'. Well, moves 17-20 were perhaps only mild examples, but they certainly demonstrated that Black had a comfortable position.

11	...	0-0
12	0-0	♖c8
13	♖ad1	

A good guideline for players of all standards is 'Study the opponent's last move carefully'. In this case, that useful rule would have made it evident to White that Black (who has just played ...♖c8) is

B

planning to attack the c-pawn by moving the knight from c6. It is perhaps a bit harsh to label the sensible developing move 13 ♖ad1 with a '?', but I would have given 13 f4 (preventing ...♘e5) a '!'.

13	...	♘e5!
14	♘d2	

14 ♖d4 may look more active, but, after 14...♘c6 15 ♖d2 ♘e5 16 ♖d4 ♘c6, Black's alternating attacks against the rook on d4 and the c-pawn virtually force White to acquiesce to a draw by repetition of position (note that the Piket-Timman encounter given earlier ended in a similar manner). A draw with Black against an opponent who had beaten two IMs in his recent past is not such a bad result, but after 14 ♖d4 can Black do better? An alert player would find 14...♗a6!, consistently increasing the pressure against the c-pawn. Then 15 ♘d2? fails to 15...♗c5.

14	...	d6

At this stage, my friend, Grandmaster Mihai Suba, came to mind. Mihai often extols the virtues of a 'hedgehog' pawn formation, such as the one I now have. For me, one of the most positive features of Black's set-up is *flexibility*, with the pieces as well as the pawns. I think that my opponent was already beginning to experience difficulties in coping with Black's numerous possibilities. For example, 15 f4 can be met actively by 15...♘eg4 or by 15...♘g6. In the latter case Black threatens 16...h6, which would force White to part with his bishop on g5, an important guardian of the dark squares.

15 ♔h1?!

White's monarch turns out to be a target on the h1 to a8 diagonal for Black's fianchettoed bishop to attack.

15 ... h6

16 ♗f4

16 ♗e3 could be answered by 16...d5!?, a recurring pawn break in games involving a hedgehog formation. Typically, there are some tactics involved, but the road through them is quite safe and clear. For example, 17 f4 ♘eg4 18 ♗g1 ♗c5! 19 e5 (this is tempting, but in reality it is good for Black) 19...♗xg1 20 exf6 ♘e3 21 ♕d3 ♘xd1 22 ♗xd1 dxc4!? 23 ♕g3 g6 24 ♘de4 ♗d4 25 ♕h4 ♗xc3 26 ♘xc3 (26 ♕xh6? ♗xf6) 26...♖c5 (planning ...♖f5, and the line 27

♗c2 ♖h5 is completely hopeless for White).

16 ... ♕c7

17 ♕b1 ♕b8

18 h3 ♕a8!

Black's army is now in a state of complete harmony. Its numerous members are co-ordinating nicely, and Black is ready to initiate a well-prepared tactical sequence.

19 ♗g3 b5!

The hedgehog has many spines. Here, one on the left flank stabs at the opponent.

20 ♗xe5

20 cxb5 ♖xc3! 21 bxc3 ♘xe4 22 ♘xe4 ♗xe4 is even worse for White than the actual game continuation, because 23 ♗f3 can be met by 23...♘xf3. That is why White captures the knight on e5. However, we shall see that this is also unsatisfactory. 20 b3, though passive, was the most tenacious defence for White.

20 ... dxe5

21 cxb5 *(D)*

21 ... ♖xc3!!

This is much stronger for Black than 21...♗xa3 22 bxa3 ♖xc3 23 ♕b4.

22 bxc3 ♘xe4

23 ♘xe4

White has no adequate continuation. For instance, 23 ♕c2 (to protect the pawn on c3) is refuted by 23...♘xd2 24 ♖xd2 ♗xg2+.

23 ... ♗xe4

24 ♗f3 ♗xf3

B

25	gxf3	♕xf3+
26	♔g1	

If 26 ♔h2, White's monarch is even more of a target for a check from the dark-squared bishop. The continuation might be 26...e4 27 ♖de1 ♗d6+ 28 ♔g1 ♕f4!, and anyone who finds a way to prevent 29...♕h2# deserves a prize.

26	...	e4! (D)

W

I calculated this key move when I played 19...b5. White is prevented from challenging Black's queen by ♕d3.

27 ♖de1

27 ♖fe1 leaves the pawn on f2 very vulnerable. A logical way for Black to exploit that is 27...♗c5, also threatening ...♕g3+.

27	...	f5
28	♖e3	♕f4
29	♖g3	

White is lost in the following cases too:

a) 29 ♔g2 ♗d6 and now:

a1) 30 ♖h1 ♗c5! 31 ♖e2 ♕f3+.

a2) 30 ♖g3 ♕h4 31 ♖e3 (31 ♖g6 ♔f7) 31...♕g5+ 32 ♔h1 ♕f4 33 ♖g3 ♕h4 34 ♖e3 ♗f4.

b) 29 ♕b3 ♗c5! 30 ♕xe6+ ♔h7 31 ♖fe1 (31 ♖g3? ♕xg3+) 31...♖d8!, threatening ...♖d2, with these ripe branches:

b1) 32 ♔f1 ♖d2 33 ♖3e2 ♗xf2 34 ♖xd2 ♗b6+! 35 ♔e2 ♕f3#.

b2) 32 ♕c4 ♗xe3 33 ♖xe3 ♖d1+ 34 ♔g2 ♖d2! 35 ♖e2 (35 ♕f1 ♕xe3) 35...♕f3+ 36 ♔f1 ♕h1#.

b3) 32 ♕a2 ♗xe3 33 ♖xe3 (33 fxe3 ♕g3+) 33...♖d1+ 34 ♔g2 ♕g5+! 35 ♖g3 ♕c1 36 ♕f7 ♖g1+ 37 ♔h2 ♖h1+ 38 ♔g2 ♕g1#. White gets mated just before he can do the same thing to Black.

In a situation where there are several 'branches', it can be taxing for the memory to retain all the calculations clearly in the mind. However, such long variations do not always have to be calculated to the very end, because they tend to flow naturally from the harmony between the pieces (including the pawns). So it is not surprising that Black triumphed in that last sequence given in 'b3' for example.

29	...	♗h4
30	♖g2	e3
31	fxe3	

After 31 f3, Black is spoiled for good choices. One simple, but strong possibility is 31...♗f2+.

31	...	♕xe3+
32	♔h2 *(D)*	

Note that, if 32 ♔h1, Black does not have to hurry to capture the white h-pawn. He could first activate his rook on an open file with 32...♖d8!. Then 33 ♖h2 ♗g3 34 ♖g2 ♗c7 35 ♕e1 ♕xh3+ 36 ♔g1 ♗b6+ 37 ♖ff2 e5 leaves White really tied up. The finish might be 38 ♖xg7+ ♔xg7 39 ♕xe5+ ♔f7 or 38 ♕xe5 ♖d1+ 39 ♕e1 ♖xe1# , with the pin on the rook on f2 rendering White helpless in both cases.

B

32	...	♗d8!

The bishop prepares to switch onto new diagonals, with deadly effect for White's exposed king.

33	♕e1	♗c7+
34	♔h1	♕xh3+
35	♔g1	♖f6!

An example of 'The threat is stronger than its execution'. White cannot prevent ...♗b6 anyway, but now, as well as having to contend with that continuing threat and his own severe time-trouble, he must be alert to spot the additional threat of 36...♖g6! 37 ♖xg6 ♕h2#. Notice that ...♖f6 also performed a prophylactic function by stopping ♕xe6+.

36	♕d2	♔h7
37	c4	

37 ♕d7 ♖g6! 38 ♖f2 ♖xg2+ 39 ♖xg2 ♗b6+ 40 ♔f1 ♕h1+ ends White's resistance.

37	...	♗b6+
38	♖ff2	♕xa3
39	♔f1	

39 ♕d7 ♕f8 is equally hopeless for White.

39	...	♗xf2
40	♖xf2	♕c5
41	♕c2	♖g6
42	♕d3	♖g4

0-1

White would go more than just three pawns behind after 43 ♖c2 ♕g1+ 44 ♔e2 ♖g2+ 45 ♔f3 ♖g3+.

Solution to Puzzle (set before game 35)

White's heroic rook immediately sacrifices itself by **1 ♖xc5!!**. The point is that, after the reply **1...dxc5**, the e5-square becomes freely available for a white knight. The finish might be **2 ♘fe5 ♗xe5** (2...♕xd5? 3 ♘e7+ or 2...♕e8? 3 ♕f6) **3 ♕xe5** (3 ♘xe5? ♕f5) **3...f6** (3...f5? 4 ♘e7+ ♔f7 5 ♕g7+ ♔e8 6 ♕f8#) **4 ♕xf6 ♖e8 5 d6!** (threatening 6 ♘e7+) **5...♕f7 6 ♕xf7+ ♔xf7 7 d7 ♖e1+ 8 ♔h2 ♖d1 9 d8♕ ♖xd8 10 ♘xd8+ ♔f6 11 ♘c6 c4 12 ♘xa5 c3 13 ♘c6 c2 14 ♘xb4** and Black can resign, since White's bishop ensures that the c-pawn's promotion will be short-lived.

Young Guns

The next position comes from the game Rowson-M.Kaminski, World Under-18 Championship, Guarapuava 1995.

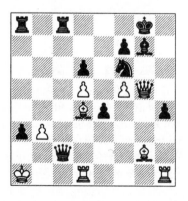

W

International Master Jonathan Rowson is one of Scotland's very best young players, and he demonstrated his alertness and calculating abilities by *not* playing the most obvious move for White here. Your puzzle is to identify the 'obvious' move, find out why it would lose, and discover (as J.R. did) how White can win instead. One game further down the road the solution awaits you.

What about other high-calibre young guns? Well, I have been very impressed by the chess talent of young players whom I have had the pleasure to work with in Belgium and in clubs and schools (particularly St Saviour's High School, Dundee, and St Columba's High School, Perth) in Scotland. I also studied a lot with International Master Jonathan Parker, a young English player who used to live in Edinburgh, and we both learned a great deal from each other. The same was true in the cases of Luke and Mark Russell from Aberdeen, or even younger players such as Alan Tate in Edinburgh. When two people listen to each other with an open mind, a lot can be learned by both parties, even if one of them has a higher rating 'on paper'.

The following game, from the 1995 European Under-16 Championship, shows England's Karl Mah (who was only 14 years old at that time, but is now a FIDE master) winning in fine style. The influence of International Master Andrew Martin, a highly original thinker who was coaching Karl, comes through strongly.

Just before we proceed with the game (which I first saw in a newspaper column), this is a natural place to mention another method, relating to newspapers, that I used for many years as a source of extra ideas. When I lived in Dundee, even as a busy teacher I generally managed to find half an hour each week to go into the library in the Wellgate Centre. There I skimmed through up to ten chess articles by regular columnists writing in certain newspapers (most libraries keep copies dating back for several years). Any specially nice games or interesting opening ideas that caught my attention were quickly jotted down in a notebook (or memorised and written down later, if I was in a hurry to catch a bus or some other event which simply would not wait for me!). After a long period, I found that I had collected a tremendous stock of useful ideas, many of which have never appeared in *Informator* and other publications that vast numbers of players focus on while sometimes not really noticing newspapers which come to their homes. For me this illustrates a moral: often what needs to be seen is near and in a simple form, and one should not miss it because of concentrating solely on seemingly grander things.

At the 1996 Cappelle la Grande Open, I was delighted to hear from Colm Daly that Joe Ryan, another Irish player to whom I had previously mentioned the 'newspaper idea', was finding it to be most useful.

Incidentally, at the same tournament I met another friend whom I had not seen for 16 years. Sweden's IM Christer Hartman was still as witty as I remembered him to be. At one point we spotted a stunning silver Rolls Royce car, and Christer immediately said 'I didn't know that the Scottish Chess Association looked after your transport so well!'.

Without further delay, it's time for action!

Game 36
K.Mah – B.Vukovič
Zagan 1995
QGD Tarrasch

1	d4	d5
2	c4	e6
3	♘c3	c5 *(D)*

White often generates some initiative through possessing the first move, similar to the advantage of having the service in tennis. In playing the Tarrasch Defence, Black is adopting a counter-attacking approach to the opening, and he aims to wrest the initiative out of his opponent's hands.

W

4 cxd5   exd5

4...cxd4, the Von Hennig-Schara Gambit, is an enterprising alternative. White's most forcing move-order is then **5 ♕a4+ ♗d7 6 ♕xd4 exd5 7 ♕xd5 ♘c6 8 ♘f3**. At move five there is nothing wrong with 5 ♕xd4 either, but, after 5...♘c6 6 ♕d1 exd5 7 ♕xd5, Black has the option 7...♗e6. I have seen WGM Susan Lalic employing that variation on several occasions. Black gets a lead in active development in compensation for the sacrificed pawn, although the theoretical antidote of 8 ♕xd8+ ♖xd8 9 e3 ♘b4 10 ♗b5+ ♔e7 11 ♔f1! looks convincing for White.

Returning to the position after 8 ♘f3, a 1994 encounter Hoeksema-Brenninkmeijer continued **8...♘f6 9 ♕d1**. It was the unanimous opinion of Correspondence GM Douglas Bryson, FM John Shaw and myself, when we discussed this variation during the 1994 Moscow Olympiad, that 9 ♕b3! is stronger and more logical than the more common retreat of the lady to d1. For example, 9...♗c5 10 ♗g5 (the greedy 10 ♕xb7?? is inadvisable, due to 10...♖b8 11 ♕a6 ♘b4 12 ♕c4 ♗e6 13 ♕xc5 ♘c2#) 10...♕a5 11 e3 0-0-0 12 ♕b5! forced the exchange of queens in Beim-Fritze, Groningen 1990. Instead, International Master Erik Hoeksema soon finds himself in hot water after 9 ♕d1. **9...♗c5 10 e3 ♕e7 11 ♗e2 0-0-0 12 0-0 g5! 13 a3** Frank Banaghan and Alice Chan, the friends who introduced me to my wife Jenny, named a chess club after 'poisoned' pawns such as the one on g5. 13 ♘xg5? ♖hg8 14 ♘f3 ♗h3 is disastrous for White. **13...g4 14 ♘d4 ♕e5!** The harmony is growing in Black's army. His queen is now pointing menacingly at the pawn on h2, which is poorly protected after White's last move. **15 ♗d2 ♔b8!** Black could have won back a pawn through capturing on d4, but he prefers not to allow White much activity. The bishop on d2 remains particularly lacking in scope. **16 b4 ♗b6 17 ♕c1** White is clearly finding it difficult to formulate a constructive plan to deal with the storm which is gathering near his camp. **17...h5 18 f4 ♕e7** White's last move seriously weakened his e-pawn, and the calm retreat of Black's queen along the e-file maintains the pressure against that weakness. **19 ♘c2 ♗f5 20 ♘a4** *(D)*

B

20...♖xd2! 21 ♕xd2 ♖d8! Joris Brenninkmeijer alertly seizes the chance to gain an important tempo before capturing the knight on c2. **22 ♕c1 ♗xc2 23 ♘xb6 axb6 24 ♕xc2 ♕xe3+ 25 ♔h1** 25 ♖f2 ♘e4 26 ♖f1 ♖d2 27 ♕c4 ♘d4 leaves White's army tied up and helpless. **25...♖d2 26 ♕c4 ♖xe2 0-1**. The sequence from moves 20-26 was, although virtually forced, nicely calculated by Black.

Notice that one does not have to rely too heavily on memory or theoretical preparation in order to achieve successful results with natural attacking systems such as the Von Hennig-Schara Gambit. Active piece play is the main ingredient characterising that opening. However, one should be aware of where the Achilles Heel lies, and, in my opinion, it is pinpointed by

9 **♕b3!**, which I mentioned earlier.

5 e4

A rare but refreshing line instead of the much more tried and tested 5 ♘f3 ♘c6 followed by 6 g3 or 6 ♗g5.

5 ... dxe4

6 ♗c4!?

6 d5 f5 7 ♗f4 ♗d6 8 ♗b5+ ♔f7 9 ♘h3 ♘f6 10 ♗c4 a6 11 a4 h6 was not convincing for White in Bronstein-Marjanovic, Kirovakan 1978.

6 ... cxd4

White has the initiative after the line 6...♘c6 7 d5 ♘e5 8 ♗f4!? ♘xc4 9 ♕a4+ ♗d7 10 ♕xc4, but 8...♗d6 looks perfectly playable for Black.

7 ♕b3! *(D)*

B

This very imaginative variation cannot be found in standard reference books such as *Batsford Chess Openings* (either edition), but, if it catches on now, we could be in for some more really hot games!

| 7 | ... | ♛e7 |

7...♛d7 8 ♘xe4 ♛e7 is messy, but probably good for White. He might continue with 9 ♔f1!? (in order to avoid ...♛b4+) 9...♛xe4 10 ♗xf7+ ♔d7. Now 11 ♗xg8? loses to 11...♖xg8! 12 ♛xg8 ♛d3+, with two branches that both end in checkmate:

a) 13 ♘e2 ♛d1#.

b) 13 ♔e1 ♗b4+ 14 ♗d2 ♗xd2+ 15 ♔d1 ♗c3+ 16 ♔c1 ♛d2+ 17 ♔b1 ♛xb2#.

However, by inserting the *zwischenzug* 11 f3! before taking on g8, White gives his king more breathing space, while the position of Black's monarch looks distinctly unsafe.

| 8 ♘d5 | ♛d7 |

Black has no satisfactory move after 8...♛c5 9 ♗f4 ♗d6 10 ♛b5+!, and a typical illustration of that is 10...♛xb5 11 ♗xb5+ ♗d7 12 ♗xd6 ♗xb5 13 ♘c7+ ♔d7 14 ♘xb5.

9	♗f4	♗d6
10	♛g3	♗xf4
11	♛xf4	

11 ♛xg7 wins, but the route chosen by White is also very strong.

| 11 | ... | ♔d8 |

White was threatening ♘c7+, but 11...♘a6 12 ♛xe4+ ♘e7 13 ♗b5! or 12...♛e6 13 ♘c7+ costs Black his queen in both cases.

| 12 | ♛e5! | ♘c6 |

After 12...f5 13 ♛xd4, White will soon bring a rook onto the d-file with deadly effect for Black's exposed king.

| 13 | ♛xg7 | ♛g4 |
| 14 | ♛f8+ | |

14 ♛xh8 ♛xg2 15 0-0-0 also wins easily for White.

14	...	♔d7
15	♛xf7+	♔d8
16	♛c7+	♔e8 (D)

W

| 17 ♛d6! | 1-0 |

Black resigned due to 17...♗d7 18 ♘c7+ ♔d8 19 ♘e6+ ♔e8 20 ♛f8# or 19...♔c8 20 ♛c7#.

An impressive win, especially by such a young player, and an emphatic demonstration of the benefits of good preparation.

Solution to Puzzle (posed before game 36)

The 'obvious' 1 ♗xf6 is a blunder, on account of 1...♛b2+! 2 ♗xb2 axb2+ 3 ♔b1 ♖a1#. However,

White alertly avoided that, and instead won with **1 ♖d2! ♛xb3 2 ♗xf6 ♛b2+ 3 ♖xb2 axb2+ 4 ♔b1!** 1-0. Black's last trick of 4 ♔xb2? ♖ab8+, which draws by perpetual check on the open a- and b-files, has been foiled.

Double Trouble

The next position arose in the game Condie-Muir at the 1982 Perth Congress in Scotland. Both Mark Condie and Andrew Muir went on to become international masters some years later.

W

White is to move, and your puzzle is to find out how he can win. The solution appears after the following encounter.

The next clash is between two really strong grandmasters. Tony Miles, who became England's first GM more than two decades ago, is playing Black. At the other side of the board is sitting Alexander Onishchuk, a very young Ukrainian man who is already making a powerful impression. His recent achievements include outright first places in the Groningen Open over Christmas 1995 and the grandmaster B-group at Wijk aan Zee soon afterwards. We join him at the scene of his latter victory.

Game 37
A.Onishchuk – A.Miles
Wijk aan Zee 1996
Nimzowitsch Defence

1 e4   ♘c6 *(D)*

W

The games of English grandmaster Tony Miles contain a treasure collection of interesting ideas. Few other top competitors regularly include the Nimzowitsch Defence in their repertoire, but Miles has frequently demonstrated that it is playable, and will probably do so again in spite of some recent setbacks with it.

2 ♘f3

It would be ridiculous to call **2 d4** a mistake, but it is true that White must be careful to avoid being tricked by a transposition into an opening that he would not normally play. For example, Howell-Miles, Isle of Man 1995, continued **2...e5 3 dxe5** 3 d5 ♘ce7 4 c4 ♘g6 or 4...d6 intending ...g6 and/or ...f5 gives a type of position which a player who usually opens with 1 e4 would not be accustomed to facing as White. Also, 3 ♘f3 transposes to the Scotch Game, but Grandmaster James Howell normally prefers the Ruy Lopez. **3...♘xe5 4 ♘c3 ♗c5 5 ♗f4** White could play 5 f4, since 5...♗xg1? (giving up a powerful, developed piece for no good reason) 6 ♖xg1 ♕h4+? 7 g3 ♕xh2 8 ♖g2 wins for him. However, after 5...♘g6 we have one kind of position in which Tony Miles revels. He has provoked White into advancing early on and leaving his king slightly exposed. **5...d6 6 ♕d2** 6 ♗xe5? dxe5 7 ♕xd8+ ♔xd8 8 0-0-0+ ♔e8 is already better for Black, since he has a powerful pair of bishops, but no problems concerning the safety of his king with the queens having been exchanged. Indeed, Black's monarch is ideally situated near the centre as the endgame comes into sight. Notice that

9 ♘b5 or 9 ♘d5 are easily dealt with by 9...♗b6 or 9...♗d6 respectively. **6...♘f6 7 0-0-0 ♗e6 8 ♘a4 ♗b6!** Simple but good. Black alertly avoids opening up the position too much with his king still sitting on the e-file. **8...♘xe4? 9 ♕e1 ♘xf2 10 ♘xc5 ♘xh1 11 ♘xe6 fxe6 12 ♘h3!** (stronger than 12 ♗xe5, which is answered by 12...♕g5+) is very good for White. If he does not win the knight on e5, then he will certainly net the one stranded on h1. **9 f3 0-0 10 a3** White wants his a-pawn to be protected, because otherwise it will be under threat from the rook on a8 after the capture ♘xb6 when Black recaptures with ...axb6. However, White has already used three tempi on moves 8-10 for the plan of removing Black's dark-squared bishop, but meanwhile his development is not increasing. This allows Black to seize the initiative. **10...♕e7 11 ♘xb6 axb6 12 ♘e2 ♘g6 13 ♔b1?** White cannot afford to use a valuable tempo in this way. Relatively best was 13 ♘c3 to restrain Black in the centre. **13...d5!** *(D)*

14 exd5 The e-pawn would not live for long after 14 e5 ♘d7. **14...♘xd5 15 ♕c1 b5! 16 ♗d2** 16 c3 b4 17 cxb4 ♗f5+ 18 ♔a1 ♕f6 19 ♔a2 (19 ♖xd5 ♖xa3# or 19 ♘c3 ♘gxf4 20 ♘xd5 ♖xa3#) 19...♘xb4+ 20 ♔b3 ♗c2+ 21 ♔xb4 ♖a4+ 22 ♔c5 ♕c6# shows a typical king-hunt. Most of White's

W

pieces are dormant near the back rank and cannot help their monarch. **16...b4 17 axb4 ♞xb4 18 b3 ♞xc2!** Nicely calculated, but the harmony in Black's army was so overwhelming that the position was crying out for a sacrifice to blast the frail shelter around the white king. Now 19 ♔xc2 loses in a variety of ways, one line being 19...♖a2+ 20 ♔b1 (20 ♔c3 ♕c5+ 21 ♔d3 ♗f5#) 20...♖fa8 21 ♗c3 ♗f5+. **19 ♕xc2 ♕a3 20 ♗c3 ♗xb3 0-1**. Notice that, just as in the case of the Von Hennig-Schara Gambit considered in Game 36, the main ingredient in Black's play was natural, attacking moves, making full use of the co-ordinated members in his army. Heavy use of memory and theoretical preparation was not needed this time. However, once again there is an Achilles Heel in Black's system, and Onishchuk finds it. As IM Douglas Bryson would say, 'Black

needs to repair it', but, if he can do so, then his original approach to the opening is no less viable than choosing one of the 'main' defencès, which have been scrutinised under microscopes in the chess laboratories of thousands of players.

| **2** ... | **d6** |

2...e5 is, of course, extremely sound, and, although it transposes to the same position as would be reached after 1 e4 e5 2 ♘f3 ♘c6, it has the advantage of avoiding the King's Gambit 2 f4, if Black is afraid of it.

3 d4	**♘f6**
4 ♘c3	**♗g4**
5 ♗e3 *(D)*	

B

| **5** ... | **a6** |

5...e6 might have been expected, but Grandmaster Miguel Illescas of Spain won convincingly as White against Miles at the 1995 Linares Zonal Tournament. Their encounter went **6 h3 ♗h5 7 d5 ♘e7?!** 7...♘e5 **8 g4 ♘xf3+** (8...♗g6 9 ♘d2! leaves Black facing the terrible threat of f4 then f5) **9 ♕xf3 ♗g6 10 dxe6 fxe6 11 e5!**, intending ♕xb7, shatters Black's position. 7...exd5 8 exd5 ♘e5 is, relatively speaking, more playable, though I know that Tony Miles considers that line to be unpleasant for Black too since he has a spatial disadvantage, but without tension in the centre to challenge White's extra space. **8 ♗b5+! c6** 8...♘d7 9 g4 ♗g6 10 dxe6 fxe6 11 ♘g5 is a nightmare for Black. **9 dxc6 bxc6** 9...♘xc6 10 e5! dxe5 (after 10...♗xf3 11 ♕xf3 dxe5 12 ♗xc6+ bxc6 13 ♕xc6+ ♘d7 14 0-0-0, the immediate threat is 15 ♖xd7 ♕xd7 16 ♕xa8+, and Black is in a hopeless situation) 11 g4 ♗g6 12 ♘xe5 is extremely unpleasant for Black, who can hardly avoid material loss. For example:

a) 12...♕c7 13 ♗f4! ♗d6 14 ♘xg6 ♗xf4 15 ♘xh8.

b) 12...♕c8 13 ♕f3.

c) 12...♕xd1+ 13 ♖xd1, and again the pinned knight on c6 is a source of big trouble for Black.

10 ♗a4 ♕c7 11 ♕e2 ♘d7?! 11...♗g6 looks better. **12 g4 ♗g6 13 0-0-0 e5** 13...♘b6 14 ♗xb6 axb6 (14...♕xb6 15 ♖xd6) 15 ♘b5! cxb5 16 ♕xb5+ ♔d8 17 ♕e8#. **14 ♕c4** Threatening 15 ♘b5. **14...♖c8 15 ♘h4 ♘b6 16 ♗xb6 axb6 17 ♖d3!** (D)

B

One threat is 18 ♘b5! cxb5 19 ♕xb5+ ♘c6 20 ♘xg6 hxg6 21 ♖c3. **17...d5** Both players would have calculated 17...b5? 18 ♘xb5 cxb5 20 ♕xb5+ ♘c6 (20...♔d8 21 ♕e8#) 21 ♘xg6 hxg6 22 ♖c3 ♔d7 23 ♖xc6 ♕xc6 24 ♕b7+, winning easily for White. **18 exd5** A powerful exchange sacrifice, justified by the fact that Black is lagging so far behind in development. **18...♗xd3 19 ♕xd3 ♖d8 20 ♖d1 g6 21 d6 ♗h6+ 22 ♔b1 ♕b8 23 ♘e4! b5** Black also loses after 23...0-0 24 dxe7 ♖xd3 25 exf8♕+ ♕xf8 26 cxd3 or 23...♗g7 24 d7+ ♔f8 25 ♕f3, logically attacking the weak point f7 and threatening ♘g5 or ♗b3. **24 ♘f6+ ♔f8 25 dxe7+ ♔xe7 26 ♘d7 bxa4 27 ♘f5+!! gxf5 28 ♕a3+ ♔e6** No better is 28...♔e8 29 ♘f6# or 28...c5 29 ♕xc5+ ♔e6 30 ♕c6+ ♔e7 31 ♕f6+ ♔e8 32 ♕xh8+ ♔e7 33 ♕f6+ ♔e8 34 ♕xh6 ♖xd7 35 ♕c6 ♕c7 36 ♕xd7+ ♕xd7 37 ♖xd7 ♔xd7 38 gxf5, with a totally won ♔+♙ endgame. **29 gxf5+ ♔xf5 30 ♕f3+ 1-0** White's pieces co-ordinate so beautifully that they force checkmate, instead of merely winning Black's queen. The finish would be 30...♔e6 31 ♕f6# or 30...♗f4 31 ♕g4+ ♔e4 32 ♘f6# or 30...♔g6 31 ♖g1+ ♗g5 32 ♕f6+ ♔h5 33 ♕xg5#. Illescas's play combined good preparation with a high level of alertness (particularly for tactics), and he went on to win the tournament.

6	**h3**	**♗h5**
7	**d5**	**♗xf3?**

Black hopes to profit from the doubled pawns which his opponent now chooses to have. However, White is being allowed to acquire too much activity and space, in effect without spending any time, since the advance d4-d5 gains a tempo by attacking the knight on c6 and forcing it to move soon.

8	**gxf3!**	**♘b8**
9	**f4**	

Threatening to push Black's pieces even further back by 10 e5.

9	**...**	**c6**
10	**♗g2**	**♕c7**
11	**♕d4!**	*(D)*

Renewing the threat of e4-e5.

11	**...**	**cxd5**

11...c5 12 ♕a4+ leaves Black with an unpleasant choice:

a) 12...b5? 13 ♘xb5.

b) 12...♕d7 13 e5 ♕xa4 (or 13...b5 14 ♕a5) 14 ♘xa4 ♘fd7 15 e6 ♘f6 16 ♘b6.

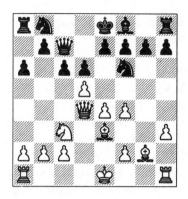

B

c) 12...♘bd7 13 e5! dxe5 14 fxe5 ♕xe5 15 0-0-0. In this last case, White has an attractive selection of follow-up ideas, including ♖he1, d6 and ♗f4, showing that the gambit of a pawn at move 13 has opened up lines for the power of his rooks and bishops to be unleashed against Black's monarch, which has not yet castled. Does 15...0-0-0 provide Black's king with a safe haven? The answer is definitely 'No'! In fact, if White is alert, he can utilise the tremendous harmony in his army to win virtually by force with 16 ♗f4 ♕f5 17 ♘b5!, and now:

c1) 17...axb5 18 ♕a8+.

c2) 17...♘b6 18 ♘a7#.

c3) 17...♖e8 18 ♘a7+ ♔d8 19 ♕a5+ b6 20 ♘c6+ ♔c8 21 ♕xa6#.

c4) 17...e5 18 dxe6.

c5) 17...♘e5 18 ♘a7+, with two branches:

c51) 18...♔c7 19 ♘c6! bxc6 20 ♕xc6+ ♔b8 21 ♗xe5+ ♕xe5 22

d6, threatening checkmate on a8, b7 or c7.

c52) 18...♔b8 19 ♘c6+! bxc6 20 dxc6 ♖xd1+ 21 ♖xd1 ♔a7 22 ♗f1! c4 23 ♗e3+ ♔b8 24 ♕b4+ and 25 ♕b7#.

Those calculations are not really too taxing on the memory, as they flow naturally from the co-ordination between the pieces involved.

On a number of occasions, I have stressed the value of looking for checks or captures, and the analysis is full of such moves. A related idea is that the moves in the calculations frequently carry direct *threats*, even if the move itself is not making a check or capture. Direct threats may be obvious to the opponent, but that does not necessarily make them easy to deal with. Of course, sometimes a threat can be strengthened by disguising or masking it, but the key point here is this: being alert to ways in which oneself or the opponent might create threats can lead to lots of fantastic combinations arising from one's calculations. A fraction (hopefully a large one!) of them will occur in actual play, thereby providing yourself and others with something beautiful and memorable.

12 ♘xd5!

A general point comes to mind here, namely that people often wonder whether or not certain pieces should be exchanged. Some exchanges are forced, but in many cases the exchange being considered is optional, and the player must assess whether or not it will improve his position. Are there any guidelines which can help us to make the decisions in such situations? Well, fortunately the answer is 'Yes', and I hope the following seven suggestions will save a lot of time, energy, and points by facilitating good future choices concerning exchanges. The mnemonic name is easily remembered because, in Mathematics, a heptagon is a plane shape with seven straight sides.

H.E.P.T.A. (which you may like to think of as: Helpful Exchanges Preferably Take Advantageously!)

1) An exchange that eliminates an actively developed piece (or pawn) in the opponent's army is normally good.

2) An exchange that eliminates a defender of the opponent's king is normally good.

3) An exchange that improves one's structure or worsens that of the opponent is normally good.

4) An exchange of a piece (in one's own army) that is lacking in scope is normally good if the piece is not required for defensive purposes.

5) An exchange normally helps to relieve the lack of space in a cramped position.

6) An exchange is normally good if one is ahead on material.

7) An exchange that helps to further one's plan at that time is normally good.

Particularly in cases 1, 2, and 7, it may sometimes be worth making a sacrifice (as opposed to just an equal exchange of material) in order to achieve the objectives described in the H.E.P.T.A. guidelines. Notice also that all seven ideas contain the word 'normally', because, although they tend to be helpful, there are exceptions in which a given idea may not be valid.

Onishchuk's 12 ♘xd5, leading to an exchange of knights, is especially appropriate in view of cases 1, 2, and 7. Why do I include number 7 there? The reason is that White's knight has cleared the way for the c-pawn to advance.

    12 ...   **♘xd5**
    13 cxd5   **♘d7**

13...♕xc2 is suicidal, in view of 14 ♖c1. For instance, 14...♕f5 15 ♖c7 (15 ♕b6 also wins) 15...♘d7 16 ♗e4 ♕f6 17 ♕a4 b5 18 ♕xa6! ♖xa6 19 ♖c8#.

    14 c4   **♘f6**
    15 ♖c1! *(D)*

White consistently prepares the further advance of the c-pawn. It was not strictly necessary to calculate long liness after 15...♕a5+, because Black's lack of development makes such excursions with the queen a luxury that he cannot afford. However, not to be lazy, here is one natural sequence which

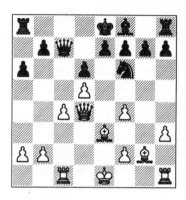

B

underlines that fact! 16 ♗d2 ♕xa2 17 ♕b6, and now, in view of the threat to take Black's b-pawn, there are only a few branches worth looking at:

a) 17...0-0-0 castles right into an attack by 18 c5.

b) 17...♖b8 18 0-0 (one of many good moves) 18...♕a4 19 ♕c7 ♘d7 20 ♗e4 (threatening ♗f5) 20...g6 21 ♗c2 ♕a2 22 ♗c3 f6 23 ♖a1.

c) 17...♘d7 18 ♕xb7 ♖b8 19 ♕c6 ♕xb2 (19...♖xb2?? 20 ♕c8#) 20 ♔e2 (threatening ♖b1) 20...♕b7 21 ♖b1 ♕c8 22 ♖xb8+ ♕xb8 23 ♖b1! ♕d8 24 ♖b7, threatening ♗a5, and Black is also unable to counter the manoeuvres ♖c7-c8 or ♗e4-c2-a4 if White chooses to win in either of those ways.

    15 ...   **g6**
    16 c5   **dxc5**

Black is also in dire straits after 16...♗g7 17 ♕a4+ ♘d7 (17...♕d7 18 c6 bxc6 19 dxc6 ♕c7 20 ♗b6! ♕xb6 21 c7+ wins for White), and now 18 cxd6 looks particularly strong (less clear is 18 c6 bxc6 19 dxc6 ♘c5!, when White must be alert to avoid 20 ♕a3? ♗xb2! 21 ♕xb2 ♘d3+). Initially 18...♕xd6 may not seem so bad, but White has 19 ♗c5!, with several main possibilities:

a) 19...b5 20 ♗xd6 bxa4 21 ♗a3, protecting the b-pawn and clearing the way for the advance d5-d6 (which unleashes the power of White's fianchettoed bishop).

b) 19...♕f6 20 ♗a3 (threatening ♖c7, but meanwhile Black cannot play ...0-0 because of ♕xd7) 20...b5 21 ♕e4, and White is in command.

c) 19...♕c7 20 d6!? (20 0-0 is also good) 20...exd6 21 ♗e3 ♕b8 22 ♗b6! threatening ♖c7.

d) 19...♕b8 20 ♗b6! ♕d6 21 ♗c7, intending 21...♕f6 22 ♗e5! winning. The white dark-squared bishop is a real star, but watch the light-squared half of the dynamic duo in the forthcoming notes to Black's 17th move.

17 ♖xc5 ♕d6

After 17...♕d7, White has the simple but strong 18 0-0, intending ♖fc1 and ♖c7. However, 18 d6! is also extremely good. For example:

a) 18...exd6? 19 ♕xf6.

b) 18...♕xd6 19 ♗xb7 ♖b8 20 ♕a4+ ♔d8 (20...♘d7 21 ♖d5 or 20...♕d7? 21 ♗c6) 21 ♖c6 ♕d7 22 ♗b6+ ♔e8 23 ♗c8 ♖xc8 24 ♖xc8#.

c) 18...♗g7 19 ♖c7 ♕xd6 20 ♕xd6 exd6 21 ♗xb7. One of the dominant, recurring features in those and other variations is the harmony and power of White's two bishops, co-ordinating with each other. The resulting effects are devastating in an open position.

18 ♕a4+! ♘d7 *(D)*

18...b5? loses to 19 ♖xb5, and 18...♕d7 19 ♕c2, threatening ♖c7, is also terrible for Black. However, even after the move played, Onishchuk has prepared a stunning continuation.

W

19 ♖c6!! ♕b8

19...bxc6 20 dxc6 and now:

a) 20...♘c5 21 ♗xc5 ♕xc5 22 c7+ ♕b5 23 ♕xb5+ axb5 24 ♗c6#.

b) 20...♖b8 21 cxd7+ ♔d8 (or 21...♕xd7? 22 ♗c6) 22 0-0 ♗g7 23 ♖d1 ♕b4 24 ♕xa6 ♗xb2 25 ♕a7 e6 26 ♗c5 ♕b5 27 ♗e7+! ♔xe7 28 d8♕#.

c) 20...♖c8 21 0-0! threatens 22 ♖d1. Then 21...♘f6 22 ♖d1 ♕c7 allows 23 ♗b6! ♕xb6 24 c7+ ♕b5 25 ♕xb5+ axb5 26 ♗c6+ ♘d7 27 ♗xd7# *(D)*.

B

The attempt 21...♘b8 to prevent White's light-squared bishop from landing on c6 fails after the continuation 22 ♖d1 ♕c7 23 ♗b6! ♕xb6 24 c7+ ♕b5 25 ♕xb5+ axb5 26 cxb8♕ ♖xb8 27 ♗c6#. Such calculations are pretty, but not really surprising given Black's lack of development.

20 ♖b6

Threatening d6 and then ♖xb7.

20	...	♕c8
21	0-0	♖b8
22	♖c1	♕d8
23	d6	♗g7
24	♖xb7	♖xb7
25	♗xb7	0-0

1-0

Black resigned without waiting for 26 ♖c8.

Solution to Puzzle (set before game 37...which seems a long time ago!)

Both sides have rooks doubled on open files. However, it is White to play, and the move he alertly spots wins by force, as calculations will show. The game went **1 ♘c6!**. 1 ♖c7 ♕d5 (1...♕b8? loses to 2 ♖xd7 or 2 ♘c6) 2 ♖c8+ ♘e8 3 ♘c6! *(D)* also wins, as follows:

B

a) 3...♕xd6 4 ♘xa5 ♖xa5 5 ♖xe8+.

b) 3...♖xb5 4 ♘e7+ ♔h8 5 ♗b4!! (5 ♘xd5? ♖xb1 is fine for Black) and now:

b1) 5...♕b7 6 ♖xa8 ♕xa8 7 ♖c8 ♖xb4 8 ♕xb4 ♕a1+ 9 ♔h2 ♘f6 10 ♕b5!.

b2) 5...♖xb4 6 ♕xb4 ♖xc8 7 ♖xc8 ♕d1+ 8 ♔h2 ♘f6 9 ♕xb6 (9 ♕b5?? ♕d6+).

c) 3...♖a1 4 ♘e7+ ♔h8 5 ♕xa1!! ♖xa1 6 ♘xd5 ♖xc1+ 7 ♖xc1 ♘xd6 8 ♖c7 exd5 9 ♖xd7 ♘xb5 10 ♖xf7.

d) 3...♖xc8 4 ♘e7+ ♔f8 (or 4...♔h8 5 ♖xc8! ♕xd6 6 ♖xe8+ ♘f8 7 ♖xf8#) 5 ♘xd5+ ♘xd6 6 ♖xc8+ ♘xc8 7 ♘xb6! ♘cxb6 8 ♕b4+ ♔e8 9 ♕xa5, although the winning process will take some time. White can, for example, manoeuvre his queen to c6 and his king to a5 to break Black's blockade of the b-pawn.

The continuation was **1...♖a1**. Black is also lost after 1...♖a4 2 ♘e7+ ♔h8 3 ♖xa4 ♖xa4 4 ♖c8+ or 1...♖a2 2 ♘e7+ ♔h8 3 ♖c8+ ♘e8 4 ♖xe8+ ♖xe8 5 ♕xa2. Then came **2 ♕xa1 ♖xa1 3 ♖xa1 ♔h7 4 ♖ca4!**. The co-ordination in White's army is superb, but Black's poor queen can hardly breathe. **4...♘c5 5 ♖a7 ♕c8 6 ♖a8 ♕d7 7 ♖d8 ♕b7 8 ♖a7 1-0.**

Whose back rank is weaker?

B

Not surprisingly, it is Black to move. What is perhaps more surprising is that he can win by force! In view of the weakness of Black's back rank, the first move **1...♕xd3** is obligatory, but it also wins the game after **2 cxd3** (2 ♕xd3? ♖b1+ illustrates the weakness of White's back rank too) **2...♖b2!**, and White can resign because of the forthcoming ...c2 and ...♖b1. That instructive combination was based on the encounter Kadiri-Pritchett, Skopje Olympiad 1972. The one difference in the actual game was that Pritchett's h-pawn was on h6 instead of h7. That made Black's position safer, but it also made his queen sacrifice even more brilliant, because, although there were many other choices besides 1...♕xd3, Craig was alert in his calculations and found the lovely finish.

Now that our thinking is even hotter after that example, it is time to be...

R.O.A.S.T.E.D.!

This mnemonic stands for Ratio Of Attacking Strikers To Enemy Defenders. It can be well explained by means of the following stunning combination played by international master, and correspondence grandmaster, Douglas Bryson in a 1976 Glasgow League encounter Taylor-Bryson.

B

It is Black to play and win. The position arose from a **Four Knights Game** after eight moves, as follows. **1 e4 e5 2 ♘f3 ♘c6 3 ♘c3 ♘f6 4 ♗b5 ♘d4** Rubinstein's variation. **5 ♗a4 ♗c5** 5...c6 intending ...♛a5!? is also fashionable nowadays. **6 ♘xe5 0-0 7 0-0?!** This is another example of the importance of preparation in certain openings. 7 ♘d3 ♗b6 8 e5 is now generally regarded as best, but instead White castles into an attack. Actually, it is quite possible through alert and logical thinking to realise that 7 0-0 is a mistake even without knowing the theory. That kind of approach will, of course, use up valuable time at the board, but it shows that unfamiliar situations are not impossible to cope with. In White's shoes, my thinking would have gone something like this: 'What will Black do if I castle? He has yet to activate his light-squared bishop, so I think he's going to free it by

playing the logical move 7...d6, which also attacks my knight on e5. Then I don't want to retreat to f3 because of the unpleasant pin 8...♗g4. Oops! 8...♗g4 is coming anyway, and my queen will be embarrassed. Back to the drawing board ... at least hopefully not the losing board! Okay, no fear or pessimism. Let's look for a good, sensible alternative to castling'. **7...d6 8 ♘d3**. So here we are in the position given in the last diagram. The game proceeded **8...♗g4 9 ♕e1**

Instead 9 f3?? loses quickly to 9...♘xf3+ 10 ♔h1 ♘xh2. However, White is still about to be roasted after 9 ♕e1. A striking feature of his situation is that it is very congested. It would require a lot of time for White's pieces to transfer to the immediate neighbourhood of his king. Consequently, the lonely monarch on g1 is mainly protected by the three pawns on f2, g2 and h2. 'Three enemy defenders...', Black could say, '...but I have five key strikers ready to attack: my knights, bishops, and queen. My rooks cannot transfer so quickly to join in an assault against White's king, but the ratio of attacking strikers to enemy defenders is 5:3. That's not bad, but let's make it better!' **9...♘f3+! 10 gxf3 ♗xf3** The ratio is increasing. It is now 4:2, since Black has sacrificed one attacking striker (a knight in this case), but one enemy defender has also been eliminated (White's g-pawn). Furthermore, White cannot afford a tempo to capture the striker bishop on c5, in view of 11 ♘xc5 ♘g4! 12 d4 ♕h4 13 ♗f4 ♕h3 and 14...♕g2#. That explains his next move. **11 h3 ♘g4!** 'Make way for my queen to get to h4, and don't let the enemy monarch out to h2' is the knight's noble and alert attitude. The quick calculation 12 hxg4 ♕h4 and 13...♕h1# (or 13...♕g3#) confirms that Black is winning the battle. **12 ♘f4 ♕h4 13 d4** Stopping the threat of ...♕g3#. From a purely mathematical viewpoint, the ratio of defenders to attackers has temporarily improved for White. However, an overriding factor is that the next move will eliminate the new defender on f4, which is the only thing standing in the way of Black's queen capturing the most vital defender, namely the pawn on h3. **13...g5! 14 ♗d7** 14 ♘cd5 actually carries a threat of ♘e7+ and then ♘f5, but 14...gxf4 15 ♘xf4 ♗xd4 16 ♗e3 ♗e5! consistently aims to eliminate the key piece on f4 which is holding White's defences together by a thread. **14...gxf4 15 ♗xg4 ♗xg4 16 dxc5** No better is 16 hxg4 f3! 17 ♘e2 ♕xg4+ 18 ♘g3 ♕h3, and 19...♕g2# cannot be averted. 16 ♗xf4 ♗f3! is also hopeless for White: his f-pawn cannot advance

to make room for other potential defenders to help. **16...♗xh3!** Black has three members of his army continuing harmoniously in the attack, but only one of White's original three defenders is left. 3:1 is the best ratio yet! Notice that Douglas Bryson was again precise in his calculations, because the move chosen is more convincing for Black than 16...♕xh3 17 f3 or 16...♗f3 17 ♔h2. **17 ♗xf4** 17 f3 comes too late on account of 17...♕g5+ 18 ♔f2 ♕g2#, and the little striker on f4 plays a role in the checkmate. **17...♕g4+! 18 ♗g3 ♕f3 0-1.**

The finish focuses on the light square g2. There is no piece in White's army which can defend it for the king, but it is attacked twice by Black. Mathematicians keep clear of ratios such as 2:0, but it is evident that Black's advantage is now infinite, since 19...♕g2# cannot be stopped.

Well, things do not get much hotter than when they are roasted, so we are nearing the conclusion of our H.O.T. adventure. The short last chapter is dedicated to you, and to all the readers who journeyed far to get here.

Do not stop and sleep just yet, unless you also intend to have a dream game...

5 N.B.

N.B. normally represents the Latin words *nota bene*, meaning 'note well'. Here, however, I also have **new beginning** in mind. Instead of thinking of this as the end of something, I hope it marks a new beginning in your chess.

Grandmaster David Bronstein, who is himself a highly original thinker, once stated 'Chess is imagination'. I would like to show you the game I had in a dream on 7 February 1996. Incidentally, the date is a popular one, because Florence Nightingale had a special vision on the same day in 1837!

The previous day, my mind had been even more on Chinese than usual (my wife Jenny is Chinese), as the fifth game of the Women's World Championship match between China's Xie Jun and her challenger, Zsuzsa Polgar of Hungary, was played on 6 February 1996. I was interested to see the Scotch Game appearing so effectively (Polgar won with White in 25 moves), and I started to think about playing something like it myself, but with a new beginning. During the night it happened! So as not to leave the names of White and Black blank, I have made the assumption that I was playing against myself!

Game 38
P.Motwani – P.Motwani
Brussels 1996
Dunst Opening

1 ♘c3

At this stage, the opening is classed as the Dunst Opening, although numerous possibilities of transpositions to other openings exist. For example:

a) 1...g6 2 e4 ♗g7 3 d4: Modern Defence.

b) 1...f5 2 d4: Dutch Defence.

c) 1...e6 2 e4 d5 3 d4: French Defence.

d) 1...d5 2 d4 ♘f6 3 ♗g5: Veresov Opening.

e) 1...c6 2 e4 d5 3 d4: Caro-Kann Defence.

f) 1...c5 2 e4: Sicilian Defence.

g) 1...b6 2 e4 ♗b7 3 d4 e6: Owen's Defence.

h) 1...♘f6 2 e4 and now:

h1) 2...e5: Vienna Game.

h2) 2...d5: Alekhine's Defence.

h3) 2...d6 3 d4: Pirc Defence.

There are other opening paths the game might travel along, including the one I played, as Black I mean!

1	...	e5
2	♘f3	♘c6
3	d4	exd4
4	♘xd4	♘f6

4...♗b4 5 ♘xc6 bxc6 6 ♕d4! is nice for White.

5	♗g5

5 e4 would have transposed into a variation of the Scotch Game that is normally reached via the move order 1 e4 e5 2 ♘f3 ♘c6 3 d4 (3 ♘c3 ♘f6 4 d4 exd4 5 ♘xd4 is also possible, although 4...♗b4 is an interesting deviation for Black) 3...exd4 4 ♘xd4 ♘f6 5 ♘c3 ♗b4. However, remembering 'allegro' back in chapter one, I like developing another piece.

5	...	h6? *(D)*

W

This position is worth a diagram, because 5...h6 looks so plausible and yet it is definitely a mistake. 5...♗e7 6 ♘f5! is also pleasant for White, so Black should prefer 5...♗b4.

6	♗xf6!	♕xf6

After 6...gxf6, Black's structure is a nightmare!

7	♘db5!	♕d8

The alternatives are also bleak:

a) 7...♗b4 8 ♘xc7+ ♔d8 9 ♘d5.

b) 7...♗c5 8 ♘xc7+ ♔d8 9 e3! (intending 9...♔xc7 10 ♘d5+ and 11 ♘xf6), not 9 ♘xa8?? ♗xf2+ 10 ♔d2 ♕f4+, mating next move.

c) 7...♔d8 8 ♘xc7! ♔xc7 9 ♘d5+.

d) 7...♕e5 8 ♘d5 (clearer than 8 f4?! ♕xf4 9 ♘d5 ♕h4+! 10 g3 ♕e4) and now:

d1) 8...♗d6 9 f4! winning.

d2) 8...♕xb2 9 ♖b1! ♕xa2 10 ♘bxc7+ ♔d8 11 ♘xa8 should also win. However, in calculating that variation, White must be alert to avoid 9 ♘bxc7+ ♔d8 10 ♘xa8? due to 10...♗b4+ 11 ♘xb4 ♕c3+! 12 ♕d2 ♕xa1+ 13 ♕d1 ♕xd1+ 14 ♔xd1 ♘xb4, when Black will soon win the stranded knight on a8, and the game with it.

8	♘d5	♗d6
9	♘xd6+

I always keep in mind the saying 'The threat is stronger than its execution', and so White might consider delaying the capture on d6. However, 9 g3 ♗e5! 10 f4 a6! is fine for Black.

9	...	cxd6
10	g3	0-0
11	♗g2	♘e7
12	0-0

White has a dream position! His pawns are healthy and the pieces enjoy plenty of scope, whereas the black doubled d-pawns are not only a structural problem (chapter three makes a guest appearance!), but they are also making it extremely difficult for the queenside section of his army to develop in a natural way.

12	...	♘xd5
13	♕xd5	♕c7
14	c3	♖e8
15	♖ad1!	

Increasing the harmony within White's army. My e-pawn would normally have advanced to e4 14 moves ago. However, it seems to have gone to sleep, so it might as well be offered as a gambit!

15	...	♖xe2 *(D)*

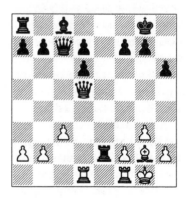

W

16 ♖fe1!

The ratio of attacking strikers to enemy defenders is now overwhelming. Black is being roasted!

16	...	♖e5

Black must have read Chapter two: he makes a tenacious attempt to hang on! 16...♖xb2?? 17 ♖e8+ ♔h7 18 ♕f5+ g6 19 ♕xf7# is far worse. White must now avoid the blunder 17 ♕xd6?? ♖xe1+ 18 ♖xe1 ♕xd6.

17	♕d4	♔f8

After 17...♕c5, White has numerous good continuations, including the simple but strong 18 ♕xc5 ♖xe1+ 19 ♖xe1 dxc5 20 ♖e8+ ♔h7 21 f4, when Black has few constructive moves left. White can win with ♗h3 whenever he wants to, or take the king for a walk first!

18	♕d3	g6
19	♗d5	

The bishop sees a very unsafe king, and wants to play an active part in White's forthcoming victory.

19	...	♖b8

Preparing ...b6 and ....♗b7, but it is too late to save the game.

20	♕f3	♖f5

After 20...f5, there follows 21 ♕f4 ♔g7 (21...g5 22 ♕f3 threatens the deadly ♕h5) 22 ♕d4 (threatening f4) and now:

a) 22...♕c5 23 ♖xe5 ♕xd4 24 ♖e7+ ♔f6 25 ♖f7+ ♔e5 26 ♖xd4 g5 27 f4+ gxf4 28 gxf4#.

b) 22...♔h7 23 f4 ♖xe1+ 24 ♖xe1 ♕d8 (24...♕c5 25 ♖e7#) 25 ♕xa7 ♕c7 26 ♖e7+ ♔h8 27 ♕d4#.

c) 22...♔f8 23 ♕h4 ♔g7 24 ♖xe5 dxe5 25 ♕e7+ ♔h8 26 ♕f8+ ♔h7 27 ♕g8#.

21 ♕e3   ♔g7

21...h5 22 ♕h6+ ♔g8 23 ♖e8#.

22 ♕d4+ *(D)*

B

22 ...   ♖f6

The alternatives were equally hopeless:

a) 22...♔f8 23 ♕h8#.

b) 22...♔g8 23 ♖e8+ ♔h7 24 ♕h8#.

c) 22...♔h7 23 ♖e8 ♖e5 24 ♖f8 f5 25 ♖f7+ ♔h8 26 ♕h4 checkmates quickly.

d) 22...f6 23 ♖e7+ ♔f8 24 ♖f7+ ♔e8 25 ♕e3+ ♖e5 26 ♕xh6 ♔d8 27 ♕h8+ ♖e8 28 ♕xf6+ ♖e7 29 ♖f8#.

e) 22...♖e5 23 f4, and White will be enough material ahead to win the game in his sleep!

23 ♖e7   1-0

Black's dormant cohorts on the left flank cannot help to counter the terrible threat of 24 ♖xf7+ on the other wing. The dream ended about there. I suppose I must have resigned, then congratulated myself on a convincing win! Fortunately it was not lost from my memory (thanks to Chapter four!), and when I played over the moves on a board the next morning I decided they were worth noting.

My wife Jenny says I should have a break. I think I will cool down after that H.O.T. journey, and I leave you with these words:

We often race, staying full of stress, heart knowing it's above the ceiling's limit;

Soften your pace, playing cool with chess, start flowing and love the feelings with it.

I hope we will meet again in my next Batsford book, which will be called **C.O.O.L. Chess**...